THE COLLEGE STUDENT'S HANDBOOK

FOR
BETTER GRADES, JOB SEARCH,
AND CAREER SUCCESS

THE COLLEGE STUDENT'S HANDBOOK

FOR
BETTER GRADES, JOB SEARCH,
AND CAREER SUCCESS

S. A. Swami, Ph.D.

Professor of Civil Engineering
West Virginia Institute of Technology

Minibook Publishing Co.
Montgomery, WV

Library of Congress cataloging in Publication Data:

Swami, S. A. (Shanmugam A.), 1928–
    The college student's handbook for better grades, job search, and
career success/S. A. Swami.
    p. cm.

    Includes bibliographical references (p.).
    1. Study, Method of. 2. College student orientation—United
States. 3. Job hunting—United States. 4. Career development—
United States. I. Title.
LB2395.S93   1990
378.1'98—dc20   89-49143
                                                              CIP

ISBN 0-941553-01-9 :

To

My Parents, Anusuya, and Jay

ACKNOWLEDGMENTS

During the course of writing this book, like most authors of how-to books, I sought and got help from a great many willing people, experts in their field of specialization who were eager to help others. I have tried to pass on their cumulative wisdom to the reader through the pages of this book. I do not claim originality to any of the techniques presented in this book.

It is with great pleasure that I acknowledge the interest of Dr. J. Sam Brill, Ed.D., Retired Academic Vice-President, West Virginia Institute of Technology, who enthusiastically came forward to write the Foreword for this book.

The financial assistance provided by the Jamey Harless Foundation of Gilbert, West Virginia, towards the publishing cost of this book is gratefully and sincerely acknowledged.

Special thanks are due to John M. Neal, graduating senior in electrical engineering, West Virginia Institute of Technology and amateur photographer, who shot all the photographs in this book.

The assistance provided by my wife Anusuya Swami and our son Jay in the various phases of this project is greatly appreciated.

Very special thanks go to all of the following, many of whose names will be found mentioned again in these pages:

Mary J. Hicks	Donald G. Brannon
Denise Hardy	John M. Parks
Julia Brown	Stephen W. Brown
Anne Repaire	Otis K. Rice
Tom Phillips	Rita Wicks-Nelson
Beverly Wattie	Paul C. Pappas
Cantrell Miller	Ronald L. Johnson
Patricia Hopkins	Mostafa Shaaban
Elvin E. Dillon	Charles F. Martyn
Una Karner	Shakuntala Ghare
Sherman Bobbitt	Richard F. McCormick
Mike Gleason	Robert C. Gillespie
Virginia P. Gray	Govindappa Puttaiah
Debra A. Dangerfield	Robert A. Marshburn
John F. Cavalier	Howard Nunley
Norma F. Lauer	Elizabeth A. Miller
Robert J. Lieb	Hattie Nunley
Robert P. Scholl	Virginia Atwater
George Smith	Nina Morton

CONTENTS

Preface:

How This Book Was Written and Why

Foreword

by Dr. J. Sam Brill, Ed.D.

PART 1.   ACADEMIC EXCELLENCE

Section 1.   Factors in Learning

Section 2.   Techniques for Learning

Section 3.   Techniques for Taking Tests, Report Writing & Effective Speaking

PART 2.   CAREER EXCELLENCE

PREFACE

How This Book Was Written and Why

The knock on my office door was feeble. I looked up. The agony on the face of the student was easily noticeable. "Sir, I studied hard, but I didn't do well on the test. Can you help me?," he blurted out in a voice that was almost choked with emotion.

This was not an isolated incident that I was confronted with during the many years of my college teaching. From my own long experience as a college student in three different countries with different educational systems and now as a college professor who has the authority and freedom to determine the grades of students in my classes I became aware of the predicament of the modern college student in today's complex academic environment. I began to view my students' academic performances in a more comprehensive way, rather than as isolated instances of their striving for better grades in particular test situations. Something in me hurt whenever I saw the sincerity and agony on their perplexed young faces when they came to me for help. I saw myself in them. They reminded me of my sleepless nights of prolonged study and my agonizing uncertainties over the outcome of tests.

I decided to do something to help students not only survive the college jungle, but also get the most benefit from their college lives and graduate with distinction. I wanted to provide them with guidance, techniques, and know-how needed for this venture, which I felt would be effective based on my personal experience. To help them, I could not think of any better way than writing a self-help book in which they could find answers to their questions about various aspects of college study and also learn techniques needed to better their academic performances. The outcome of that decision is this handbook.

As I started researching and writing on academic excellence for college students, I sought the help of many academic professionals, experts in their own fields of specialization, to give specific guidelines to study the divergently different basic and applied subjects which the modern college student needs for the completion of his/her academic program. A special feature of this book is that cumulatively more than 600 years of college teaching experience are reflected in two chapters, namely Chapter 10 and 11.

College and career! They have come to be two sides of the same coin for millions in the United States of America, as well as in most countries of the world today. Though the ultimate purpose of education should be to learn, develop, and grow intellectually and emotionally, it has become necessary for many, young and old, to use college education as a means to find a job. That being the case, it is vital for the college student and for anyone who plans to go to college to become aware of all the facets of college education and their relevance to a successful career.

Though many sources of information are available on the various aspects of college education and career choice, they are far too specialized and scattered for meaningful use by today's college student towards integration of his/her college life with a successful career. The link between college and career is not fully understood by most students and as a result they find themselves groping for direction after graduation. Many are forced to take any job that comes along due to their ignorance of job search techniques. There is a vital need for the college student to know the various techniques not only for studying and getting good grades but also for getting the right job and being successful at it once it is found. It is the purpose of this book to serve this need.

Necessarily, this book is more pragmatic than academic. It is designed as an easy and ready reference book for the use of college students of all majors. It is primarily a self-help book, and, as such, to get the most out of this book, the student must learn to put into practice the relevant techniques and suggestions presented therein.

The book is basically divided into two parts: Academic Excellence and Career Excellence. Academic Excellence is further divided into four sections:

Section 1. Factors in Learning
Section 2. Techniques for Learning
Section 3. Techniques for Taking Tests, Report Writing and Effective Speaking
Section 4. Contributing Factors in Learning.

The principles of effective learning culled from educational psychology form the basis for the various techniques of study presented in this book. Besides, factors that either affect learning negatively or contribute to it positively are also included, such as motivation, self-image, student stress management, time management, and goal achievement to mention a few.

The second part, Career Excellence, is further divided into two Sections:

Section 5. The Twilight Zone
Section 6. The Grand Strategy.

Section 5 deals with career development, the right job, how to write an effective resume, job search strategy and how to take interviews. Section 6 deals with factors contributing to career success, a 4-year plan for action, and the "secrets of success" in personal and career life.

While the book fills the college student's need for a total handbook for academic and career excellence, it also can serve him/her as a tool for success in life in general.

College Freshmen Orientation advisors will find this book very useful for their introductory classes to acquaint students with what lies ahead for a successful college and career life, and to help them prepare for their academic and career challenges when they begin college.

Montgomery, WV
January 1, 1990

S. A. Swami

FOREWORD

To The New College Student

by
by Dr. J. Sam Brill, Ed.D.,

Dr. J. Sam Brill, Ed.D.,
University of Southern California,
Vice President for Academic Affairs (Retired),
West Virginia Institute of Technology

The best thing about the future is that it comes only one day at a time.

—Abraham Lincoln

You are entering a special time in your life, one which promises much, requires much effort, and yet provides an opportunity for personal growth and development, a freedom of choice, and a demand for personal responsibility which you may never have experienced before. You will question and be questioned. You will examine and be examined. You will judge and be judged. You will work and you will play hard. You will encounter frustration and at times elation. Somehow through this total experience you will learn a great deal about many things, and you will also learn a great deal about yourself, who you are and what you believe in and value. Hopefully, you will learn how to learn and how to keep learning throughout life.

The study of how we learn has been a fascinating topic of concern to educators and psychologists for many decades. Strangely enough, the results of most efforts at understanding this phenomenon have been directed towards only one side of the teacher-learner notion—the teacher. While an understanding of learning theories can no doubt be of great benefit to teachers, such knowledge would seem to be of even greater benefit to those who learn. It is in keeping with this philosophy that this book has been prepared.

This book is devoted to the task of learning, particularly that learning associated with the classroom. As intended by the author, this book is primarily a "how to succeed" manual, targeted towards you the student in a most pragmatic manner, but also dealing with factors in learning and taking tests drawn from educational psychology, years of personal teaching experience, and much sound common sense. The author has eclectically chosen from the various approaches to learning psychology, selecting those elements which he has observed seem to work or to produce success, without belaboring you with particular theories or often dissenting viewpoints of different psychological opinions. The topics are limited to four and include techniques for improving learning in the various situations which you as a student will encounter as you pursue your college education. The intent is always to assist you and enable you, the student, to take charge of the learning process.

Prior to utilizing this book, it seems most appropriate that you should reexamine why you feel it is important to achieve a college education. You must attach some value to this experience if you are to be successful. By this I do not mean the economic value of a resulting job, although that obviously has value, but rather what change or improvement in your life can result from such an education. Let me suggest to you as a model to start your thinking, a set of objectives proposed by Paul L. Dressel, a noted educator, in an article entitled "The Meaning of a College Education" published in The Journal of Higher Education a few years ago. I will paraphrase these somewhat to better suit our purpose:

1. You should know how to acquire knowledge and how to use it.
2. You should have a high level of mastery of the skills of communication.
3. You should be aware of your own values and value commitments, and you should be aware that other individuals and cultures hold contrasting values which must be understood and to some extent accepted for satisfactory interaction.
4. You should have awareness, concern, and a sense of responsibility regarding contemporary events, issues, and problems.
5. You should see your total college experience as coherent, cumulative, and unified by the development of the broad competencies already indicated, and by the accompanying realization that these competencies are relevant to your further development as an individual, and to fulfillment of your obligations as a responsible citizen in a democratic society.
6. You should be able to cooperate and to collaborate with others in studying problems, formulating solutions to them, and taking action on them.

You must realize that these are long-term objectives and that you will not achieve them immediately but over the course of your college education. Don't become discouraged. As Lincoln states in the quote above, the future comes one day at a time. Develop a set of questions based on your objectives to help determine your progress from time to time. For example; Are you learning how to acquire knowledge and how to use it? Is your level of communication skills improving? Are you becoming more aware of other cultures' values and in turn, your own? Are you keeping up with contemporary issues? Are you learning to work with others in problem solving situations? If you are conscious daily of your long-term goals, as you progress you will find yourself developing as an individual and your college experience becoming a coherent, cumulative, and unified experience.

As I mentioned in the opening paragraph, to achieve success in your college experience demands a personal responsibility greater than any you may have experienced. This book can help you assume this responsibility and avoid many of the pitfalls and problems of learning with which you will be faced. Keep it close to your study area for easy reference. All of those who have contributed to this book have participated in situations similar to those which you are now facing, with many of the same feelings of inadequacy, uncertainty, or general unsureness which you may experience. Their advice is based upon both their experience as students and years of teaching students at the college level. It is their hope and that of the author that you may profit from these suggestions. Use them to develop both your mind and life to its fullest potential. Remember, your mind and life are the only ones that you will ever have. Best wishes for your success.

PART 1

ACADEMIC EXCELLENCE

Section 1

Factors in Learning

Chapter 1

ALL ABOUT GRADES

"The greatest wealth that one can have in this world is learning. Through learning everything that is desirable becomes achievable."

Thiruvalluvar,
3rd century B.C philosopher,
poet, and saint of India,
Author of "Thirukural"

TOPICS

1. The Importance of Learning
2. Knowledge is Power
3. What is a Grade?
4. The Importance of Good Grades
5. Are Grades an Index of One's Scholarship?
6. Variations in the Award of Grades
7. Role of Professor's Bias in Awarding Grades
8. High Grades and Your Future Life
9. Interpretation of Grades

THE IMPORTANCE OF LEARNING

Never before in the history of civilization have we had a greater need for learning. Today we live in a technological society that has linked all corners of the world with an unprecedented network of communication and transportation. High technology and mass production offer many of us a standard of living undreamt of by previous generations. However, while today's world has so much to offer for the pleasure and enjoyment of a person, it also demands that he/she know much more about the world than previous generations—both for survival and employment. Today's world has evolved into a system of complex activities of many facets and levels, and to find employment in this complex society one must have a certain level of formalized education and training through schools and colleges.

Learning, per se, is to gain knowledge through study and experience. Schools and colleges aim to provide opportunities and facilities so that the student can help himself/herself to attain a certain degree of competence in the subject matter chosen for study.

While it is possible to find a job without going through a formalized educational program, the fact remains that monetary remunerations and job security are much higher for the jobs that need specialized knowledge and training. It is obvious that there is no need to over-emphasize the importance of learning, in general, and of college education, in particular.

KNOWLEDGE IS POWER

Among the many sources of power for a human being, nothing is more unique than knowledge. It was a superior knowledge of military science and strategy in warfare that made the diminutive General Napoleon Bonaparte successful in his military ventures. In a game of chess, success undoubtedly belongs to the player with a better knowledge of the game.

In the modern business world, the knowledge of the product they make and sell comes first as the key element for the companies and corporations not only for making a profit but also for their very survival.

The same is true for a person as far as knowledge and success are concerned. Specialized knowledge is the order of the day. When you acquire specialized knowledge your career prospects improve. College is the right place to get started on acquiring this basic ingredient of your future success. It is the learning aspect of acquiring knowledge that we are primarily concerned about in this book. Learning takes time and effort on the part of the seeker of knowledge, and as such it is worthwhile to know the various techniques of learning appropriate to the subject matter.

WHAT IS A GRADE?

Webster's Dictionary defines a grade as "a stage in a process." It can be one of the successive levels of a school or a college course that usually represents a semester's or a year's work. It can also be a mark indicating a particular grade, such as a student's accomplishment of a particular piece of work.

Grading is a crude attempt on the part of the instructor to assign a level of classification to those on the receiving end in formalized education, which has been necessitated by the marked individual differences in student groups in the average classroom. It is supposed to reflect the level of achievement or scholarship in the subject matter of the course. Grade per se is but a symbol used to measure the learning process artificially, and as such it may or may not be an accurate measure. The most important thing for you to be aware of is that the grade with all its limitations is the controlling factor in your student career, and you must take it seriously.

THE IMPORTANCE OF GOOD GRADES

There are seven important reasons why you should strive for high grades:

1. Admission to a college of your choice is largely dependent on good grades. Almost all colleges and universities across the country have admission standards which place heavy emphasis on the student's grades. Whereas a student with mediocre grades is likely to be rejected by many colleges, the student with all round high grades gets numerous invitations from reputed institutions.

2. Again, admissions to professional colleges such as medical, engineering, and law, are dependent on the student's high grades in

the qualifying or entrance examinations. The same is true for the admission to graduate education leading to the master's and doctorate degrees where the acceptance standards are, in general, very high. Among other things, in these cases, high grades play a major role in determining the future education of the student and in fulfilling his ambitions and desires as far as higher education is concerned. High grades have the potential to make his dreams come true in so far as giving a shape to his professional future.

3. Graduation from high school or college requires a certain minimum grade point average which may vary from one institution to another. However, the fact remains that without the minimum passing grades no one can "make it" through the school or college after entering it. Of course, to graduate with honors and distinction one needs to get the highest possible grades consistently to meet the school's requirements for their achievement.

4. Not all students are fortunate enough not to need any financial aid or loan to get them through the college years. Almost all colleges have some form of financial aid varying from a small student loan to a direct grant of several thousand dollars to deserving students. High grades are a major factor in qualifying for scholarships and grants, and many loans require a minimum grade point average.

Even for the seemingly small jobs around the campus such as a laboratory assistant, paper grader, secretary for a department, or resident assistant in the dormitories, decent grades are required to show seriousness, sincerity and hard work on the part of the student. Do not brush these jobs aside as insignificant. I have seen over the years that students who take them seriously and do a good job are ones who become successful in their later careers. These jobs serve as a training ground to develop the success potential of the student.

5. Grades serve as a feedback for the student in his/her progress towards his/her cherished goal, the graduation, especially in the pre-senior years, whether in the high school or the college or even in the advanced graduate program. Looking at past grades the student is able to plan better for the semesters ahead and reschedule his plan of study, if needed. They indicate his/her strengths and weaknesses in the various academic programs. They serve as a prior warning signal to alert the student of the need for a better strategy in his/her approach to the courses he needs to master.

6. The purpose of learning has taken a new meaning in the modern technological era. It is geared towards obtaining a "diploma" or a "degree", which in turn serves as a passport to a job. Of course, having a job is a matter of survival for many and as such its importance can not be understated. The first thing a potential employer looks at, though he may not admit it, is the high school or college grades. The grades tell him more about you than you can tell him about yourself in the interview. They serve as an index to locate your potential strengths and weaknesses from his view point for the optimum utilization of your knowledge and training.

7. Another important reason to aim for high grades is their impact on you subjectively. Good grades can make you feel good. Psychologically speaking, consistent good grades can increase your self-confidence and help build a positive self-image.

ARE GRADES AN INDEX OF ONE'S SCHOLARSHIP?

Yes and no! Grades are the reflection of a complex combination of many factors such as the student's grasp of the subject matter, his/her attitude to learning, the techniques of preparation for the test, techniques of taking the test, ability to communicate on the test, skill of writing, emotional stability during the test, and above all, the bias of the teacher. This is the reason why you often come across the situation where a seemingly knowledgeable and hard-working student gets a poor grade and the happy-go-lucky person who spends most of his/her evenings on activities other than studying ends up with a high grade. Certainly the latter knew something that the former did not, and it has been reflected in the grade.

This is exactly the subject matter of the first part of this book. The purpose is to present to you a complete picture of all the factors that influence the grade, so that you can optimize your time and energy not just to get higher grades but also to graduate with a sense of pride and accomplishment in your scholarship and true learning.

VARIATIONS IN THE AWARD OF GRADES

There is no universal standard in the award of grades by teachers, though they follow certain guide lines either provided by the institution or by themselves. In general, most teachers go by the point system whereby they count the points accumulated by the student throughout the semester through quizzes, tests, home-assignments, laboratory reports, and other means outlined by the teacher at the beginning of the semester. Letter grades are assigned based on the points accumulated. A is excellent, B is good, C is fair, D is poor but passing, and F is a failure to pass the course.

Though this looks nice and logical on paper, the point-system is heavily biased by the methods of awarding points and the type of test employed. It is the teacher who generally decides what type of testing is appropriate for the subject matter tested and makes up the test. Again, the teacher's personal decision shows up in his method of evaluation of the test and in assigning "partial-credits" for incorrect answers.

ROLE OF THE PROFESSOR'S BIAS IN AWARDING GRADES

Professors are human beings and as such there are bound to be differences in their functioning as teachers. Teaching is role-playing like any other profession. The professor reacts with the external world—in this case the students—through his/her personality. His/her attitudes and emotional experiences in and outside of the classroom have a profound influence on the professor's method of testing and evaluating the student's learning. It is not uncommon often to see a professor, however well qualified and adept in the art of teaching, accused of being hostile to one or a group of students, showing undue favoritism in the grading of tests and in giving the final grades.

Of course, you don't always have the option to choose a course and the professor, but whenever there is a choice, go for the professor who is more humanistic and shows genuine concern for his/her students.

HIGH GRADES AND YOUR FUTURE LIFE

Do high grades obtained in the high school or college make a person become successful in his/her future life? This is a constantly debated question for which there is no definite answer. Persons with poor grades in the school years have been known to become successful leaders in business and politics, and on the same token some with high grades have turned out to be miserable failures in the personal, family and financial aspects of their lives. However, persons with high grades very often do become quite successful, and persons with low grades sometimes do not make a significant mark in life after school.

Life is a continuous process of learning. For that reason the day of graduation is appropriately called the day of commencement. Those who learn the laws of success and apply them in their lives, knowingly or unknowingly, are the ones who become successful, and this, precisely, is what you are expected to do after graduation. There is no better time to inculcate the habit of learning than in your high school and college days. Behavioral psychologists affirm that good habits reinforce your positive personality and contribute to your physical and mental well-being. Thus, working for high grades systematically in your school and college years has the potential to influence your future life by developing habits conducive to success.

Another thing you must be aware of is that the final grade sheet at your graduation, whether you like it not, is like a branding iron for a horse, which is stamped with it for life. Every time you try for a new job, your grade sheet is looked into, as well as your experiences and accomplishments, by the potential employer. The good impression a high grade sheet makes, or the poor impression a low grade sheet makes, need not be overemphasized.

There is yet another element in going for high grades which you may not think much of at present. Someday when you will be talking to your children or grand-children about the importance of their going to school and getting good grades, you can proudly cite yourself as an example. Nothing impresses children more than seeing their own parents and grand-parents as good role models.

INTERPRETATION OF GRADES

By Robert P. Scholl, Jr.

**Robert P. Scholl, Jr., M.A.,
W V College of Graduate Studies,
Registrar and Director of Admissions,
W V Institute of Technology**

College like any other institution of learning measures and records the performances if its participants. How one performs is a matter of record and is normally kept in the Registrar's Office at the college or university.

Semester Grade Report

To understand student records we must first start with the semester or quarter grade report.

Typically, colleges and universities produce a semester or quarter grade report much like the example below. It contains three specific items of interest to the student:

    (a) grades in each class for the particular marking period,

    (b) grade average for the current term, and

    (c) a cumulative of the student's grade point average.

To arrive at the student's grade point average, we use a system of quality points. Numerical values are assigned to each letter grade.

A = 4 quality points per semester or quarter hour
B = 3 quality points per semester or quarter hour
C = 2 quality points per semester or quarter hour
D = 1 quality point per semester or quarter hour
F = 0 quality points per semester or quarter hour

CLASS	SEM. HOUR	GRADE	QUALITY POINT	COMPUTATION
World Civilization	3	B	9	3 (grade of B) × 3 (sem. hrs.)
Music	2	C	4	2 (grade of C) × 2 (sem. hrs.)
Freshman Composition	3	B	9	3 (grade of B) × 3 (sem. hrs.)
Physical Education	1	A	4	4 (grade of A) × 1 (sem. hrs.)
General Biology	4	C	8	2 (grade of C) × 4 (sem. hrs.)
Prin. of Sociology	3	B	9	3 (grade of B) × 3 (sem. hrs.)
	16		43	= 2.688

To calculate the student's grade point average we divide the total semester hours attempted into the total quality points. Using the example in Figure 1 the student's average would be 2.688 (43 quality points divided by 16 semester hours = 2.688.

College Transcript

In addition to the semester grade report, the student's total record of his/her performance, semester by semester, is entered on a college transcript. The college transcript is the student's confidential record of his/her performance and cannot be released to anyone without the written consent of the student. Note the two examples in Figures 2 and 3 which have been provided by the American Association of Collegiate Registrar and Admission Officers.

To graduate, the student must achieve a minimum grade point average of 2.00 (C) in all college work attempted. This would include his current college plus, if he/she is a transfer, his/her work from the previous college. A college might also require the student to have a 2.00 (C) on course work taken at their institution. In addition, many colleges require a student to have a 2.00 (C) in their major or professional courses. For example, a Business major would include all business courses, a Nursing major would include nursing courses plus laboratory sciences, while an Engineering major would include engineering, math, and physics.

Each college has a policy unique to their institution, so you should refer to the college catalog under "requirements for graduation" to familiarize yourself with your particular major.

Graduation with Honors

Students who achieve a cumulative academic average as determined by the college are granted the distinction of graduation with honors. The student is recognized at commencement and their transcript is noted with the level of achievement.

Summa cum laude   3.750

Magna cum laude   3.500

Cum laude   3.250

Keep in mind that these averages reflect one college's level of honors. You will find variations between colleges, so check with your college to see what grade point is required.

The D & F Repeat Rule

One of the more significant changes which benefits the student is the D & F Repeat rule. A student who earns a D or F grade no later than the semester in which a total of 60 hours were attempted may repeat the course and have the original grade deleted from their cumulative grade point average. The student can only utilize the repeat one time in any particular course and it must be repeated prior to their earning the baccalaureate degree. You should check with your college regarding their D & F Repeat policy.

NAME OF COLLEGE

CITY, STATE

DEPT.	COURSE	COURSE DESCRIPTION	GRADE	CREDIT HRS.	QUAL. POINTS
HIST	105	World Civilization I	B	3	9
ARTX	141	Music	C	2	4
ENGL	101	Freshman Composition	B	3	9
PHED	101	Physical Education	A	1	4
BIOL	101	General Biology	C	4	8
SOCI	221	Prin of Sociology	B	3	9

STUDENT NAME

DATE	STUDENT NO.	ADVISOR	SUMMARY	HOURS EARNED	HOURS ATTEMPTED	QUALITY POINTS	POINT AVERAGE
			CURRENT SEMESTER	16	16	43	2.688
			CUMULATIVE	33	33	94	2.848

GRADING EXPLANATION

A • EXCELLENT - 4 POINTS   W • WITHDRAWAL
B • GOOD - 3 POINTS   X AUDIT   =
C • AVERAGE - 2 POINTS
D • PASSING - 1 POINTS
F • FAILURE - 0 POINTS
I • INCOMPLETE - 0 POINTS

Figure 1. A typical semester grade report

AACRAO SAMPLE UNIVERSITY
State Center, USA 9999

STUDENT
NAME   Student, John D.

STUDENT
NUMBER   999-99-9999

DEGREE(S)
CONFERRED: Requirements not yet completed

CURRENT
PROGRAM   Geography

DATE   June 22, 1984
PRINTED

PAGE
NO. 1 of 1

DEPT	COURSE	COURSE TITLE	CREDITS	GRD	DEPT	COURSE	COURSE TITLE	CREDITS	GRD
		Transfer Credits Accepted From State College 1980-81					SPRING SEMESTER 1983		
					GEO	325	Europe	3.0	C
					GEO	574	Aerial Photo	3.0	C
SOC	101	Intro to Soc	5.0		APS	321	Basic Stat	3.0	C
MAT	101	College Algebra	5.0				SEM TOTAL 9 Cr Ernd 18.0 PE 2.00 GPA		
HLT	101	Personal Health	4.0						
MUS	101	Intro to Music	3.0				FALL SEMESTER 1984		
PHY	281	Aerobic Dance	2.0		HEC	238	Sex Roles Amer	3.0	C
		Total Credits Accepted 19 Credits			GEO	351	Pop & Settlem	3.0	D
					POS	101	Govt & The Ind	4.0	F
							SEM TOTAL 6 Cr Ernd 9.0 PE 0.90 GPA		
		FALL SEMESTER 1981					ACADEMIC DISMISSAL		
HST	190	Sources & Lit	3.0	C			Undergraduate Total		
ENG	166	Medieval Engl	5.0	D			85 Cr Ernd 116 PE 1.76 GPA		
PSY	100	Hum Grow & Dv	3.0	C					
PSY	106	Educational	3.0	D					
		SEM TOTAL 14 Cr Ernd 20.0 PE 1.43 GPA					***********END OF TRANSCRIPT***************		
		SPRING SEMESTER 1982							
ENG	417	Lit Fr Adoles	3.0	C					
SED	320	Teach Engl	5.0	C					
ENG	586	Chaucer	3.0	C					
SED	301	2nd Student Teach	5.0	D					
		SEM TOTAL 16 Cr Ernd 27.0 PE 1.69 GPA							
		FALL SEMESTER 1982							
FHD	381	Adolescence	3.0	D					
GEO	223	Economic	3.0	F					
GEO	302	Africa	3.0	C					
GEO	588	Geogr Methods	3.0	C					
		SEM TOTAL 9 Cr Ernd 15.0 PE .25 GPA							
		ACADEMIC SUSPENSION							
		READMITTED ON PROBATION INTO THE DEPT OF GEOGRAPHY							
		FALL SEMESTER 1983							
GEO	328	Latin Americ	3.0	C					
GEO	370	Arctic & Alp	3.0	B	TRANSCRIPT IS VALID				
GEO	381	Geomorphlogy	3.0	C	ONLY IF UNIVERSITY				
GEO	595	Computer Cart	3.0	C	SEAL AND SIGNATURE				
		SEM TOTAL 12 Cr Ernd 27.0 PE 2.25 GPA			OF THE REGISTRAR ARE AFFIXED				
		***CONTINUED ON NEXT COLUMN ***							

I CCORDANCE WITH THE FAMILY EDUCATIONAL RIGHTS AND PRIVACY ACT OF 1974, AS AMENDED, THIS INFORMATION IS RELEASED ON THE CONDITION THAT YOU WILL NOT PERMIT ANY OTHER PARTY TO HAVE ACCESS TO THIS INFORMATION WITHOUT THE WRITTEN CONSENT OF THE INDIVIDUAL WHOSE RECORD IT IS.

Figure 2. A typical college transcript

STUDENT NAME:	Student, John D.	AACRAO SAMPLE UNIVERSITY	DEGREE(S) CONFERRED:	B. S. Geography

STUDENT NAME: Student, John D.
STUDENT NUMBER: 123456
DATE OF BIRTH August 9. 1962
PAGE NO. 1 of 1

AACRAO SAMPLE UNIVERSITY
State Center, USA 99999

DEGREE(S) CONFERRED: B. S. Geography
June 3, 1983
Cum Laude

DATE PRINTED: 04/04/84

DEPT	NUMBER	COURSE TITLE	CREDIT HRS	GRADE		DEPT	NUMBER	COURSE TITLE	CREDIT HRS	GRADE
		COLLEGE LEVEL EXAMINATION PROGRAM						FALL QUARTER 1982		
		August 1980				MATH	105	College Algebra	5.0	B
		Natural Science				GEOG	328	Latin America	3.0	A
		Biological	10.0	P		GEOG	370	Artic and Alpine	3.0	B
		Physical	10.0	P		GEOG	381	Geomorphlogy	3.0	A
		Humanities	10.0	P		QTR TOTAL		14.0 Cr Ernd 48.0 PE 3.43 GPA CUM 3.55		
		English	6.0	P				DEANS LIST		
		Soc Sci & Hist	10.0	P						
								WINTER QUARTER 1983		
		Transfer Credits Accepted				PSYCH	101	Gen Psychology	5.0	A
		From State College				GEOG	325	Europe	3.0	B
		City, State 1980-81				GEOG	574	Aerial Photo Interp	4.0	A
		71 Credits Accepted				MUSIC	101	Enjoying Music	3.0	A
						QTR TOTAL		15.0 Cr Ernd 57.0 PE 3.80 GPA CUM 3.61		
		FALL QUARTER 1981						DEANS LIST		
HIST	190	Sources and Lit	3.0	A						
ENGL	166	Medieval Engl Lit	5.0	B				SPRING QUARTER 1983		
PSY	100	Hum Growth and Dev	3.0	C		ECON	200	Economics I	5.0	B
PSY	106	Educational	3.0	A		HECE	238	Sex Roles in Amer	3.0	A
QTR TOTAL		14.0 Cr Ernd 45.0 PE 3.21 GPA CUM 3.21				GEOG	351	Population & Settl	3.0	A
		DEANS LIST				POLS	101	Govt & The Individ	3.0	B
						QTR TOTAL		14.0 Cr Ernd 48.0 PE 3.43 GPA.CUM 3.58		
		SPRING QUARTER 1982						DEANS LIST		
HIST	170	American Civil	5.0	A						
GEOG	223	Economic	3.0	A				REQUIREMENTS COMPLETED FOR BS 060383		
GEog	302	Africa	3.0	A				X-X-X-X-X-X-X-X-X-X-X-X-X-X-X-X-X-X-X-X-X-X-X-X-X-X-X-X		
GEOG	588	Geographic Methods	3.0	A						
QTR TOTAL		14.0 Cr Ernd 56.0 PE 4.00 GPA CUM 3.61						TOTAL UNDERGRAD 188.0 Cr Ernd 503.0 PE 3.58 GPA		
		DEANS LIST						**********END OF TRANSCRIPT*********		

CONTINUED ON NEXT COLUMN

TRANSCRIPT IS VALID
ONLY IF UNIVERSITY
SEAL AND SIGNATURE
OF THE REGISTRAR
ARE AFFIXED

IN ACCORDANCE WITH THE FAMILY EDUCATIONAL RIGHTS AND PRIVACY ACT OF 1974, AS AMENDED, THIS INFORMATION IS RELEASED ON THE CONDITION THAT YOU WILL NOT PERMIT ANY OTHER PARTY TO HAVE ACCESS TO THIS INFORMATION WITHOUT THE WRITTEN CONSENT OF THE INDIVIDUAL WHOSE RECORD IT IS.

Figure 3. A typical college transcript

Chapter 2

MOTIVATION: THE PSYCHOLOGICAL FACTOR IN LEARNING

You can only lead a horse to water or take a bucket of water to the horse; It is for the horse to drink.

—Western Proverb

A genuine desire to learn is the key to the achievement of high grades in any course. Learning itself is an active process. It is not a passive absorption of facts and figures, or the mere reading of books and notes, or listening to lectures with a view to reproduce what has been read and heard.

TOPICS

1. Learning—A Subjective Experience
2. The Three Factors in Learning
3. Motivation—The Psychological Factor
4. Intrinsic Motivation
5. Cognitive Motivation
6. Extrinsic Motivation
7. Triggered Motivation
8. Reasons Why Students Do Not Get Motivated
9. First Test Syndrome
10. Freshman First Semester Blues

LEARNING—A SUBJECTIVE EXPERIENCE

Learning is a subjective experience on the part of the learner and every bit of true learning adds up to his/her intellect in the same manner that tiny droplets of water accumulate in a bucket, so imperceptibly but yet increasingly. True learning is the knowledge acquired through understanding which becomes a part of one's intellect. It is an enriched experience stored in the memory cells of the brain available for recall at a later time.

In humans all learning is instigated by one or more of the following factors:

1. Necessity (need)
2. Curiosity
3. The desire to excel
4. The joy of learning for learning's sake.

The old adage that necessity is the mother of invention aptly portrays the very foundation of learning. Psychologist Abraham Maslow recognized the hierarchy of needs in the human behavioral plane, starting from one's own survival to the point of self-actualization. At this point the individual raises himself/herself to the highest possible level of physical and mental achievement, in line with his/her innate potentials. Fulfillment of these needs necessitates learning as a means and sets the human being in a perpetual state of continuous learning.

Curiosity is an innate characteristic of all bioorganisms, more so in humans. Behind the action of exploring the environment lies the survival instinct, guiding and learning to avoid real or imagined threats. Behind curiosity lies another innate instinct noticeable distinctly in humans—the desire to excel. It is this desire to excel that instigates the person to take up activities conducive to learning. In my book Self-Excellence, it has been pointed out that only human beings have it in their power to bring about a secondary evolution through conscious and wilful effort—a state of betterment of the self, physically, emotionally, and intellectually, using the innate instinct to excel.

Learning results in the acquisition of knowledge and skill, which, of course, are desirable. Apart from this, the very process of learning itself is capable of inducing a sense of joy and elation in the learner. It is this element of joy that perpetuates learning for its own sake. Reading as a hobby has its roots in this element.

THE THREE FACTORS IN LEARNING

Learning emanates from the survival instinct, and as such it can be noticed as an activity in all bioorganisms in their interaction with their respective environments. Activity is brought about by an intangible innate element in the organism which psychologists call the motivation. Motivation is the psychological component of the learning process and constitutes the primary factor. The other two factors in the learning process are the physiological and the environmental which mainly condition the quality and the degree of learning. They are discussed elsewhere in this book.

MOTIVATION—THE PSYCHOLOGICAL FACTOR

Motivation is the very heart of your learning process. It is the propelling force that gears you up to take your study seriously. It lets you go after your goals in your learning. Motivation sustains and directs your interest and efforts in all the various activities which result in learning. It lets you take up hard work, long hours of studying and burning the so-called "midnight" oil, sacrificing the immediate pleasures and comforts, and makes you feel good about yourself.

Basically, two kinds of motivation are recognizable from a psychological point of view: intrinsic and extrinsic—originating from the inside and outside of the person's mind respectively. Two other forms of recognizable motivation, cognitive and triggered, are also briefly presented below.

INTRINSIC MOTIVATION

The first law of behavioral psychology is that all bioorganisms act at their own self-interest, which is all the more valid in human beings. The desire to take on a particular activity is ignited in the individual when he/she feels an innate liking for the activity or when one perceives a direct benefit to the self. It is important that you realize this fact. In it lies the key to getting high grades and graduating successfully.

There are some courses that may not interest you at all, whereas you will be naturally drawn to some other courses. This aspect of a person's nature is rooted in one's inherent inclinations which is hard to describe or define, other than saying that it is innate for that person. Nevertheless the inherent inclinations are paths of least resistance for the person in the choice of activities. In activities that are in line with your inherent inclinations you will be naturally motivated and you will enjoy doing them no matter how hard they appear to others. Besides, the activity itself becomes a source of joy and you are easily bound to it. Educational psychologists call this intrinsic motivation. It emanates from the affective or feeling part of the human mind, and as such it is purely subjective. Only you will know what you naturally like.

COGNITIVE MOTIVATION

There will be many courses and activities, such as turning in home assignments and reports, which you will have to go through during your student years, whether you like them or not. But when you realize that they are needed for your graduation, and when you constantly keep in view your goal to graduate and fulfil your career plans, it becomes a part of your self-interest. Once your self-interest is associated with the course or activity, it provides the motivation for you not only to complete the task, but even to excel. This form of motivation emanates from the cognitive or perceiving part of the human mind. I prefer to call this cognitive motivation, which is motivation you create by putting a task into perspective with your goals and plans for the future. It is a strong ally to intrinsic motivation and it provides a synergistic effect in achieving high grades.

EXTRINSIC MOTIVATION

Rewards

The factors that motivate you to learn but which are external to the learning activity itself are referred to as extrinsic motivation.

Praise from peers, teachers, and parents, and rewards in the form of money, scholarships, exemptions, social approval and increased job potential are but a few of the external sources of motivation. Though by themselves they are no match for the intrinsic and the cognitive motivations, they do play a positive role in your learning process.

Punishment

On the same token, negative factors such as punishment, blame, and penalty for not learning are not only poor external motivators, but also can kill the enthusiasm of the student—the vital ingredient needed for effective learning. Professors genuinely interested in the progress of the student's learning do not resort to them.

Rivalry

Rivalry between individuals as a form of extrinsic motivation must be avoided because it invariably leads to resentment, jealousy, and an excessively competitive spirit which eclipses the pleasure in the learning activity. Group rivalry is not bad as it tends to generate some stimulation among members of the group. But the major drawbacks are in the need for a leader of the group to function effectively, and the possibility of some members of the group not being motivated at all.

Self-rivalry or the rivalry in the form of competition with one's own past record is the most desirable form of motivation. However, this is purely subjective in the sense that it is for the student to induce himself/herself to take up the challenge of bettering oneself. This is one aspect of self-excellence which is discussed elsewhere in this book.

TRIGGERED MOTIVATION

There is yet another form of motivation which occurs spontaneously for an individual. An event or a person that can induce an emotional outburst can trigger motivation for action and achievement. It is not uncommon for students suddenly to get motivated and become serious in their studies when they are under the spell of love. Meeting celebrities who had been the object of hero-worship could trigger some motivation for achievement in the field of specialty of the celebrities. Failure in a test in a course that is the favorite subject of the student can also trigger motivation to do better in the next test. In all these cases, it is the emotional element awakened in the individual that is responsible for bringing about a positive change.

REASONS WHY STUDENTS DO NOT GET MOTIVATED

Wrong Major

There are several reasons why a student is not motivated to study harder and work for high grades. The foremost reason is that the student is not interested in the subject matter of the course, or the course major for which he/she has been signed. This often happens when the parental wish overrides the student's natural inclinations in the name of "guidance". For example, when a parental desire for their son/daughter to become a medical doctor or an engineer clashes with the young one's desire to become an accountant, a powerful conflict occurs in the mind of the student. When he/she cannot openly rebel for fear of incurring the displeasure of the loving parents, all attempts to conform and study are to no avail due to the mental block.

If you are in such a situation, talk to your academic advisor and a student counselor to get the message to your parents, along with your telling them directly. It is important that you choose a major because you like it, or at least because you think you will like it.

Negative Self-Image

A negative self-image on the part of the student often prevents him/her from achieving the highest grades. He/she decides, based on some past unpleasant experiences, that he/she cannot get good grades in a course, and so what is the use of working hard in that course. What the student does not realize is that he/she has a tremendous intellectual potential which is waiting to be released through his/her self-effort. It is the faulty attitude towards oneself lacking in self-confidence that reflects in the lack of interest in the subject matter of the course, which in turn, leads to a poor grade. The methods of improving your self-image are discussed elsewhere in this book.

FIRST TEST SYNDROME

The first test in a series of tests counted for the final grade is critical for the student. A high score on the first test tends to boost up the morale and also his/her interest in the subject matter. However, a low score has the potential to undermine the self-confidence of the student and also diminish his/her interest in the subject matter. Teachers who care about their students are sensitive to this fact. Many among them have a policy of dropping one bad test from a series. Such a policy greatly helps the student to try to make amends and improve himself/herself on the next test, and minimizes the agony of a bad start. Of course, you do not always come across professors who care. When you are faced with such a situation, the right thing to do would be to take on a positive attitude that you can do better on the next test and keep studying unmindful of the first test result.

FRESHMAN FIRST SEMESTER BLUES

The first semester in college is a traumatic experience for some students. Away from the security and comfort of parental cushion, the need to face the realities of living alone in the dormitory and taking care of personal chores can be devastating to them. Though it may look simple to others, it is an emotional experience for them until they get used to the new way of life. Some take longer than others. It is during this time that their ability to concentrate on academic matters, home assignments, and tests falls to its lowest ebb. Student counselors can be a great help in restoring their confidence in themselves during this stressful time.

Chapter 3

STUDENT STRESS
AND
HOW TO MANAGE IT

"A mind that is in a state of agitation is far from being in a state of preparedness for learning. It is the still water of the lake that reflects the beauty of the moon."

—Eastern Proverb

TOPICS

1. Effect of Stress on Performance
2. Financial Stress
3. Psychological Stress
4. Health Stress
5. Techno-phobia and Techno-Stress
6. Interpersonal Relation Stress
7. Commuter Stress
8. Handicapped Student Stress
9. Late Starter Stress
10. Married Student Stress

EFFECT OF STRESS ON PERFORMANCE

Not all students go through the formal learning process in schools and colleges under ideal and equal conditions. Many have severe financial and other problems while trying to study and compete for high grades. The impact of these extraneous problems on the student results in his/her mental discomfort of varying degrees, depending on the magnitude and severity of the problems, commonly known as student stress. Nevertheless, the student's progress of learning in a course or a program of study is judged mainly through intellectual achievement demonstrated by tests and reports. Unfortunately, the stress in the emotional part of the mind has a profound influence on the cognitive part of the mind which is associated with all learning processes. This stress induces bodily and mental tension and impedes the activity of learning.

Thus, it is apparent that a student under constant stress of one kind or other is more likely to suffer and not be able to put forth his/her best performance, though he/she may normally be a good student.

Hence, it is important that a student who aspires for high grades should become familiar with all the negative forces that prevent him/her from achieving his/her goal and take proper steps to ensure the most favorable conditions conducive to learning. Following are the nine different types of stress most often encountered by students sometime or other during their learning years:

1. Financial stress
2. Psychological stress
3. Health stress
4. Techno-phobia and techno-stress
5. Interpersonal relation stress
6. Commuter stress
7. Handicapped student stress
8. Late starter stress
9. Married student stress.

FINANCIAL STRESS

Fortunate indeed is the student who has no financial problems, either due to parental grace or his own efforts. Some scholarships and fellowships also can make a student financially adequate and alleviate financial stress. He/she can devote substantial time and effort to learning and the betterment of grades.

However, if you are one of those who must work and go to college at the same time, then you must be aware of the fact that your work time is carved out of your study time. It is not just the time-sharing; working, depending on the type of job, saps the energy needed for study and the associated tasks. The net result is reflected in poor grades in tests, poor quality reports and poor attention in the classroom lectures, thus pushing you away from scoring high grades.

Supplementing your finances through a work-study program administered by your college is not that bad. Such a program is specifically designed to help needy students, and as such a hard-working student should be able to go through the work-study without undue damage to his grade point average.

Low-interest, long-term student loans from banks and other sources are the best alternative to working for those whose finances fall short of their needs for college education. A commitment to a long-term loan often works as an extrinsic motivation to do well in the courses and graduate with honors in order to land the best possible job.

PSYCHOLOGICAL STRESS

Psychological stress is purely subjective and is felt by the individual as frustration, anxiety, fear or a phobia, all of which have a detrimental effect on the learning process. They are related to the self-image and the value-system of the student. A student with a positive self-image has less problems in adapting to the educational system. He/she enjoys the various activities associated with learning. On the other hand, a student with a poor self-image has more problems in adjusting to the learning process. Self-image is discussed more in detail in the next chapter.

Anxiety and Fear of Tests

It is natural for anyone to feel a sense of anxiety at approaching tests or examinations. Anxiety is an emotional response that is vague and undefined due to the unspecific nature of the outcome of the test.

It is the fear of failure that becomes the source of stress for students who can not accept failure as part of the learning process. You usually learn more about yourself through failure than through success, and without a reasonable knowledge of yourself, any sustained success is not possible. Though psychological in origin, the stress manifests itself somatically. In extreme cases, a student-blackout and/or profuse perspiring are noticeable before or during a test.

Of course, these are abnormal reactions in a student indicative of psychological stress. It is advisable that such a student should seek help from counselors or psychologists who are professionally trained to alleviate the negative effects of stress. What you have to bear in mind is that when a test becomes a potential stressor, it corrodes the ability to learn and stands in the way of achieving high grades. It also takes the pleasure out of the learning process.

Dislike or Fear of a Teacher

The process of learning in formalized institutions like schools, colleges, and universities is built on the premise that the teacher in a classroom setting plays the role of a leader and provides efficient leadership to the aspiring student in his/her progress in learning. A healthy emotional link between the teacher and the student is an essential element in the learning process. Unfortunately, this has often become the weakest link in many a class, and the student nurtures secretly or openly a feeling of dislike, animosity, or fear of a teacher for various reasons. No matter what the reason is, the student will not be in a position to apply himself/herself fully to his/her course work, and as a result, not only do high grades become elusive, but also a general dislike for the subject matter of the course is likely to develop.

Of course, you can not always drop the class and avoid the teacher at your will and pleasure. A required course for your graduation taught only by the teacher whom you don't like puts you in a tight spot. There is nothing much you can do about this. Accept what you can not change and adapt to the situation as well as you can. Try to establish personal contact with the teacher by asking questions related to the subject matter, preferably in his/her office. Most teachers are more receptive in their own offices than in the classrooms. These personal contacts help to reduce your stress and concentrate on learning in that course.

HEALTH STRESS

You may not normally have major problems with your health during your college years, but there may be times when calamity may strike in the form of a personal injury sustained from playing a friendly game of football or baseball, or from an automobile accident. It may also come in the form of an illness of short or long duration and you may be forced to miss a few days or weeks of classes and tests. The uncomfortable feelings in your mind and the physical pains in your body make it impossible for you to concentrate and study. Together with the missed classes they make you slip behind in your learning.

Under these circumstances you should try to do what you can. Most colleges have clear policies regarding missed classes due to injury or illness. Check with the administration office of your college and do what is necessary to satisfy their regulations, such as obtaining a medical certificate as a legitimate excuse for not attending classes. The most important thing is that you talk to the teachers of the missed classes and try to make up for the missed lessons, assignments, and tests. Most teachers will be sympathetic to your plight and try to help you out. Nevertheless, the mental strain that you go through in all this has a direct influence on your learning and grades. You may not be at your efficient best to get top grades. You have to learn to accept such inevitable situations in your life and adapt suitably to their demands.

TECHNOPHOBIA AND TECHNOSTRESS

With computers, personal to mainframe, entering our educational system from kindergarten to college, a new era of technologically oriented learning has dawned. Key-boards, monitor screens, disk drives and printers associated with the learning through computers have begun to occupy more and more office and classroom table spaces. Their contribution in the student's learning process is an acknowledged fact, and their place in our educational system is firmly established.

However, a few inherent drawbacks in the use of computers as far as the student's learning process is concerned may be pointed out here, relevant to the theme of this book. Foremost is the frustration that develops following an unresolved problem when the student does not know how to proceed further; worse yet is when he/she does not know what mistake he/she has made, but the computer refuses to proceed and keeps beeping or blinking at him/her!

Some people have an unfounded, but innate, dislike or phobia for the use of technological equipment. If you are one of them, it may affect your grades in a course where the use of computers has been prescribed. Just like any other phobia, this may look trivial to others but is real and painful to the phobia-sufferer. This is aptly called technophobia.

Computer Addiction

On the other end of the scale, another problem emanating from the computer is computer-addiction. When a person gets addicted to the computer screen and spends long hours in front of it, he/she develops a tendency to shrink away from other humans on the emotional plane. He/she would rather spend the leisure time in front of a computer screen instead of socializing with people. His/her interpersonal relationships tend to become poor, and many young marriages have been found to be on the rocks for this reason. The stress induced by the computer addiction is called technostress by behavioral psychologists.

INTERPERSONAL RELATION STRESS

Stress due to interpersonal relation could be a major problem for most students during their school and college years. It is a factor to be aware of for the aspiring student determined to be successful after graduation. A genuine respect for the self and the other person constitutes the basis for effective communication and long-standing relationships with peers and others. A healthy friendship is an outcome of good interpersonal relationship.

A student who shies away from others and keeps a low profile is a candidate for loneliness, which can be stressful in itself. Making

friends is an important aspect of one's student-life. It has a subtle contribution to your developing a self-excellent personality. Boy-friend/girl-friend problems are indicative of the conflicts in their relationship, which in turn can negatively affect progress in learning and grades.

COMMUTER STRESS

Many a student who has chosen to live off campus often finds himself/herself at a disadvantage, particularly with time management. Precious time is often wasted in peak hour traffic or in finding a parking space around the campus. Dependence on the automobile to reach the classroom also presents other problems. It is important that you should avoid, or at least minimize, the need to drive to and from classes and use that time effectively for learning. You need to mobilize every minute of your available time not only for study-related activities, but also for relaxation and socializing with your friends.

HANDICAPPED STUDENT STRESS

Seldom do we realize the stress experienced by a handicapped student in his/her pursuit of an education. The physical handicap puts a lot of strain on these students to carry out even the routine tasks of reaching the classrooms, laboratories, etc., besides competing with the rest of the class for high grades. However, many are driven by a strong will to succeed. If you are handicapped in anyway, do not feel disheartened on any account. All people, even those who seem to have everything going for them, have their own limitations. A positive attitude that you can make it, an indomitable will to go through your life one day at a time, and a burning desire on your part not just to pass but to excel will take you along the path of progressive learning and lead you to the coveted goal of graduation with distinction.

LATE STARTER STRESS

Students who come to college after a short or long break since their high school graduation may generally find the first semester very rough—even traumatic. They have to make adjustments and adaptations in many aspects of their life. Since they might have forgotten some of the basics in the academic area, they need to study doubly hard to catch up with the rest of the class. Finding themselves taking classes with people who are many years younger than they will be a new experience. However, the late starters have in general one thing in common—a desire to get a college degree in a major they have set their mind on. When this desire is strong enough it will provide adequate motivation to weather the difficulties of getting started.

Also, the intervening years spent in the real world either on a job or other pursuits have made them realize the importance of a college education. For these reasons, late starters in general are able to overcome the initial hurdles and become successful in their college education. If you are a late starter, my suggestion for you is to keep working systematically and regularly on your lessons and assignments until you have no gaps in your fundamental understanding. In the meanwhile, do not pay much attention to the grades you get on the tests.

MARRIED STUDENT STRESS

Married students have to attend to two different fronts at the same time—and as such their time is to be shared or managed between their studies and spouses, and with their family if they have children. Needless to say, it could be stressful to some, particularly when their financial stability is low. It is not uncommon for one of the spouses to work on a job to put the other through college. It places added strain on the working spouse, if he/she also has to cook and do the household chores. There is no standard solution to married student stress. Each couple must work out a satisfactory agreement between themselves as to how best manage the college years for the sake of a better future.

Chapter **4**

LEARNING, SELF-IMAGE, AND SELF-EXCELLENCE

"There is no value-judgment more important to man no factor more decisive in his psychological development and motivation—than the estimate he passes on himself".

Nathaniel Branden,
author of "The Psychology of Self-Esteem"

TOPICS

1. Self-Image
2. Learning and Self-image
3. Self-Image and Interpersonal Relations.
4. Self-Image and Self-Esteem
5. Positive Mental Attitude
6. Self-Confidence
7. Self-Discipline
8. Self-Psychoanalysis: Know Yourself
9. How to Improve Your Self-Image
10. Self-Excellence

SELF-IMAGE

Dr. Maxwell Maltz points out in his book "Psychocybernetics" that the key to success in any of your undertakings lies in your self-image. What is this self-image? Psychologists refer to it as the latent undefined perception of the self by the self. It is the subjective view of yourself with which you interact and react with the outside world. It reflects the emotional, intellectual, creative and spiritual components of your personality. A positive self-image implies a well-adjusted and confident personality, capable of adaptation to the realities of the environment. A negative self-image, on the other hand, implies a lack of emotional stability and self-confidence in interacting with the outside world, often resulting in conflicts at the conscious or subconscious levels of the mind. Every unresolved conflict in the mind is a potential source of stress which can prevent the psychological maturation of the person, thereby influencing his or her personality traits.

Self-image is not, fortunately, a fixed or constant identity. Like a tree it keeps growing and changing though the process is not perceptible. Emotional experiences which leave indelible marks on the consciousness and cognition play a key role in the molding and shaping of the self-image. It is amenable for analysis only subjectively, but to others it reveals itself as the personality in an objective sense.

LEARNING AND SELF-IMAGE

In as much as you are unique in your physical structure, you are also unique in your psychological make-up, giving you the uniqueness of your self-image. It is important that you recognize this fact because in it lies the secret of self-improvement through self-effort, towards the fulfillment of your goals and aspirations in life, including getting better grades and graduating with distinction.

Educational psychologists have observed that those with a positive self-image display a healthy attitude towards learning itself, formal or informal, and consistently get good grades. They adapt themselves more easily to the system and accept the rigors of the learning process with pleasure. On the other hand, those with a negative self-image have been found to have problems in their adaptation to the rigors and routines of the learning process and they do not derive a sense of self-satisfaction from their involvement. Negative self-image prevents the individual from utilizing his or her full potentials, and prevents him or her from putting forth maximum effort.

SELF-IMAGE AND INTERPERSONAL RELATIONS

The influence of self-image is nowhere more obvious than in the sphere of interpersonal relations. There is a need for everyone to interact with others in the course of daily living, whether it is at home, the office, the classroom, or outside, in a meaningful manner. Modern living itself implies some form of interpersonal relations for everyone, and that is the basis of organized social living. Yet, many people undergo tremendous stress in interpersonal relations. Conflicts with parents at home, with friends during dating and with peer groups are reflective of the person's inability for meaningful interaction with others, which stems from his or her self-image.

A positive self-image has the potential for a sound and realistic relationship with others, whereas a negative or a weak self-image becomes a source of stress for the individual in dealing with other people.

SELF-IMAGE AND SELF-ESTEEM

Self-esteem is the respect that one develops for oneself. It is the subjective worth of the person in his or her own eye. Self-esteem develops through the feedback one gets from others for the behavioral responses in the past, and it is cumulative in the sense that it is the net result of all previous responses. It is closely linked with the sense of values of the person, which, in turn, has its roots in his or her socio-cultural and religious environments during the formative years as a child. Later, the emotional experiences in day-to-day living provide modifications on the person's worth as a human being, and there emerges the self-image with its own self-esteem. A positive self-image and high self-esteem go hand in hand, in as much as a negative self-image and low self-esteem do.

In the learning process, getting high grades enhances the self-esteem, thus contributing to a positive self-image, whereas low and failing grades have the potential to induce low self-esteem and a poor self-image. Psychologist Nathaniel Branden, in his book, "The Psychology of Self-Esteem", mentions that man's need for self-esteem is inherent in his nature. That being the case, it is only natural that a student should take every effort to go for high grades, which can result in high self-esteem and reinforce a confident self. Also, educational psychologists have observed that those low in self-esteem tend to be reserved, easily upset, timid and lacking in self-confidence. People with positive self images and high self-esteem are usually successful in whatever they choose to do and are able to enjoy life to the fullest. For this one reason alone, it is worth developing a positive self-image and high self-esteem.

POSITIVE MENTAL ATTITUDE

Psychologist F. A. Fredenburg asserts that there is probably no more important concept within the realm of social psychology than that of attitude. Attitudes refer to a person's convictions as to whether something is good or bad, acceptable or not, and worth going along with or not. What makes attitude important is the emotional appeal inherent in it. Attitudes are generally formed from past experiences of pain and pleasure associated with activities and from faiths and beliefs derived from childhood environments and exposures. Attitudes tend to be highly resistant to change, more because of the personal component—like and dislike—than because of factual information.

During the first year at college many students are suddenly exposed to ideas, beliefs, facts, and attitudes that are in sharp conflict with their childhood views. It is inevitable that they undergo a reevaluation of their attitudes during this stage of their development. There is nothing wrong in this as far as you, as a college student, are concerned because college serves as a testing ground for old faiths and beliefs. However, you should be on the alert to develop new attitudes based on facts and knowledge and not on peer pressure alone. It is the positive mental attitudes towards study, career, and life itself that are going to pave the way for your success in these areas and enrich your life.

SELF-CONFIDENCE

Self-confidence is the conviction that one is competent to think, to judge, to know, and to correct one's errors. Easy as it sounds, self-confidence does not come by itself easily. It is an acquired state of mind obtained through knowledge (learning) and experience. This means that one must be willing to apply oneself to a task and keep an open mind to learn from the outcome. It is the cumulative effect at the psychological level from the past successes and failures that manifests itself as self-confidence for that person.

It is essential that you should become aware of this fact, because in it lies the key to getting better grades on your tests and graduating with distinction. Remember that self-confidence is founded on both successes and failures which constitute the cumulative experience. It is your willingness and a positive mental attitude to take them in the same stride and learn from them that will slowly but steadily make yours a confident self.

SELF-DISCIPLINE

Another psychological component of a person of great significance in achieving academic excellence in college and career excellence later in professional life is self-discipline. Self-discipline is the manifest indication of motivation which serves as the driving force for a person to work towards goals. Efficient time management and undertaking arduous tasks with willingness are easily possible for the self-disciplined. In fact, without self-discipline, achievement potential in human beings has no meaning.

Self-discipline is a subjective phenomenon and as such it cannot be infused by others. However, when a person is motivated by whatever means, extrinsically or intrinsically, self-discipline shows up in his/her activities.

SELF-PSYCHOANALYSIS: KNOW THYSELF

Since the center stage of your life revolves on the "I" concept, it is essential that you learn more about "I". "Who am I?" is not just a philosophical question but it has a lot of meaning particularly in the modern technological era of multitudinous career potentials. While there may not be one single satisfactory answer, you should at least try to find out what your strengths and weaknesses, likes and dislikes, inherent inclinations, and your own value-system are. The inherent inclinations of a person carry the seed of success in them. When a person undertakes an activity for which he/she has no natural inclination, it is unlikely that he/she will excel in that direction.

This fact is worth remembering when you choose majors for your college study as well as careers for your future life.

HOW TO IMPROVE YOUR SELF-IMAGE

Can self-image be improved? Subjective psychologists say "yes". The following 5 step-technique, when practiced consistently and with faith, can do a lot to improve your self-image:

1. Have faith in yourself as a human being whose potentials are no less than anybody else's.
2. Suggest to yourself that you can do what others can do.
3. In your conversations avoid using statements like,
   "I can never do things right"
   "I always go wrong"
   "I commit too many mistakes"
   "I am hanging in there"
   "I am not that good-looking".
   Instead, always use the positive side only.
4. Develop a creative hobby based on something you like best and spend at least half an hour everyday on this activity. Self-discipline yourself to practice this EVERY DAY. Soon you will become proficient in this hobby of yours and acquire greater skills as days pass by, and a sense of achievement will be a natural outcome. Nothing can give a greater boost to your self-image than this single act of yours.
5. Learn to respect other people and their opinions. Modify your behavior towards others by always being courteous and polite. Remember the law: respect begets respect. Respect

from others will push up your self-esteem, thereby your self-image.

SELF-EXCELLENCE

To excel is an innate human need. Civilization is itself a constant manifestation of the progress of man in the application of his physical and mental prowess to better his environments in which he can not only survive but live well by successful adaptation. This adaptation is considered as a secondary evolution of the human being from his birth to death by Hans Selye, the author of "Stress of Life". Going to schools and colleges with a view to get a formal education is nothing else but a process of adaptation in the secondary evolution of the person. The learning acquired is expected to make him/her suitable for whatever role the learner has set his/her mind on during later years. Successful adaptation brings him/her health and happiness while failure to do so leaves him/her sick in body and unhappy in mind.

You have it in your power to influence this secondary evolution to a considerable extent during your school and college years through willful adaptation to student life and striving for excellence—excellence of body and mind. The totality of body-mind improvement for successful adaptation is called self-excellence in my book "Self-Excellence". It is the reflection of the self-image which is capable of meeting the challenges of life and dealing with them constructively. It is a subjective and self-realized state of being, physically and mentally. It includes the homeostasis of the body, equanimity of the mind, and the creativity of the intellect. Your learning potential is at its best during such a state of self-excellence.

Self-excellence is not a static process. It is continuous and dynamic. It is a way of life. Efforts toward keeping the body in excellent physical health, developing a confident self-image through positive mental attitudes, developing the intellect through planned continuous education, and developing sound interpersonal relations constitute the basics of self-excellence.

Chapter **5**

LEARNING, NERVOUS SYSTEM, AND MEMORY

"Cognition is the process of knowing. It is also the product of the act of knowing. Cognition includes thoughts, bits of information, memory elements, as well as mental symbols and the processes by which those symbols are acquired and manipulated".

Philip G. Zimbardo,
author of "Psychology and Life"

TOPICS

THE THREE QUESTIONS

To learn is to gain knowledge or understanding of whatever that is sought to be learned. Learning is a subjective experience on the part of the learner and as such no one can do it for another. Educational psychologists define learning as the experience of knowing. That which is once experienced is held in the memory for relatively short or long periods of time, making it available for recall any time during this period. Memory is the greatest gift that Mother Nature has provided. Memory alleviates the need to learn again what is learned once. However, we do tend to forget what is learned once, sometimes slowly, sometimes quickly. Then, there arise three questions:

1. How do we experience learning?
2. How do we remember?, and
3. How do we forget?

The answers lie in the physiological domain of the individual in his/her nervous system. Hence, let us briefly review the relevant factors of the nervous system that have a bearing on learning, remembering, and forgetting.

THE FIVE TOOLS OF LEARNING

We learn about the world around us by means of our senses. It is generally considered that human beings have five primary senses: sight, hearing, touch, smell, and taste. Modern scientists have added to the list the secondary senses of pressure, heat, cold, and pain.

There are several steps in the process of sensing. When a stimulus acts on the nerves in one of the sense organs, nerve impulses from the sense organ travel to the brain. In the brain, the impulses are interpreted as a feeling or a sensation. Though all of these sense organs are important for the functioning of the person as a whole, the two so-called higher senses—vision and hearing, are the most important from the point of view of learning and getting high grades. It is important for you to have an overall understanding of the process of how a stimulus from the outside world reaches your brain, how it provides the "experience", and how it is stored and retrieved as "information" when you need it. The secret of learning, remembering and forgetting is entombed in this knowledge.

NEURONS AND SYNAPTIC TRANSMISSION

Anything that you read or hear, in order to become a part of your knowledge, must reach your brain. The stimulus acts on the nerves of the sense organ and is carried as nerve impulses from the sense organ to the brain through a series of connected nerve cells called neurons. The neurons and their fibers constitute a network that covers the entire inside of the body and all of the skin. They have star-shaped bodies with two kinds of long cytoplasmic fibers projecting from them. Messages or impulses to the cell body are carried by the nerve fibers known as dendrites. From the other side of the cell body there extends a long, thick nerve fiber which ends in slender, branching threads of protoplasm. These nerve fibers are called axons. Axons are enclosed in flattened cell sheaths. They carry messages away from the cell body.

Neurons that carry messages from sensory organs to the central nervous system are sensory neurons; those that carry messages from the nervous system to the muscles or organs are motor neurons. The long fibers of neurons are arranged in groups or bundles commonly called nerves.

The continuity of nerve impulse transmission from one neuron to the adjacent one is effected through what is known as a synaptic connection or simply as a synapse. The narrow space between the terminal membranes of the linking neurons is referred to as the synaptic gap. The nerve impulse, due to a stimuli from the outside world or from the brain, travels in only one direction from neuron to neuron by the instantaneous release of a neurotransmitter, a chemical released by the transmitting neuron which carries the message to the receiving neuron across the synaptic gap.

THE HUMAN NERVOUS SYSTEM

Our ability to learn about, understand and react to the world around us depends on our nervous system as a whole. The brain and spinal cord compose the central nervous system; whereas, the cranial and spinal nerves constitute the peripheral system.

In fact, the nervous system is a control and communication system that originates and coordinates our physical reactions to the environment. It also controls the involuntary muscles and organs such as the heart and lungs through an autonomic nervous system. The autonomic system is concerned with the bodily changes which accompany the emotions. The nerves that bring nerve impulses into the central system are called afferent nerves, and the nerves that conduct impulses to the reacting organs and muscles are called efferent nerves.

THE BRAIN

Central to the nervous system is the brain, the most complex and specialized organ of the body. All human learning, remembering and forgetting take place in the brain. It guides our movements, interprets the senses and above all, enables us to think.

The brain is made up of the cerebrum, cerebellum, pons and medulla. The cerebrum, the main part of the brain, is divided into right and left halves, called the hemispheres. The outer surface of the cerebrum is the cortex. It is wrinkled in structure and irregularly shaped, with deep furrows that help to increase the brain's surface area. The forebrain, located in the front of the cerebrum, is the site of the most complex functions of human thought and action. These functions include memory, judgment, reasoning, speech and the formation of words. The forebrain is also considered to be the seat of emotions and the personality traits. The interpretations of the senses of sight, hearing, taste, smell, and touch are carried out in the cerebrum.

Also, on the cerebral cortex lies the motor area where motor impulses arise, which cause contractions of voluntary muscles.

The midbrain controls vision and eye reflexes, involuntary muscle activities, and motor responses of the head and torso. The hindbrain consists of the cerebellum and pons and is located behind and below the cerebrum. The hindbrain coordinates muscular activity and amplifies cerebral stimuli on their way to the muscles.

The thalamus lies within the lower part of the brain. It is an important relay center for both motor and sensory impulses. The hypothalamus, one of the most important parts of the brain, is situated below the thalamus and close to the hypophysis (Pituitary gland). Various autonomic functions are controlled from centers in the hypothalamus. It is a regulatory center for both the sympathetic and parasympathetic divisions of the autonomic nervous system.

Many neuropsychologists consider the hypothalamus as the body-mind bridge, the elusive connection between matter (the molecules of the cells) and non-matter (the consciousness pervading the cells) of the body. The hypothalamus responds to the surging emotions, considered to originate in the limbic system of the brain, by activating the pituitary gland, which, in turn, activates the other endocrine glands. The corresponding state of mind is reflected in the pattern of the brain-waves, such as an emotional or agitated state, and the varying degrees of a relaxed state, including sleep. The brain is always active, whether you are awake or sleep. It stops functioning only at death.

LEARNING AND BRAIN WAVES

Ability to learn is intimately linked with the emotional state of the person. A physically and mentally relaxed state is conducive for learning. The most relaxed waking state is referred to as the alpha state. During this state the brain sends out electrical impulses predominantly in the range of 8 to 13 cycles per second, known as alpha waves.

Brain waves of frequency higher than 13 cycles per second are indicative of an agitated or emotional state of the mind. 'They are called beta waves. When a person is in a highly agitated or emotional state of mind, such as under the influence of anger, fear, or grief,his/her intellectual ability to learn or respond to the outside world in a rational manner is very much impaired. Emotions cloud the reasoning process and no true learning is possible during such a state. It is important that you be aware of this fact when you aspire for high grades. You should always aim to keep yourself in the relaxed alpha state during your study hours, no matter what part of the day you are working at your lessons.

Brain waves lower than 7 cycles per second are indicative of a drowsy or sleepy state. Waves of frequencies from 3 to 7 cycles per second are called theta waves and those lower than 3 are known as delta waves. Theta and delta are not waking states and as such are obviously not suited for learning. Deep meditative states also produce brain waves of theta and delta rhythm.

MEMORY

Memory is the ability to recall events, information about previous experiences, or what has been learned before—a few minutes ago or many years ago. Memory of an event involves four phases:

1. Experiencing (encoding)
2. Storage
3. Retaining, and
4. Retrieval.

In short, to remember is to reinstate what has been previously learned. It is still a puzzle to modern science how we retain some of what has been learned and forget all else. It is generally believed that a change in the neural pathways in the brain must take place before learning may occur. The pathway is called a memory trace or an engram by neuro-psychologists. Modern research seems to indicate that ribonucleic acid (RNA) may be the physical basis for memory. According to this view, when learning takes place, an alteration of RNA molecules may occur in the cortex of the brain.

Some distinct aspects of the human memory have been recognized. In spite of the scanty knowledge about them, you can effectively use them in your learning and improve your overall memory when you become aware of their existence.

TRANSIENT MEMORY

Transient memory is the immediate recognition of the continuous sensorial information that reaches your brain through the five senses, just long enough for instant use in perception of the external world during your waking state of normal living. It is the built-in ability of the brain to make sense of one's own environment for effective adaptation. The perceived information is then almost forgotten so that the body's cellular energy may be conserved, and not wasted on trivial information not needed any longer than the time needed for its use—no more than a quarter-second, such as walking through a room but not remembering the color of the walls of the room.

SHORT-TERM MEMORY

Information perceived as needed a little longer by the brain for possible recall is held in a short-term storage. Finding an unfamiliar telephone number from the pages of a directory, holding it in the memory and dialing the number is a classical example of the use of short-term memory. After the dialing the number is usually lost to the brain and is forgotten. The short-term memory lasts from two to thirty seconds—just long enough to permit us to carry on the desired task and respond to the filtered input in other appropriate ways. Then it decays very rapidly if it is not further processed.

LONG-TERM MEMORY

There seems to be a buffer or a filter system in the brain beyond the short-term memory which provides a means of protecting the long-term memory from having to handle too much information. The buffer acts in a selective manner. It will handle only a limited number of items of information. However, the process is not random. Some information is favored over others. Familiarity, interest, emotional experience, concentration and repetition are but a few factors that seem to be responsible for such a selective process. Information getting through the buffer system gets implanted in the cells of the cerebral cortex and is available for recall for a long term. The retention of information over a period of time is largely dependent on a process that is called rehearsal. In familiar language, it means repetition, practice, or drill. Rehearsal prevents decay and loss of memory. The long-term memory is relatively more permanent and enduring, capable of lasting for months, years, perhaps the life time.

While we still do not know how exactly the long-term memory takes form, neuro-psychologists concur that a neural path is established through the synaptic gap of the neurons of the filter system in the cerebral cortex of the brain during rehearsals. The neural path is akin to a path of least resistance in the retention and decay characteristic of the brain.

PHOTOGRAPHIC MEMORY

Some individuals seem to possess imagery that is almost like actual perception in clarity and accuracy which psychologists call eidetic memory, commonly known as "photographic memory". Does photographic memory help in learning? Educational psychologists do not think so. Actually, eidetic memory obstructs clear thinking, rather than helping it. Persons with such a memory can reproduce what they have seen, but it is difficult for them to use this information in an analytic or synthetic manner. Abstract thinking and creative imagination require flexibility in thought which are not provided by eidetic memory.

FORGETTING

Forgetting is the loss of the ability to remember and recall. It is considered to occur primarily due to the decay of the memory trace over time in the brain and to some extent due to the interference from other experiences. Absence of recall of the stored information over a long period of time seems to be the primary cause of forgetting for most people. Organic causes can also compound the forgetting.

HOW TO IMPROVE YOUR MEMORY

Since memory is a function of the organism, it is limited by the inherited structure of the organism. However, for human beings the capacity for long-term memory is virtually limitless. By improvement of memory, therefore, we mean simply improvement in the techniques of learning and methods of memorizing and recall. They are presented in detail elsewhere in this book under effective study techniques.

It may be pointed out here that very often the problem lies in the lack of comprehension of the subject matter under study rather than in the memory. Comprehension implies the total understanding and grasping with the intellect, thus making the learning a meaningful experience. Poorly comprehended ideas and concepts seem to decay fast and get lost in the memory much sooner than wellcomprehended subject matter.

Section 2

Techniques for Learning

Chapter 6

STUMBLING BLOCKS TO LEARNING AND HIGH GRADES

"It cannot be, when the root is neglected, that what should spring from it will be well ordered. It never has been the case that what was of great importance has been slightly cared for, and, at the same time, that what was of slight importance has been greatly cared for".

Confucius (556–479 B.C),
Chinese saint and philosopher

TOPICS

1. Physiological Factors
2. Attitudinal Factors
3. Environmental Factors
4. Behavioral Factors Inside the Classroom
5. Behavioral Factors Outside the Classroom
6. Academic Factors
7. Personality Factors

When you aspire to graduate with high grades and distinction you must become aware of all the factors that act as stumbling blocks in your pursuit, which prevent you from reaching your goal. While you may not be able to eliminate all of them completely, you can at least manage them effectively—by doing something within your power, which can make the difference between low grades and high grades. These factors are presented in this chapter.

PHYSIOLOGICAL FACTORS

Vision

More than eighty percent of your learning is effected through your eye, the sense organ of vision, and as such it is of paramount importance that you pay attention to maintain a keen vision. Few eyes are perfect. Most have slight defects. However, fortunately many of these slight defects can be corrected by means of eye-glasses or contact lenses. Myopia or short-sightedness is one of the most common of such slight defects. Because of the fact that in the course of your college study you will be using your eyes so much for reading, it is most important that even the slightest defect should be remedied as much and as quick as possible.

Defective vision can also cause headaches which could adversely affect your concentration in your studies, thereby leading to poor grades. Have your eyes tested by a doctor and follow his instructions for better vision.

Hearing

The ear, the sense organ of hearing, comes next only to the eye in its importance in your learning process and response to external stimuli. Talking and listening are the foundations of learning and social behavior. A normal ear is capable of detecting the four types of auditory sensations—pitch, loudness, tone, and timbre or the quality of the sound.

Any defect in your hearing will affect your performance as a student for obvious reasons. If you have reasons to doubt your hearing ability, you must have it checked with your doctor for correctional measures.

General Health Problems

Minor and major health problems of various types can hit you any time from known and unknown sources. Their effect is always the same as far as your learning is concerned—to interfere with your efficiency of learning. Whereas you may be able to manage minor illnesses yourself most of the time, you may have to seek medical attention for the serious ones which may keep you away from your classes for an extended period of time. Of course, there is nothing much you can do about such a calamity except accepting it as your ill-luck, but don't let it undermine your self-confidence. By paying attention to preventive health management techniques you will be able to alleviate most of the minor health problems.

ATTITUDINAL FACTORS

Attitudinal factors are psychological in origin. Whereas motivation is a positive psychological factor, the following attitudes of indifference on the part of the student are detrimental to effective learning and they act as stumbling blocks to achieving high grades.

Indifference to the Purpose of College Education

Many students do not realize and appreciate the true purpose of their college education. Some think of it as a recreational activity funded by their parents to have a good time while they are young. Seldom do they realize that colleges and universities are temples of learning where one is trained to equip oneself with knowledge needed not only for survival but also for enrichment of one's life. Such knowledge will shape the individual emotionally and intellectually into a mature person who, in turn, can enrich the society where he/she lives and works.

When the student becomes indifferent to this lofty purpose of college education, the desire to excel diminishes and a sense of drifting through with least effort for getting just the passing grades necessary for graduation takes over. Motivation takes the back seat and the student can not realize the need to put forth his/her best foot forward.

Indifference to the Human Potentials

Unlike other organisms of the animal world, man is endowed with enormous inherent potentials for learning, creativity, and adaptation. However, motivated self-effort is needed to unlock this potential through systematic and consistent learning. College education provides the ideal climate for the acquisition of this knowledge. However, when you are indifferent to this great human potential that is dormant in you, the seriousness of approach to college education is lost and you will not be in a position to put forth your best efforts.

Indifference to the Purpose of Living Itself

A healthy attitude towards life itself is necessary for all people who desire to lead a healthy, happy and successful life for themselves. Life is an one-time phenomenon as far as you as an individual is concerned. In order to make the most of your life, it is necessary for you to make it goal-oriented as well as task-oriented. What kind of goals? The goals should be such that working towards them will provide opportunities for your own self-expression and creativity, leading to self-fulfillment. Simply put, your goals should be emotionally satisfying to you.

However, when one not only does not have a positive attitude but also develops an indifference towards goal-oriented living, there is nothing much for that person to look forward to as worthwhile in life. How can such a person aim for high grades and graduate with distinction, which in itself is such a goal?

ENVIRONMENTAL FACTORS

Light

The physical environment greatly influences the effectiveness of your learning. The place of study should be well-lit to prevent eyestrain. Studying long hours in a poorly lit room will affect your vision in the long run. Also, it can affect your concentration. It is worth investing in a table lamp which can be adjusted in height and position to provide you with optimum light without glare and without casting a shadow on your work space as you write.

Noise

Noise in the place of study is a powerful stimuli that can easily undermine your concentration. Students living in dormitories and other places where noise is inevitable should take every effort to find a quiet place in study lounges and specially provided low-noise areas where they can study whenever they so desire. Noise per se is not bad. It is the intensity of it that is often disturbing. The human mind is capable of shutting itself off from external stimuli when it is functioning at high levels of concentration. This is the reason why you find that college union study areas and coffee shops are popular places of study for many students.

Music

Mild music in general is a natural relaxant and can help you to get started in a study session. However, continuous listening to music can weaken your concentration and jeopardize serious study. You are the best judge to know as to when and how to use music to your best advantage.

Temperature

Temperature, too warm or too cold, in your place of study is another environmental factor that can adversely affect the effectiveness of your learning. Proper clothing and controlled heating or cooling of the place can easily mitigate this problem.

People

Frequent interference from other people can sometimes be a major disturbing factor. It is mainly situational. However, one can easily take preventive measures to keep away from others by going to the library or elsewhere to carry out studies and assignments.

BEHAVIORAL FACTORS INSIDE THE CLASSROOM

Classroom Ethics

No other place is more contributory to human learning than the formal setting of a traditional classroom. It is not just that the teacher is supposed to teach and the student is to receive the words of wisdom in the classroom. Since individual instruction is almost impossible in the modern era of mass education, the grouping of students in one class is a necessity. Thus, there arises a need for basic ethics in classroom interaction, providing at the same time for a climate of effective learning. However, sitting in a class does not mean effective learning, nor does it guarantee high grades. What, then, are the factors that prevent the student from high grades related to classroom instructions? They are presented below.

Cutting Classes

The number one enemy for the serious student is "cutting" classes—the deliberate action of not showing up for the classes. Not being able to come to class due to a genuine reason is not implied by this. Most professors have a policy on unauthorized absenteeism. Whether they have a policy or not, the class cutter is running the high risk of a poor impression on the professor, which has a certain influence in the assignment of the final grade. Also, cutting classes widens the gap in the student's knowledge in that subject area which is bound to affect his performance in the tests and assignments.

Inattentiveness and Mind-wandering

Lack of concentration in listening to what the teacher is discussing in the class prevents the student from understanding the subject matter even though he is physically present. "Mind-wandering" is the most common student problem. Such is the nature of the mind. It is akin to a rider's ability to keep the reins of a horse, preventing the animal from wandering as it pleases. Disciplining oneself to listen to the teacher is both the function and purpose of classroom instruction. The secret of getting high grades is hidden in this self-discipline inculcated in the classroom.

Boredom

There is nothing more wasteful of one's energy than sitting bored in a classroom where others are listening and taking notes. Boredom is indicative of the person's lack of involvement in the learning process and a lack of enthusiasm. Cognitive motivation is the cure for boredom, but it must be brought about by the student himself/herself. If you have signed up for a course, then you should take every effort to make the most of the classroom time by getting interested in the subject matter of the course.

Not Asking Questions When One Should

During the course of the classroom lecture and discussion, it is natural that you will miss many things the professor has mentioned or you might not have understood what he/she said. It is important that you raise your hand to ask him/her to repeat or explain what you had missed. A small question on your part at the right time will save you later on hours of searching and finding out on your own. Also, a concept well understood in the classroom helps you to go ahead in your learning.

Not Taking Notes

Sitting and listening to the professor in a classroom, of course, is fine in your learning process. However, only a small percent of what the professor said is retained by your memory. When you go home and try to recall what all he/she mentioned in a lecture, you will find vast gaps in your recollection. You may remember how your brain's short-term and long-term memory systems work, which we had discussed earlier in this book. As an aid to the memory, if you were taking notes during the course of the lecture and noting down everything that the professor put on the board, you will find that you can recall for further analysis a far greater percentage of the matter discussed. Also, during note-taking your concentration is two-fold, both the senses of audition and vision being active. When you are aiming for high grades, you can not afford to overlook the importance of taking notes, no matter which class you are in—a descriptive subject like history or a conceptual subject like mathematics.

Not Turning in Assignments

Doing the out-of class assignments is an integral part of your learning. It provides understanding and reinforcement of the concept or topic under investigation. Most professors assign some credits to the outside assignments which are counted towards the final grades. Some give assignments but do not collect or grade them. Whatever is the policy, you should pay full attention to the assignments and do as you have been instructed. Systematically doing the assignments and keeping a record of them provides an excellent reference for that course which you can review before the exams. On the same token, by not turning in the assignments and not doing them at all you are robbing yourself of an excellent opportunity for learning and getting high grades.

Lack of Respect for the Professor

Classroom instruction is not a mechanistic process. Neither the professor nor the students are robots meeting in a classroom for the exchange of signals. Learning is most effective only when the student has respect for the professor. In an age when the professor can be dragged to a court of law by the student for a low grade received in a course, the element of respect for the professor in a classroom has, of course, quietly taken the back seat.

BEHAVIORAL FACTORS OUTSIDE THE CLASSROOM

Oversleep

It is important that you should get a good night's sleep before starting the next day. There is a considerable variation in the number of hours of sleep that is needed for various individuals; six to eight hours are generally adequate. You are the best judge to know your requirements, and as such adjust your daily activities and schedule them such that you get your minimum hours of sleep and no more. Oversleep is a potential time waster which you could and should avoid. The time wasted is usually at the expense of your effective time for study. Oversleep is habit forming. It will interfere with your class schedules in the morning. There is no excuse for missing classes due to oversleep. A little self-discipline and an inexpensive alarm clock are the simple remedies.

Eating

The quantity and the quality of your eating has a direct bearing on the efficiency of your studying and learning. While it is important that you eat a meal balanced in proteins, fats, carbohydrates, minerals and vitamins, you should avoid eating too big a meal. Your meal should be of such type and quantity to provide you with just enough calories to meet your energy requirement of the day and no more. The fat part of the meal should be unsaturated and low in cholesterol. Substitute fruits for pastries and desserts. Include more vegetables and fibers in your diet and cut down on red and smoked meats and pork. Go for fish and poultry instead. By paying attention to what you eat, when you eat, and how much you eat, you can keep yourself slim and trim. Besides, you can be very active mentally and physically. Heavy meals and hard to digest foods such as fats slow down your mental and physical processes, preventing you from working at your full capacity.

Alcohol, drugs and smoking

If you want to lead a creative and happy life, to enjoy all that life has to offer and to live long enough to visit many places of interest, you will do well to keep away from these triple killers.

Alcohol has ruined the lives of too many people, directly or indirectly. All drugs, except those medically prescribed and supervised in their use, lead to drug addiction, which, in turn, leads to physical and mental health problems. Cigarette smoking as a habit is no different from any drug addiction. Cigarette smoke contains nicotine, tar, and carbon monoxide. They act on the membrane walls of the alveoli, the tiny air sacs of the lungs, with long-term detrimental effect to the physical health of the smoker. To be short, as a serious student desirous of getting the best out of your college life, you owe it to yourself and to the bright future you are seeking to say "No" to alcohol, drugs, and smoking.

Too Much of Sports and Parties

It is good to play or watch sports of your liking for relaxation and for physical fitness. However, spending too much time on them is a drain on your effective study hours. It is all the more important for students who are "on the team". The long hours of practice sports, and the travel and play times are all done at the expense of their learning periods, not to mention field injuries which compound the problem. Besides, the stress of competitive sports is not conducive for effective learning. As a result, their grades slip by and graduation becomes difficult.

However, it is not all that bad for student-athletes who can approach studies and sports with a proper sense of balance in their priorities. Effective time management for his/her various academic and sports activities holds the key for success in studies and enjoyment in sports.

Social parties of peer groups and friends add pep to college life. They also provide opportunities for interpersonal relationship and relaxation. However, they must be kept within bounds both in time and content of the party. A party that runs late on a Sunday night does more harm than good for the participants.

There must be sports and there must be parties—you choose them for fun and relaxation, but don't let them rob your study time.

Dating

The college environment provides ample opportunities for both men and women students to meet members of the opposite sex for effective and meaningful interpersonal relationship, which often results in dating. Dating, in order to be a rewarding and enriching experience, should be approached with mutual respect. However, it has the potential to become an explosive drama and emotional trauma. It can also adversely affect the mood and studies of a person involved in an unpleasant situation. An aspirant of better grades should be aware of the impact of dating on his/her studies and take preventive measures to handle dating with care and respect.

Dating is intended to pave the way for getting to know the other person more and better so as to explore the possibility of longstanding friendship of mutual trust, and the compatibility of personalities. The cherished goal of dating is its culmination in mutual love and perhaps marriage at a future date. Obviously morals and ethics play a key role in the dating process, besides a genuine sense of caring for the feel-

ings of the other person. Dating often runs into turbulence because of the violation of the subtle principles of ethics, morals, and trust by one or both the partners.

On the positive side, when the dating matures into steadiness during the college years, the dating couple tend to take studies and life itself more seriously. Their grades certainly improve and they look forward to graduation with zeal and enthusiasm.

Too Much TV

Watching television has become an integral part of modern living. Many superb educational and scientific programs can be seen on television; so also, many programs of genuine entertainment. However, if one is not selective about the program and gets into the habit of watching all sorts of programs and games, one is likely to develop an addiction to the TV screen. Such an addiction is a non-productive activity and can consume an enormous amount of the student's off-class time, part of which, of course, should have gone for studies and doing assignments. You can easily visualize the devastating effect of TV addiction on your learning and grades when you deprive yourself of valuable, and effective study hours. There is no excuse for a student to place TV ahead of his learning schedule.

ACADEMIC FACTORS

Too Many Credit Hours

Another stumbling block for most above-average students is their greed to carry a few more credit hours than their optimum. They do so partly because of a delusion that they can complete the course curriculum earlier than the listed time frame in the catalog, and partly because they underestimate the time needed for assignments, laboratory reports, and term papers in the various courses. They don't realize that an extra three credits of overloading is literally carved out of the effective time apportioned for the other courses. The result is devastating on the whole. The student will not be able to do full justice to all the courses and the effect is distinctly noticeable in slipping grades. It can also result in a feeling of discomfort and mental stress.

If you find yourself in this situation, do not linger on until the end of the semester. Drop the overloading course or courses before the deadline for dropping without affecting your grades. All colleges have a policy and a deadline for dropping courses during mid-semester. Do not hesitate to take advantage of the deadline for dropping. Resume your normal load at which you are comfortable. You will, then, feel at ease and will be able to perform at your best since the pressure has been lessened.

Wrong Major

We have already discussed about the effect of a wrong major earlier in this book. Here, it should be pointed out that a wrong major acts as a stumbling block preventing the student from putting forth his/her best effort for learning. A wrong major implies the denial of opportunity for the natural unfolding of the student's potentials in the right direction.

PERSONALITY FACTORS

Procrastination

Of all the personality factors procrastination, the tendency to put off intentionally what can be done today, is the single most important factor which affects the grades directly. Many a good student falls a victim to this trait. Postponing working on long assignments, term papers, and laboratory reports makes things worse day by day as fresh assignments accumulate and the student finds himself/herself fighting on many fronts at the same time. Needless to say, he/she will not be able to put forth his/her best in all directions at the same time and something has to give way. Obviously, the grades are jeopardized.

If you are a procrastinator, there is some good news for you. Psychologists consider that the so-called personality traits, such as procrastination, are changeable through self-will and determination and through cognitive motivation. By cognizing the ill-effects of pro-crastination on your grades, you can motivate yourself to get rid of this stumbling block between you and high grades. It is the greatest gift that you can give to yourself, and you will feel yourself a different person. Getting rid of procrastination is a giant step towards self-excellence and future success.

Carelessness

Another trait of a student which has a tremendous significance in his/her grades is carelessness. It is nowhere more pronounced and profound in its impact than in tests and examinations. The so-called "silly" or "careless" mistakes in tests are more often a reflection of the personality of the student rather than being "silly" because there is no such thing as a silly mistake.

Consistent silly mistakes are a kind of learned carelessness without paying due attention to correctness of the learned material, and it forms into a habit. It is this habit that needs to be broken and replaced by a sense of attentiveness.

Impatience

Learning in general is a slow and steady process. It depends largely on the comprehending ability of the learner as well as the subject matter. Conceptual subjects could be hard to comprehend for the first time for most people and may require repeated attempts to learn. This is where patience is needed. Patience implies not getting frustrated at initial failures to understand, and constantly trying with the same zeal with which one started in the beginning. Patience implies not skipping pages of reading material after an enthusiastic beginning. Patience implies finishing an assignment once it is taken up. Patience also implies going over the finished task, be it report writing, problem-solving, or taking a test or examination.

Fortunately, patience is a cultivable virtue. Besides the learning situation, it has a direct bearing on your future success in the career world and in dealing with people.

Chapter 7

TIME MANAGEMENT AND GOAL-ACHIEVEMENT

"This automatic creative mechanism within you can operate in only one way. It must have a target to shoot at".

Maxwell Maltz,
author of "Psycho-Cybernetics"

TOPICS

Time Concept: The Seven Principles of Time Management
1. Time and Activity
2. Time and Money
3. Time Budget
4. Time for Planning and Review
5. Waking Time
6. Time Pressure and Stress
7. Human Biological Time Clock

Goal Setting and Achieving: The Seven Principles of Success
1. Goals and Emotional Satisfaction
2. Goals and Measurability
3. Goals and the Master-plan
4. Goals and the Time-Budget
5. Goals and the Sacrifice
6. Self-Discipline and the 3 D's
7. Goal-Feedback Relationship

A freshman entering a two or four-year college program or a graduate student registering for a master's or Ph.D. program naturally expects to complete the desired program in the specified time scale. It is implied in this expectation that he/she will be carrying a minimum load recommended by the academic advisor each semester, and that the student will be able to complete the signed-up courses every semester. In other words, a predetermined goal or goals have been built into the program, which, of course, is for the student to achieve using his/her available time and effort effectively. It will be worthwhile to review the principles of effective time management and goal-setting. With a basic understanding of these principles, it will be easy for you to work out a time schedule in relation to the goals desired and take appropriate steps to achieve them semester by semester through a system of sub-goals.

TIME CONCEPT: THE SEVEN PRINCIPLES OF TIME MANAGEMENT

1. Time and Activity

There is no such thing as time. It is a conceptualized entity which derives its meaning from the consciousness of activities by a person. Without consciousness there is no time. Time and activity go hand in glove such as thirty minutes of walking, studying, resting, etc. You must realize that it is the activity that you are engaged in that results in the desired effect and not time per se.

In order to get a result that you seek such as the completion of writing a report, you have to initiate the cause; that is, the activity of writing for a length of time. This results in your completed report. This in essence is the principle of cause and effect applied to time and activity. The point to remember is that you have to initiate the cause through an activity and the result will simply follow. Time then is the duration of the activity and, thus, it does not have a separate existence of its own.

2. Time and Money

For all practical purposes time is on a par with money. Both can be invested, expended, and wasted. Unlike money, time is available to you just one day at a time as the gift of life, and it is up to you to utilize it for your maximum benefit. While a person can choose to accumulate a substantial amount of money, no one can accumulate time. It can only be used more efficiently.

Time spent on studying and learning is obviously towards your goals and, as such, it is a good investment. Time spent in normal sleeping, eating, getting ready to go to classes and in other chores of daily routines can be considered as a necessary expenditure. Time spent in oversleeping, and in non-productive activities which are neither planned towards your goals nor for the maintenance of your bodily and mental health is a shear waste of your life energy. Time is obviously more valuable than money; lost money can be recovered, but not lost time.

3. Time Budget

Budgeting your time is the key in time management. Since the available time every day is a limited quantity, it is of paramount importance that you budget out your time to the various activities which you have planned for the day. Budgeting prevents the waste of your precious time on trivial and non-productive pursuits and lets you invest your time on goal-achieving activities.

4. Time for Planning and Review

Effective time management rests on the small amount of time spent on planning the time budget and reviewing the efficiency of the budget execution. On the face of it this principle may not appear very important, but I want to emphasize to you that it is my observation over the years that those who have learned and applied this simple principle to their daily activities have been successful not only during their college years, but also in their careers and professional lives. Five minutes of planning in the morning before starting your day and five minutes of review before going to bed is probably your most productive activity keeping you oriented towards success.

5. Waking Time

Time is meaningful only during your waking hours. It implies two things. One is that meaningful activities such as studying and learning can be done only when you are fully awake and alert, and the other is that spending longer hours in bed than needed for the body's well-being is done at the expense of your productive activities. Over-sleep means time lost on two fronts. On the same token, carving out one hour of waking period from routine sleep without detrimental effect on your health is doubly beneficial if it can be invested in a productive activity.

6. Time Pressure and Stress

Time pressure can induce psychosomatic responses. When the time and activities are not properly matched, that is, trying to accomplish too many things in too short a time, so-called time-pressure occurs and the unaccomplished activities induce frustration. Frustration is a common occurrence with students trying to catch up with missed lessons and assignments. Regardless of its source, frustration is an uncomfortable, unpleasant and disturbing experience. It acts on the mind producing discomfort and a state of tension, commonly referred to as stress.

Minor frustrations are normal human reactions and are not harmful to the well-being of a person. However, persons with low frustration tolerance are easily affected by stress and can develop stress-related ailments such as migraine headaches, peptic ulcer, high blood pressure, asthma, and skin rashes to mention a few.

7. Human Biological Time Clock

There is a biological time clock built in the human organism—and for that matter of fact in all bioorganisms—which regulates the body's cellular activities from the very conception of life to death. We do not know how the mechanism works; but we do know that our bodies' periodic functions such as sleep, wakefulness, hunger, thirst, etc., are regulated involuntarily through our nervous system. When we plan our activities without violating the body's natural functions, particularly sleep, the efficiency will be high. It is essential that you realize this fact in planning your study schedules to get the most out of your waking time.

GOAL SETTING AND ACHIEVING: THE SEVEN PRINCIPLES OF SUCCESS

1. Goals and Emotional Satisfaction

The term "goal" is highly personal. To be meaningful to the goal-seeker it should have an emotional connotation. Working toward a goal and its eventual achievement should be a source of pleasure and pride. Many a goal remains a goal and never achieved for want of this emotional element. One person's goal need not inspire another person to accept it as the goal for himself/herself. It is for this reason that the goals of parents as well as organizations often fall short of achievement.

For the goal to be meaningful, it is necessary that you believe in that goal and identify yourself with it. No goal is worth working for or achieving if it is not emotionally satisfying or intellectually rewarding to you. Motivation has its roots in this emotional element. When it is your goal to graduate with distinction, you will feel throbbing enthusiasm running through your veins to overcome all the hurdles on the way.

2. Goals and Measurability

Any goal is achievable only when it is measurable on a time scale and in terms of tangible results. When a goal is set, it is your activities that will take you towards the goal. How effectively you are moving towards the goal can be judged only by some measurable results on short-term and long-term basis. Any unforeseen difficulties and the rigidity of the planned activities can be gauged under this dual measurement, which, in turn, can make room for adjustments. The goal should be flexible enough to accommodate modifications but rigid enough to become a meaningful reality.

On the same token a note of caution must be exercised in the case of too flexible a goal. Such a goal easily loses its original objective and becomes side-tracked to reach nowhere.

It is not uncommon to find students getting side-tracked into working on a part-time or full-time job or "being on the team" and never arriving at the goal of graduation, let alone getting high grades.

3. Goals and the Master-plan

A master-plan for your life or for the intended years in college is a course of creative actions designed to take you to your desired destination. Each element of the master-plan constitutes a goal in itself. It is imperative that all the individual goals must be integrated into a sequential network on the time scale so that the orderly pattern of their achievements will lead you to the ultimate goal.

Once the goals are well defined and delineated, you should concentrate on one at a time until you achieve the objective of that goal. From an effective management point of view, it is better if you can organize your goals into three groups: immediate goals, short-range goals, and long-range goals. Immediate goals concern themselves with things to be done for the day and within the week. As for as your graduation is concerned, the semester goals can be considered as short-term goals, whereas graduation and commencement the long-term goals.

4. Goals and the Time-Budget

The 5-minute strategy planning at the beginning of the day which we mentioned a while ago is your key to daily time management in relation to your goals. It is very important that you realize the fact that you live only one day at a time. It is up to you to invest, spend, or waste the precious minutes and hours at your disposal. Once you are conscious of your immediate goals, budgeting the time for the various activities that are needed for their achievement becomes possible.

For greater effectiveness, put your strategy on paper in writing in a list of activities and their allotted time, prioritized for the day, and keep it right in front of you for periodic perusal during the day. You will be amazed at the amount of things you can do in a single working day, when you begin it with a "5-minute strategy planning" session.

Weekly goals and their budgeted time organized on the same pattern as the daily goals can take care of fluctuations and deviations that might happen during the week, without losing the direction.

5. Goals and the Sacrifice

A certain amount of sacrifice of personal comforts and conveniences of routine living is inherent in any goal-seeking mission. For instance, you might like to spend long hours in bed during week-ends, watch television, play your favorite game of football or tennis, and attend a party of beer, dance, and music which goes on until the small hours of the morning. If you keep your weekly and the semester goals in view, you will certainly realize the need to divert at least some of your week-end hours to studying for the impending tests the following week, the assignments due on Monday and doing some research for the term paper due in the following weeks.

I do not mean to imply that it should be all work and no play. On the contrary, you must have both. It is up to you to workout a judicious balance of your activities so that you can sacrifice some of your immediate "enjoyments" for the sake of long-term benefits through effective time management. I want to assure you of one thing. Even though it appears as if you are actually giving up a part of your "good time" for the sake of a goal, the truth of the matter is that you will get more enjoyment doing the goal-oriented activity because it is your goal and choice. It is a basic law in behavioral psychology that anything you do at your self-interest is a stimulating experience.

6. Self-Discipline and the 3 D's

Motivated action on your part provides the connection between your budgeted time and the desired goal. Without the element of action or execution, the time and goal have no meaning. Thomas Edison said that genius is one percent inspiration and 99 percent perspiration. The same is true in goal-oriented activities: Success is one percent inspiration and 99 percent perspiration. It is the action on your part that makes goals realizable.

Goal-oriented actions have their origin in your self-discipline—the single most important factor that you must be aware of. The secret of self-discipline lies in a 3-dimensional mental element constituted of desire, dream and determination. When your goal is an outcome of your desire, dream, and determination, you will find yourself motivated with enthusiasm to undertake activities towards your goal, however hard or insurmountable they may appear to be. Studying text books, problem solving for the course-work, carrying out laboratory experiments, and writing reports and term papers are among the many goal-oriented, time-budgeted activities on your part. When executed with gusto, the fruits of the activities accumulate and your ambitions of getting high grades and to graduate with distinction are certain to be fulfilled.

There is another side to planned action. Action has the potential to dissipate emotional stress and frustrations besides becoming a source of pleasure when it is initiated voluntarily. By the law of cause and effect, an initiated action must result in a reaction which is the outcome toward the goal or the goal itself. Regulation of time-budgeted activities, then, is the royal highway to success in the goal-oriented student-life.

Planned action has yet another benefit to the individual. It boosts his/her morale and reinforces the positive self-image, which, in itself, is a contributor to success.

7. Goal-Feedback Relationship

Many a goal-setter never achieves the goal—not for the lack of planning and hard work but for the lack of a feedback system in the goal-seeking activities. Feedbacks are indicators of the outcome of the activities so far carried out. Their message is loud and clear. They indicate whether you are on course, off the course or deviant from the course of your mission. Your performance in the quizzes, mid-term tests, lab reports etc., and the comfortable or uncomfortable feeling you get in learning a course are the feedbacks which you should not ignore. They let you know whether you are proceeding on the right track at the right speed or whether you need to modify or increase your efforts.

Almost all colleges provide an opportunity during the semester after about half-way to with-draw from the courses in which your performance is not to your anticipation. There is nothing wrong in dropping a course when things don't go well, and also when overloading is felt as a hindrance to the overall performance. Withdrawal is nothing else but a strategy modification in your goal-oriented mission.

Chapter **8**

EFFECTIVE STUDY TECHNIQUES

"What we need, therefore, is not a synthesis but a dynamic interplay between mystical intuition and scientific analysis".

Fritjof Capra,
author of "The Tao of Physics"

TOPICS

1. Prerequisite Factors:
   Reading Ability   Concentration
   Study-Habit Formation   Enthusiasm
   Unit Budgeting of Time   Organization

2. Study Techniques for Descriptive Subjects
   SQ3R Method
   Whole to Part Method (Gestalt Principle)
   Part to Whole Method
   Skimming and Scanning
   Fast Reading
   Overlearning
   Cramming
   Distributed Studying
   Mnemonic Devices
   Summary-Question Method

3. Study Techniques for Concept-Oriented Subjects
   Visualization
   Thinking through Sketches
   Equation Analysis
   Equation Charts

4. Study Techniques for Problem Oriented Subjects
   Visualization
   Free-body Diagram Analysis
   Model Problem Analysis
   Collection of Solved Problems.

In this chapter various study techniques are presented, which are suited for the different natures of the subjects under study, along with the prerequisite factors governing the application of these techniques. Seldom do students realize the role played by the prerequisite factors in the comprehension and absorption of the material that is being studied. The study techniques themselves are meaningful only when practiced along with these factors, and together they have a synergistic effect in your overall learning.

PREREQUISITE FACTORS

Reading Ability

Ability to read ranks foremost among all factors that contribute to comprehension and understanding of the material under study. For the freshman entering college it is a skill carried over from the high school. Whereas good reading is an asset for further learning, bad reading becomes a stumbling block in your progress. It is important that you take every step to improve your skill at reading, if you feel that you are deficient in this area.

Silent reading is preferable as you move up in your studies. Loud reading in the early years of schooling is intended primarily for correct pronunciation. The habit of reading aloud impedes the speed of reading. Since fast reading is essential for certain types of assignments you will be better off practicing silent and fast reading and becoming good at it.

The main reason for habitual slow reading is the lack of a bank of vocabulary. Vocabulary building is a continuous process and the best way is to stop at every new word you encounter and look it up in the dictionary. Keeping handy a good dictionary at your study table for immediate reference is a must when you aspire to get high grades and graduate with distinction. Though stopping reading in the middle of a page or a sentence and seeking the meaning of a word in the dictionary appears a slow process, it is not only the right method but also the best method to build your vocabulary in the long run.

Undoubtedly there are other rewards in the process. Discovering the new meanings of many words that you come across for the first time opens up the door for a better understanding of the ideas and concepts under reading. Also a sense of intellectual pleasure generally follows, of which you may or may not be aware. New words enrich the power of your expression, besides enhancing your comprehension of ideas and concepts.

Study-Habit Formation

It is a behavioral trend in us that the customary types of acting tend to persist. This is what we commonly refer to as the force of habit. This applies to both right and wrong habits, and it is at your best interest to form right habits that are contributory to learning. When habits are bad it takes additional effort and motivation to mitigate their negative effects before you can settle down to learn.

The habit of choosing the same time and place to study is a powerful contributor to effective studying. If you use the college library as your place of study, taking the same table at the same location at the same time will make you feel at ease with the environment. Your mind will quickly reach the so-called alpha state of relaxation, which is the most conducive and receptive state for effective learning.

Unit Budgeting of Time

From a practical stand point it is beneficial to start your study session with a 5-minute visualization period. During this period you project in your mind the stretch of time at your disposal for study and divide it into units of 30 minutes. For example, if you plan to study from 7.00 p.m. to 10.00 p.m. it is equivalent to 6 units of 30 minutes each. Depending on your need you may allocate a certain number of units such as 3 units for Mathematics, 2 units for English, etc., in your study plan for the evening.

For more efficient learning you should include a 5-minute relaxation period in each time unit. In other words, you study for 25 minutes at a stretch and take a relaxation break for 5 minutes. It does not mean that you leave the table every 25 minutes, but simply implies that you relax your stiffened muscles in locked up physical postures during your study. Educational psychologists have observed that the rate of absorption of the studied material slows down considerably after about 20 minutes of intense concentration. This is the rationale behind the 30 minute unit budgeting of your study time with a 5-minute relaxation.

Concentration

Concentration means one-pointed attention to whatever task a person is applying himself/herself. In the case of a student, it implies that the mind is focused on the activity of studying. Since studying is a psychophysical activity occurring during the waking state of the person, it is of utmost importance that the interference due to all external stimuli other than the ones related to the activity of studying be held to the minimum. Besides, the state of health of the physical body and the emotional state of the mind affect your concentration. You can imagine how well you can concentrate when you are dead tired after a strenuous football game, followed by a heavy meal and an emotional state of unabated anger at your team's poor performance that evening.

We saw before that when your brain emits electrical impulses from 7 to 13 cycles per second, called alpha waves, your body is totally relaxed and your mind is at its creative best. Such a state is generally known as the alpha state of relaxation. Alpha state is naturally conducive for concentration and learning. It is attainable at will by systematic training. By paying proper attention to your physical health and diet, you can train yourself to get to the alpha state of relaxation during your study sessions. Practicing a 5-minute meditation at the start of the study is ideal for inducing psychophysical relaxation of the alpha state.

Lack of concentration reduces the efficiency of your efforts at studying. The net result is spending more time at the study table and not assimilating what is studied. Poor grades are often the outcome of this correctable malady.

Enthusiasm

Enthusiasm is the very essence of living. It is the lingering fragrance of self-excellence. When you approach any activity with enthusiasm you are bound to succeed. That is a law of success. It is all the more true in your studies. Anything studied with enthusiasm is absorbed and retained in the brain cells; on the same token, anything that is not studied with enthusiasm does not make an impact and is lost to the memory. Herein lies your key for better grades and successful graduation.

Fortunately, enthusiasm is a cultivable habit. It is a reflection of the positive self-image and positive attitudes in life. When you become conscious of making the most of your valuable life, it is inevitable that you will become enthusiastic in anything you do. Enthusiasm promotes concentration and makes the learning process as enjoyable as any of your leisure time activities.

Organization

It may appear too common-place a suggestion but it is the organization of thoughts and activities that precedes the successful culmination of all human endeavors. In fact, learning itself implies developing an ability to organize by systematic planning and effort. Thus, organization becomes an automatic prerequisite in the process of studying to learn and get high grades. You can easily see for yourself the power of organization manifesting itself in the home-assignments, reports and tests of your fellow students, when you compare the grades earned by those who are generally well-organized and those who are not.

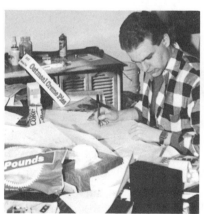 

With the prerequisites in place, we can now consider the various techniques suited for studying different subjects. It is important to recognize that the nature of the subject material under study can vary widely and as such no one technique will be suited for all. Some subjects may be descriptive, whereas some others may be either concept-oriented or problem-oriented; some may be design-oriented as in the case of many engineering subjects. Hence, for optimum learning you should become aware of the various study techniques and their appropriate use. They are presented in the following sections.

STUDY TECHNIQUES FOR DESCRIPTIVE SUBJECTS

SQ3R Method

SQ3R Method is in fact five strategies rolled into one: Survey, Question, Read, Recite, and Review. Two educational psychologists, Morgan and Deese, are credited with the formulation of this technique which has now been recognized as one of the most effective learning tools ever devised for a student.

In an initial survey you skim over the material in order to get an overview. The idea is to avoid jumping into detail before you know what is covered and where the details will be leading. You remember facts better if you get to know the general theme first. Often you will find it difficult to make much sense of what you have read for want of a knowledge of the theme. During the initial survey make a mental note of all the topics covered by chapter headings, titles and subtitles, tables, figures, any listed summaries and conclusions, etc. This will help to bring to focus in your mind the central theme of the subject matter. As you go along this reconnoitering survey, be watchful for key words and phrases that tend to repeat.

On the basis of this initial survey, next attempt to ask some questions about the material. What are the main points of the section or chapter? What is the order of development of these points? What appears to be the central theme? What appears to be totally new to you, etc. Asking questions immediately after the survey stage can further help in orienting you to the learning material and funnel the flow of your thoughts towards the main theme.

The third stage, reading, describes the process of actually reading the material thoroughly, now paying attention to the details. Most students start right away with reading the details and as a consequence get lost to the theme, often unable to even guess where anything is leading. You can see for yourself the power of the preliminary survey and question stages; they allow you "to see the beach and not just the grains of sand".

Reciting is the fourth stage. Reciting is reading or saying the material out loud. It leads to better retention of the material, which in turn ensures active attention rather than passive reception. It also ensures that your learning has reached the degree necessary for recall rather than only recognition. Educational psychologists believe that the effectiveness of such recitation, even in the absence of a check on accuracy, lies in the opportunity it provides for practice in retrieving the information—the strategy that will be most effective for you later on during your tests.

Finally, review what you have so far learned. Can you answer the questions asked initially? Can you remember how the material was organized? Have you figured out the central theme of your reading material? Review is both a critical evaluation and a judicial reexamination of the material of your study. Review enables you to direct your attention to parts which you might have missed earlier and provides reinforcement to the process of remembering.

Together as SQ3R these five strategies have a synergistic effect on your learning and comprehension; you get the most of your reading material through this technique than from any other.

Whole-to-Part Method (Gestalt Principle)

This is a powerful tool in providing comprehension of the material under learning. The Gestalt principle is that the whole is different from the sum of its parts and that in many ways it determines the character and behavior of the parts, instead of the other way around. A proper understanding of the material you have taken up for study will be possible only when you view it from the point of view of the totality or whole of the material. For example, studying the motion of a car on a highway curve with a view to understand its safe speed during the motion will be meaningful only when you study it along with all the forces acting on the car, such as the centrifugal force, weight of the car, etc., along with the geometry of motion and the slope of the pavement cross section.

Another example would be the analysis of the behavior of an individual. The behavior within the comforts of one's own home or within the confines of a hostile crowd is understandable and meaningful only when you can proceed from the whole to the part. It is the totality of the environment that influences the individual's behavior more than anything else.

The important thing for you to recognize is that for learning to be effective you should develop the skill and habit of looking at the total configuration of the subject matter first and then study the material. This is similar to focusing the lens of your camera on an object without losing the context of the background to provide the right perception.

Part-to-Whole Method

In the learning process often one encounters a situation where there is no logical unity or continuity in the material. Also, there are situations where the study of a part you are doing now may be related or linked to a topic which you may be learning at a later date. In such cases, you should resort to studying the material on hand as an entity by itself through the SQ3R Method. Your professor is your best guide in letting you know of the nature of the material assigned to read and its place in the course treatment of the subject. Eventually when your learning is complete with respect to the parts, then a comprehended whole will emerge. Such is the case for subjects or courses which indicate a prerequisite in the college catalog.

Skimming and Scanning

Skimming is to read, study, or examine superficially and rapidly. Obviously it is a technique for light reading where you don't aim at the comprehension of concepts. Skimming is ideally suited for an initial survey of any material taken up for a deep studying. It has a place where voluminous reading is encountered, particularly during a short time. Newspapers, magazines, and novels read for an overview can be skimmed profitably.

Scanning as a technique of studying is a misnomer. On the one hand, it can mean an intensive examination of the material and, on the other, it can also mean making a wide sweeping search of the study material looking for key words and phrases such as preparing for a subject index for a book. In spite of the misleading terminology, scanning has a definite place in reading—particularly in fast reading.

Fast Reading

Earlier in the chapter we emphasized that the ability to read is a valuable asset to anyone who aspires to get high grades and graduate with distinction from college. As a technique, fast reading includes skimming and scanning as we discussed above and implies a strong vocabulary on your part. With the explosion of published materials and textbooks, you will find that you will have need for fast reading in many of your courses. It can spell the difference between a high or low grade in courses dealing with voluminous reading material.

Overlearning

Your learning of a material appears complete when you can recall the material or the concept of it without error. It would seem that there is no point in studying it further. However, educational psychologists have found that further practice, called overlearning, is necessary to prevent forgetting what is learned. It has been found that remembering is directly related to overlearning. Besides, continued overlearning makes one proficient in the recall of the material learned. This is the secret behind the seemingly incredible feat of repeating with increased proficiency the large amount of course material by most teachers of schools and colleges, musicians, stage performers and others of similar vocation. In fact, perfect practice makes one perfect.

As a technique, overlearning is a powerful weapon in your arsenal in your combat for high grades. Overlearning requires that you keep reviewing the learned material on a periodic basis, preferably once every day.

Cramming

Cramming means studying hastily in preparation for an examination. It is an attempt to acquire control, usually for the purpose of immediate reproduction, of a relatively large amount of material in a comparatively short time. A summer school course of five or ten weeks which is normally covered in a quarter or a semester is equivalent to a cramming process in the case of certain subjects. Weekend cramming for a test on the following Monday is a familiar technique for some students.

The question often debated is "Does cramming contribute to learning?" For certain types of examinations and certain life situations of transient nature cramming may be justified, and it does have a place in the modern competitive job-oriented society. However, where real permanence of learning is desired cramming is of little value. True learning is a product of maturation, of enlargement of meaning, of comprehension, and of assimilation. For such an outcome, of course, time is necessary.

Distributed Studying

This, in fact, is the very opposite of cramming. By distributing your available time for studying a subject over six days of the week is superior to allocating it to two or three days a week. The latter, still, is better than having one study session per week for the same total time. Experimental evidence has consistently shown that continuous study over a single long period results in poor assimilation and the interest in the material under study would begin to wane under an unduly prolonged studying period.

By a judicious combination of unit budgeting of time which we have discussed earlier in this chapter and distributing the budgeted units for the different subjects you have taken up for study, you should get the most return by way of true learning. As a part of this technique, if you can accommodate a brief daily review of the earlier materials studied in each subject, it will enhance your assimilation and lead to a systematic overlearning. Your ability for recall of the learned material in each subject would naturally reach its peak and it is your greatest asset as a preparation for the tests which you may be taking subsequently.

Mnemonic Devices

Mnemonic devices are contrivances basically intended to assist memory. They are suited only for items of information which do not lend themselves to meaningful associations. Mnemonic is pronounced "nemonic" with the first letter "m' silent. It is derived from the Greek word for remembering. The idea behind mnemonic strategies is to use old knowledge as an anchor or context for new knowledge. Mnemonics that are useful in learning are basically techniques for associating the new with the old.

A crude example of a mnemonic device to recall the seven colors of natural light is a coined-word "vibgyor"—each first letter of the word standing for one color of the spectrum namely violet, indigo, blue, green, yellow, orange, and red respectively.

Q = C I A is another example of a mnemonic device to help the student remember the equation for the rate of quantity of water flowing in a channel, making use of the familiar abbreviation CIA (Central Intelligence Agency). Once the equation is brought to memory, the student substitutes C for the coefficient of runoff, I for the intensity of the rainfall in inches per hour, and A for the catchment area in acres. Mnemonic devices are most effective when they are invented by yourself to fit the situation and the material under study. They are useful in closed-book tests where you have to depend largely on your memory.

Summary-Question Method

This method primarily is helpful to test the effectiveness of your learning at the end of a study session. It can be applied literally for all learning situations. After a topic or a reasonable amount of material has been studied first you should write a summary of what you have learned during this session. Then you should write your own questions on the subject matter from every conceivable angle possible as if you are setting questions for a test. Now you should start answering these questions to make sure that you have completely comprehended the material. Though it looks easy on paper, it won't be so when you actually try the questions; you will find a lot of misunderstood material which may need further studying.

STUDY TECHNIQUES FOR CONCEPT-ORIENTED SUBJECTS

Studying a concept-oriented subject is, of course, very different from studying a straight-forward reading material. Often you will find that the topics in subjects like mathematics, physics, chemistry, philosophy, etc., can not be just "read" and understood, as you might do in English or history. The methods more suited for their study are as follows:

1. Visualization
2. Thinking through sketches
3. Equation analysis
4. Equation charts.

Visualization

Visualization is forming a mental image of the concept of the subject matter taken up for learning. Repeated reading may be necessary to form a picture in the mind. Close your eyes and concentrate on the idea or concept in your mind. Contemplate on the concept and relate it to your earlier reading of it. The mental image may be very vague and often you may not have a "picture" in your mind's eye. Nevertheless, the concept will begin to crystalize in your mind and you will begin to have a "feel" for it. You can test your understanding using the summary-question technique discussed earlier.

Thinking through Sketches

A visualized concept can be further translated into a sketch in some instances which has the potential to become an aid to clear understanding. There is no hard and fast rules of making sketches in the learning process; they are purely individualistic. Though modern educational systems have not taken sketching seriously as a tool in learning, its rightful place in a learning situation should not be overlooked. You should remember that before the letters and words emerged to describe a phenomenon, the early civilizations had employed sketches in one form or other as a means of learning and communication.

Equation Analysis

In science-oriented subjects, engineering, and mathematics, it is common to derive and use many equations for understanding a phenomenon or a concept and to solve problems. In these cases, your learning is dependent on your understanding the basic equations and how they are derived. In these equations, there will be symbols representing different factors that influence the subject matter under study. Equations can not be just read as one would do in the case of an essay. An analysis of each of the equations from the fundamental is necessary for clear comprehension of the topic.

Equation Charts

Writing your own equation charts after understanding them in each subject is a good technique for study, particularly for overlearning. Such a chart also serves as a summary for the subject area covered and will be very helpful for revising the subject before a test. Equation charts compiled by you imply that you have understood all the factors in them. Copying equation charts from another student defeats the very purpose for which it is prepared. It should be your own.

STUDY TECHNIQUES FOR PROBLEM-ORIENTED SUBJECTS

Studying certain subjects particularly in science and engineering involves first the understanding of the fundamental principles and then using them for problem solving. Though the "real-world" nature of the problem may be different the basic principles underlying them may be the same. Following techniques have been known to be very effective in handling problem-oriented subjects:

1. Visualization
2. Free-body diagram analysis

3. Model problem analysis
4. Collection of solved typical problems.

Visualization

Visualizing a problem and figuring out its possible solution using the Gestalt Method (Whole to part) or any method is undoubtedly a technique well suited for many subjects which are more problem-oriented. Visualization is particularly more effective in design-oriented subjects where the designer can visualize the various aspects of the problem to choose the optimum solution. Creative visualization goes one step further in that it offers not just one optimal solution but can show many different ways of solving a given problem. However, visualization is a subjective technique and as such it can not be explicit; you have to try yourself to experience its efficacy.

Free-body Diagram Analysis

Unlike visualization, free-body diagram analysis is specific in its application. Free-body diagram concept is readily applicable to physical world problems where many forces are involved in the state of rest or motion of a physical body. They are widely used in applied physics and engineering problems. The term "free-body" refers to the conceptualization of a specific body of known mass with physical dimensions in relation to all the forces acting on it for static or dynamic equilibrium. Free-body diagram is an objective technique which serves as the starting point for the comprehension of a problem.

Model Problem Analysis

Model problems are those that typify problems of similar nature with minor variations. Learning to solve a model problem provides the key to solve similar problems. Often model problems are worked out in detail by the professor in the classroom or they are seen worked out in textbooks. It is important to pay special attention to model problems because they are milestones in the true learning of a student.

Collection of Solved Problems

Collecting solved problems from outside sources as well as by the student himself/herself is a technique of study resorted to by serious students with an eye on high grades. Undoubtedly this is a sure means to have a grip on the subject matter under study. Of course, merely collecting solved problems will not solve your problem of taking a test; but, it can make you face the test with confidence when you review them periodically. And, that is the winning difference.

Chapter 9

HOW TO STUDY YOUR TEXT BOOK AND CLASSNOTES

"Besides lectures, textbooks are probably the next most valuable learning resource available to students. As with lectures, your task with textbooks is to find the meaning of material for which you are responsible".

Thomas M. Sherman and Terry M. Wildman,
authors of "Proven Strategies for Successful Test Taking"

TOPICS

NEED FOR A TEXTBOOK

A textbook to a student serves a similar purpose as that of a crutch to a walking-impaired person. The latter is an aid to walking; the former is an aid to learning. The textbook provides the substance and direction to the subject matter you are seeking to learn. Since textbooks are usually written by experienced masters in that field of knowledge, they carry a certain amount of authority and provide confidence to the new learner. The textbook also serves as a source of reference on matters pertaining to the topic of the book. It is now almost universal to prescribe a textbook for most of the courses taught in colleges and universities. The dependence on textbooks is likely to be more in the freshman and sophomore level courses than at the upper class and graduate levels.

Then again, the degree of adherence to the textbook varies according to the nature of the subject as well as the method of teaching of the individual professor. Some professors use the textbook only to assign homework problems and some use it for reading assignment only. Some may prescribe a textbook but may never use it; it is left to the student for making effective use of it.

Irrespective of the professor's commitment to the textbook, it is at your best interest to have a textbook and to know how to make the most use of it to widen the horizon of your learning.

INITIAL ACQUAINTANCE WITH YOUR TEXTBOOK

When you buy a textbook the first thing to do should be writing your name and address in indelible ink preferably on the inside of the front hardcover (or soft cover). This gives you a chance of getting back your textbook in the event it is lost, hoping that the finder may turn it in to the lost-and-found office of your college or return it to you directly.

The author of the textbook you have bought is, for all practical purposes, your consultant on topics presented in the book. Therefore, it is good for you to know his name and credentials. Look at the title of the book and associate the author and the title together such as "Foundations of Theoretical Soil Mechanics by M. E. Harr".

Then note the year of copyright, the year of publication and the number of the edition, if any. Also look at the name of the publisher. These can be found on the back of the title page at the beginning. Nowadays all books published in the United States of America by reputed publishing companies carry an individual identifying number called ISBN (International Standard Book Number) which can be seen behind the title page in front, and at the outside of the back cover of the book.

Browsing through the whole book is an important step in getting acquainted with it. Glance through the preface, table of contents, chapter arrangements, footnotes, figures, tables, bibliography, glossary of terms and index. This will give you an idea of the coverage of the book, and in general, what is in the book. The table of contents lets you know the number and names of chapters in the book, together with the page numbers. It shows the order in which the chapters are arranged. Getting familiar with the table of contents helps you locate quickly a topic or subject presented in the book.

Besides the table of contents, the index found in the back pages of the book is an important tool for reference and research. It lists the names of topics and sub-topics discussed in the book in alphabetical order, together with the page numbers. Thus it makes it easier and quicker to locate a subject matter if it is discussed in the book.

A glossary of terms and terminology, also found usually at the end of the book before the index, is a useful section. The meaning and, sometimes, a brief explanation of unfamiliar words, phrases, and scientific terms are given by the glossary. Its importance lies in its usefulness to comprehend the precise meaning of new and unfamiliar terms in learning a new subject.

GETTING READY TO STUDY THE TEXTBOOK

A systematic and an orderly approach to your textbook is a prerequisite if you want to optimize the time you spend with your textbook. Keeping yourself mentally and physically fit and alert is the foremost factor implied in all learning processes. The choice of your time of study should be such that you start studying after a good rest from any strenuous physical activity. A mind free from strong emotions like anger, fear, and grief will be able to comprehend the subject matter of study better than one in a state of agitation. The ideal state of mind for learning recognized by educational psychologists is equanimity of mind. Your ability to keep all your personal problems away from your study table is an asset to you in the learning process.

We have discussed elsewhere about the importance of doing your studies in the same place and at the same time. This habit restores the mind quickly to a receptive state for learning. Studying your textbook under such conditions will be naturally very productive.

Keep two different color markers, preferably yellow and orange, handy before you start reading the textbook. Be sure that your place of study is well lit and ventilated.

STUDYING THE LESSON IN THE TEXTBOOK

As you turn to the lesson in the textbook, be sure of your purpose in doing so. Depending on the subject matter, it may be a reading assignment for additional learning, or it may be to consult the section and do a problem, or it may even be just to clarify something you have not fully understood, or it may be to find the answer to a specific question. Having such an aim to start with helps channelize your efforts towards that goal.

The various study techniques we discussed in the previous chapter are at your disposal to effectively study the lesson. The SQ3R technique (Survey, question, read, recite and recall) or its suitable modification to suit your need is the best way to approach the lesson taken up for study.

Delineate the chapter or section and survey it visually without making a serious attempt to read, but with a deliberate slowness, observing the headings, subheadings, figures, tables, equations, etc., within your delineated area. Repeat this twice or thrice. The visual impact introduces a sense of familiarity in your memory process of the territory you have reconnoitered.

Now formulate a series of questions on the topic based on your survey and also list other questions which you wish to answer. Let the questions be simple but many. These questions serve as the individual steps of a ladder. Conquering one by one will take you to the goal you have set for yourself at the beginning. Have the questions written on a separate sheet of paper and hold it in front of you for follow-up.

Now start reading paragraph by paragraph, or section by section, as you are able to. Go to the next paragraph or section only after you have reasonably comprehended the subject matter you have read. Consult your question sheet and see whether you can answer any of the questions in your list. Scribble the answer under the question when you find it. In this manner, proceed further until you have finished reading the delineated section and found all the answers for your questions.

The next step is to reinforce your learning. Put away the question sheet and try to recite to yourself, audibly or inaudibly, in your own words. If you are able to visualize the subject matter and recall accurately the substance you may consider that you have done a good job of studying the lesson of the textbook. Otherwise, you may go over the lesson one more time and have another recall test.

You will find that the time taken for the first round of reading and finding answers to the questions is considerably more, but with subsequent repetitions, when you become more and more familiar with the concepts, your comprehension increases and the time taken becomes less and less.

If your lesson is non-descriptive and concept-oriented or mathematical, you may still start with the survey-question-read technique but you must consider the part-to-whole or whole-to-part techniques for appropriate comprehension. If you meet equations of any kind, mathematical or chemical, instead of reading them you must derive them or at least write them as given in the text after understanding them. You should repeat and recall them until you are able to get them straight.

When problem-solving is associated with the textbook lesson, you will be better off working out by yourself not only the example problems given in the text, but also as many other problems as possible, assigned or unassigned by your professor.

IMPORTANCE OF COLOR MARKING

Some people consider color marking on the textbook pages a bad practice. However, more and more educational psychologists recognize that using a color marker to highlight a word, phrase, or an equation in the middle of a sentence or a page produces a "spot-light effect" which increases the visual impact. Of course, indiscriminate marking across every line defeats the very purpose of the color marking. Marking must be confined only to key words, phrases, and equations which are important for the comprehension of the subject matter.

All colors are not suitable for the highlighting effect. Yellow, orange, and pink are ideal. Other colors in light shades can be made use of for contrasting effect.

UNDERLINING AND MARGINAL NOTES

It is not a bad idea to underline words, phrases, and even full sentences which appear to be important as you keep on reading. However, as in the case of color marking, indiscriminate underlining over large sections of the text loses its significance and defeats the very purpose of doing it.

Writing notes and comments on the margin of the textbook is perfectly alright, as long as it is your textbook. However, if you contemplate selling your textbook after you have completed the course you will be better off not to disfigure the pages by color marking and underlining or with notes written all over the margins, which will reduce the resale worth of the textbook.

SECRET OF RETAINING WHAT YOU HAVE STUDIED

In general, quick learning and quick forgetting go together. However, well-understood at the time of learning, a subject matter starts slipping out of the memory cells in the brain steadily thereafter. The degree of permanence of retention depends on the dual components of review and recall. If the matter is reviewed periodically, preferably everyday, and recalled for some practical application, the degree of retention in the memory bank is very high. Retention is best when the material learned is logical in character and is appealing to the emotional nature of the learner.

Studying through repeated review retards forgetting and reinforces the retention capability. This process is recognized by educational psychologists as "overlearning" which we have already discussed before under study techniques. We also mentioned before that your professor's skill of repeating endless amount of classroom material is achieved through this simple process of overlearning. This is the secret you can take advantage of by applying it to your studying of the textbook.

IMPORTANCE OF TAKING NOTES IN ALL CLASSES

Few people realize the importance of taking notes in any formal classroom environment, particularly in higher educational settings such as in colleges and universities. Its importance increases as you go up the ladder to senior and graduate level courses, where the volume of material covered increases multi-fold.

Purpose of Taking Notes

Taking notes has a purpose and a function. The primary purpose of taking notes is to follow the professor in his trail of lectures, which will help to keep you introduced to the topics and areas of importance in the course material or textbook as presented by him. You should be aware of the fact that two different professors using the same textbook may present the course quite differently from each other, except in highly structured and outlined courses. Even there the professors have enough freedom to exert their individuality in the kind of course treatment and tests. Taking notes gives a preliminary but a permanent track record for you to work further on. It provides the direction and order of subject treatment presented by your professor.

Functions of Taking Notes

The obvious function of the classnotes is to supplement your textbook. In reality it serves as a second textbook for the course. It covers the areas not covered by the prescribed textbook but covered by your professor. It is this aspect of the classnotes that makes it not only a paramount learning aid but a vital tool in your quest for better grades.

Taking notes also serves another function—of being an aid to concentration in listening. It increases the percent absorption of what is heard from the professor's lecture. It is but natural that your concentration will wax and wane during the lecture hour and your mind will drift slowly away from the classroom if you don't take any notes at all. Though you sat through the lecture your comprehension of the material presented can become poor, and when you go to your room to study the topic of the lecture, you may even find that you can recall only a fraction of what was presented. If you did not take notes there is nothing for you to fall back on to recapture the subject. On the same token by taking notes, you have a frame-work of what went on in the class. You will be able to use this framework as the basis for expanding your learning.

Aid to Memory

During note taking, your brain gets input through your ears and eyes, keeps it in the short-term memory and sends commands through the nervous system to keep writing the input received in the form of notes. Of course, writing with your hand you can not match the input received one to one all the time. However, the simultaneous occurrence of these functions in your psychophysical system opens up a neural pathway from your brain to the output—that is the resulting handwritten notes. Most of the stored input in the brain cells quickly decays and is lost to the memory. Later, when you start studying your notes, it becomes the input to the brain, and attains the power to trigger some of the lost memory; it serves as a tool to reconstruct the input (the original classroom lecture) in the memory cells.

Through note taking you are sure not to miss the dates of the tests and quizzes announced in the class, and also you won't miss any take-home assignments and their due dates for submission.

Getting Tuned

Note taking has another important point in its favor. It helps you get tuned to the method of teaching of the particular professor and his/her expressions. Often-times you may be able to sense his/her logic of presentation and the sequence of expressions, and even guess a few possible test questions based on his/her verbal expressions during the lecture. Such a tuning puts you right ahead of other students in the class. What else can be a better way than this to get the most learning from a teacher?

During note taking, it is quite likely that you may have missed or partially noted many things the teacher had mentioned. This situation promotes the opportunity to ask questions about the missing links in your notes. Since genuine learning starts with asking valid questions, note taking may be considered a training ground to formulate questions on the topic and answer them through SQ3R and other techniques.

HOW TO TAKE NOTES IN CLASS

Though there are no hard and fast rules for taking notes, you will be able to take and maintain a set of good notes for each course by adhering to the following simple methods. It is essential that you keep a separate notebook or file for each subject. Start the note taking with the date of lecture on a fresh page. Use a pen or pencil to write your notes. Pencil is better; you can correct any mistakes later easily. Start the page with a heading or an appropriate title for easy identification; make it in bold letters and underline or colormark it.

Listen and Write

As the professor starts lecturing, be attentive to his words. Try to make sense of what he/she says and then begin to write on your paper the key words and phrases which the professor uses. Don't try to write verbatim what he/she says. You don't even have to write full sentences. Catching the core of the central theme of the lecture should be your aim at this time. Of course, you will miss many bits and pieces. It does not matter as long as you are able to keep the central topic in view and note the main ideas.

Copy Everything from the Board!

Be sure to write in your notes everything the teacher puts on the board, and the messages he/she addresses to the class such as the announcement of forthcoming test dates, assignments, reports, term papers, etc.

If the professor is a prolific writer on the board, it makes note-taking easy. On the other hand, if the professor is primarily a talker who seldom uses the board, you have to be alert to keep up with him/her to listen and write simultaneously.

There are some professors who use overhead projectors for the most part of their lectures. Once a theme, or an equation, or a picture is projected on the screen, the professor builds his/her lecture around the projected material. Note-taking is sometimes easy and sometimes difficult in such cases, depending on the subject matter. However, since you have both a visual and audio input from the professor, you can write your notes based on them.

If the professor writes an equation or derives it on the board, be sure to copy it. Otherwise there is no point in trying to copy long equations projected through overhead or slide projectors. Note only the page number or the source of reference from which it was taken.

As you are taking notes be generous space-wise in writing and drawing sketches. Since you are going to review and rework the notes with the help of textbooks and other reference materials, you will find it convenient and easy to work with the outline notes you have taken from the class if it has ample elbow room for additions and insertions.

If the subject matter calls for lots of sketches and diagrams, you will be better off using plain unruled paper for notes taking. On the other hand if the subject matter is descriptive in its contents, use of college ruled paper should be adequate for the purpose.

Color Markers for your Notes

Effective use of color markers for your notes will enhance your comprehension and visual impact. You can take advantage of this simple but effective technique by making it a habit in your classnotes preparation.

Use of Symbols and Shortcuts

It is not possible to write everything the professor is saying during the course of a lecture session using long-hand writing. It is not the purpose of note taking either. In order to grasp as much of the material as possible, it is better that you resort to using symbols, shortcuts, and abbreviations integrating them into your notes. With practice you will be able to take fast and accurate notes. In Figure 4 are shown some of the commonly used symbols, shortcuts, and abbreviations. You can devise many of your own which add to the efficiency of your note taking:

+	plus, positive	**w/**	with
−	minus, negative	**w/o**	without
↑	increase, higher, up	**wh/**	which
↓	decrease, lower, down	**re**	reference
=	equal, same	**sp**	special, specific
≠	different, not equal	**Q**	question
〉	more than, greater	**A**	answer
〈	less than	**e.g.**	for example
→	toward	**i.e.**	that is
←	from	**aprx**	approximately
∴	therefore	**etc**	and so on
		aro	as a result of

Figure 4. Symbols, shortcuts, and abbreviations

HOW TO STUDY YOUR CLASSNOTES

The notes written in the classroom during a lecture are in general far from being complete to be an aid in your learning. They need to be worked on to give them a status next to your textbook. The following 4 steps are in general applicable to all classnotes; yet, they are amenable for modification to suit your particular need.

Step 1. Review and Reconstruct

Once you have a set of raw notes from any class lecture your aim should be to get back to it as soon as possible, preferably the same evening so that most of the lecture is still fresh in your memory. The first step is to review the notes carefully and reconstruct them for missing links and details. You may not be able to do it from your memory alone. Do not hesitate to take help from a fellow classmate or anybody else who can be of help.

Step 2. Dovetail to the Textbook (or Reference Book)

Refer to the textbook or reference book and look for the section and page numbers dealing with the subject matter of your class notes. Note this section and page numbers in your classnotes appropriately next to the topic of heading so that in future you will know where to look for the original in case of doubts and for further references. This method of dovetailing the classnotes to the textbook or reference book will not only save you a lot of time, but will make your notes an integral part of your text material.

Step 3. Fill in and Expand

Having reviewed and reconstructed your notes, now read the textbook or reference book to learn more about the subject matter. Fill in and expand the classnotes using material taken from the textbook so that the modified notes is complete and readable by itself. Keeping the original note taking spacious will be helpful for this purpose.

Step 4. Summarize

The next step is to summarize in your own words the subject matter of the classnotes and the material learned from the textbook. Write it under the notes of the day. If the classnotes deal with methods of problem solving, it will be a good idea to have at least one model problem solved and kept as a part of the classnotes.

In addition to these four general steps, there are two other steps which are applicable to theoretical and problem-oriented subjects. They are as follows: collection of equations and collection of model problems.

COLLECTION OF EQUATIONS

As your notes keep expanding, if you note more and more equations in the subject area it will be a good idea to pay special attention to them. You can assign numbers to the equations in your classnotes in an arithmetic order starting from the first day's classnotes. The equation number is useful both for identifying an equation and for quick reference. If the same equation has a number in the textbook, you will be better off in noting that number next to the equation in your notes and tie those two numbers together to avoid confusion.

In addition to the summarizing step, you can assign a few blank pages either in the front or at the back pages of your notes for the equation collection. You can write the numbered equations found scattered in your notes on these pages creating an exclusive section of equations pertaining to the subject matter of the classnotes. Now write the corresponding page number of your own classnotes for each of the equations listed in your collection for ready reference.

COLLECTION OF MODEL PROBLEMS

Very few students realize the importance of a collection of model problems in their notes. A model problem serves to illustrate the main principle or a core concept and presents the methodology of solving the problem using an example. An understanding of the model problem increases your comprehension of the principles involved. The more model problems you collect and understand, the deeper will be your learning. It is a royal path to getting better grades.

Model problems can be picked up from many different sources. Many are worked out fully in the textbook itself. Many professors put on the board many model problems as an effective tool for explaining concepts. There are a few specialized publications such as the Schaum series of worked problems in literally all college level courses. They can be bought for a nominal cost at your college bookstore or you can check them out from your library. However, you must take the special effort of going through the problems in your area of interest and select representative problems for your valuable collection.

Chapter 10

HOW TO STUDY BASIC SUBJECTS

"The study of science teaches young men to think . . . The study of classics teaches them to express thought."

J. S. Mill,
English economist, philosopher, and
political theorist (1806–1873)

TOPICS

How to Study:
      English (Communication Skill)
      Mathematics
      Physics
      Chemistry
      Biology
      History
      Psychology
      Philosophy
      Sociology
      Economics
      Music

HOW TO STUDY COMMUNICATION SKILLS (ENGLISH)

By
Virginia P. Gray
&
Debra A. Dangerfield

Virginia P. Gray, Ph.D.,
Bowling Green State University,
Professor of English and Drama,
WV Institute of Technology

Debra A. Dangerfield, M.A.,
Marshall University,
Professor of English,
WV Institute of Technology

Like all other disciplines, the student of communications must first utilize all resources available. The ability to communicate orally or written must be practiced often. Basics are learned from preschool on, but unless constantly used they degenerate to nothing. Even a personal journal where private thoughts can be kept will give the opportunity for expressing ideas, knowledge and feelings. Typically on most college campuses, the student has access to a multitude of resources: the campus library, a writing or editing lab, computer and video aids, a personal dictionary and thesaurus, a grammar handbook, a MLA style sheet, textbooks, books of famous quotations, and most of all the college professor. The proper utilization of all these at the appropriate time will enhance learning and the proper study skills.

The student who is successful in communicating recognizes the importance of *all* forms of skills—reading, writing, listening, and speaking—to communicate ideas, knowledge and feelings. Effective time management allows the student the efficient use of his/her time, thus producing a balanced schedule for college activities. The student should read both fiction and nonfiction (books, magazines, and newspapers). He/she must not become excluded from day-to-day facts and events such as those found on the television news, if nothing else, because these facts teach the individual how others feel about important events.

The student should read for a purpose, recognizing the authenticity and validity of the material as he formulates his own interpretation of the written word. Part of this interpretation is based on his ability to analyze the written material for perhaps inferences, analogies, or symbolism. Through writing, the student generates his/her own ideas, either from personal experiences or from vicarious experiences, into an organized work so that his readers understand his/her purpose and thus communicate. Using prewriting tactics such as limiting or narrowing the subject, brainstorming, categorizing ideas, outlining, and adapting to the audience help the student overcome anxieties associated with developing communication skills. The student develops an eye and an ear for the proper sentence sense necessary for the editing of both written and oral communication forms.

Along with the recognition of written forms of communication are the spoken forms requiring both successful listening and speaking skills. Listen to what others are feeling and be able to appreciate their ideas. This type of listening gives the student the knowledge to influence others in their final decisions. The successful listener is attuned to the purpose or objective of the speaker; thus he/she learns to concentrate on the delivery so that comprehension is achieved. The speaker through his intonations, expressions and delivery teaches or persuades his/her audience by carefully organizing the strategy for communication, just as he/she would for the written form.

Communication skills are basically taught in schools, but only an effort by the individual can polish and refine these skills. Learn to proofread and find mistakes such as local cliques and vague expressions. The student must learn to listen to what he/she says to avoid misunderstandings. An increased vocabulary will make words work for the communicator.

Overall, the successful communications student must strive for quality through *all* forms of communication. Communication does not end with the study of English. It goes hand in hand with life, association, and success. If the individual is to live a complete life, he/she must write and speak in a method that can be understood by the audience to be reached at that moment in time. Only through communication can one generate original thought, and only through original thought can one be truly successful in life.

HOW TO STUDY MATHEMATICS

By
John F. Cavalier
&
Norma F. Lauer

John F. Cavalier, Ph.D.,
Virginia Tech.,
Professor of Mathematics,
WV Institute of Technology

Norma F. Lauer, Ph.D.,
Auburn University,
Professor of Mathematics,
WV Institute of Technology

Mathematics is a term that causes anxiety in many students. Usually these fears and concerns are due to inadequate preparation of the student. The anxiety can be intensified by other students, parents, or the content in a particular course. Students should keep in mind that mathematics must be learned in small doses. Large doses can intensify anxieties and "kill" the grade and the will to study.

The following paragraphs summarize procedures that will help most students effectively study mathematics. These paragraphs outline how to study, how to prepare for a test, and briefly, how to take a test.

To learn the material and to do well in a mathematics course, the student should:

1. Have adequate preparation for the course. If the student is uncertain about this, an instructor or advisor should be consulted. Sometimes it is necessary to take a prerequisite to be adequately prepared.
2. Carefully read the text, think through all details, and work all examples. As this is done, the student should focus on learning definitions and formulas. Describe new concepts in familiar words to help gain a better understanding. Similarly, work through class notes and examples. This is a slow, but necessary, process to understand the material.
3. Diligently work all assigned exercises. This will provide an understanding of the different techniques and computational procedures involved and will reinforce definitions and formulas. If it is impossible to do all problems on the day assigned, work at least one problem of each type before the next class meeting and complete the rest as soon as possible.
4. Study with classmates. A discussion with other students is often overlooked in the learning process, but can prove valuable in reenforcing material already mastered and clarifying areas not understood beforehand.
5. Design and give a self-test. A self-test will help prepare for an in-class examination. Select a few problems that include formulas and computational procedures that are likely to be on the in-class test. Grade your "test" to identify areas that need more study and to help increase speed and accuracy in the testing situation.
6. Stay current with assignments and seek help from an instructor or knowledgeable student. This suggestion can not be overemphasized since new mathematics is "built" on what has been previously learned.

These six steps will better enable a student to learn the material and to do well on tests. One final suggestion is helpful during the test. Students should work the easier problems first and skip problems whose computational procedures are not readily apparent. Students often find that initial test anxiety fades during the test and that when they return to these problems, they are better prepared to solve them.

If these study guidelines are followed, a student can be successful in a mathematics course. An immediate indicator of success is certainly the grade received, but a more important indicator is how well a student does in future mathematics courses and in work requiring reasoning, logic and maturity. These guidelines, when applied with conscientious effort, will lead to success in studying and mastering mathematics.

HOW TO STUDY PHYSICS

By
Robert J.Lieb

**Robert J. Lieb, Ph.D.,
University of North Carolina,
Research Physicist,
U S Army Ballistic Research Lab**

Physics involves the study of the nature and interactions of matter. It is the most fundamental of the sciences, and, in a sense, the simplest. All of us have a "construct" within us that we have put together to explain the universe. Some constructs are intricate and accurate, some are simple and accurate, and all constructs have biases, inconsistencies and errors. An approach to the study of physics that seems to have the most success is one which uses this construct as a basis for understanding. Once a clearer understanding is developed, modification of the construct occurs as the learning takes place, which facilitates further learning. This "holistic" approach encourages self-reliance and fosters self-learning while guaranteeing that the learned information will be internalized and put to an efficient use.

The physical approach to using the above concept can be varied and individualized. There are three principal areas in which learning can be divided. They are the lecture/demonstration, the laboratory, and problem solving. A suggested method of approach to learning in these principal areas is explained below. The techniques employed can then be modified to best suit your individual application.

The lecture/demonstration is the arena in which ideas and concepts are introduced. Generally, the approach is to state or show the nature of the problem, provide methods by which solutions to the problem are approached, and explain proper interruption of the results obtained. The involvement of the student in this area is essential to the successful completion of the course. Many students feel that they need not attend lectures, or that they can catch-up later. This is almost never the case. Interaction among students and with the instructor dramatically increases the effectiveness of the lecture/demonstration. A common experience among students is that the concepts and information learned are not apparent until after the course is finished when the personal construct has been revamped and a new awareness is realized.

The laboratory provides hands-on experience and often is the most exasperating part of the study. Students not used to scientific methods may experience difficulty in the process of extracting essential information from the experiment, properly organizing that information, and drawing the valid conclusions. The process sharpens observational skills, develops procedural and reporting skills, and reinforces concepts introduced in the lecture portion of the course. The laboratory is also the means by which the concepts of error, precision, and human interaction with the physical measurement are introduced. All these activities are of critical importance in the development of our understanding of how we fit into the universe.

The most important area of study in physics is problem solving. This is where most of the real learning takes place. Our concepts are developed and changed by small increments that result from an appreciation of such solutions. There are several steps that facilitate the process. These steps are designed to help foster problem definition, and avoid the pitfalls that often frustrate the student.

1. **Read the problem through completely.** Do not attempt to solve part of the problem without understanding how that part relates to all the other parts.

2. **List all the information given and identify what is specifically being asked.** This helps order the information in your mind and actually begins the solution process.

3. **Always carry the units associated with the numbers throughout the entire problem.** This helps to keep quantities from being confused, familiarizes the units, and helps to make sure the answer makes sense. Transform all units to a common system.

4. **Locate available resources to solve the problem.** These may be equations, concepts, laws-of-nature, etc. Express the resource as an equation, and solve for the desired quantity. This will crystallize the concept and make clear what needs to be done.

5. **Substitute the information from the list constructed from Step 2 into the solution generated in Step 4.** Be sure to carry units along, and cancel out or combine where appropriate.

6. **Check to be sure the answer makes sense.** If a good concept of the problem has been developed, a guess about the nature of the solution should be possible. If there is a mismatch between the answer and the guess, something is wrong and needs to be resolved. Check to be sure the units are correct, as well. Many errors are discovered via dimensional analysis. If "seconds" are calculated for the answer when "meters" are requested, an error has occurred.

7. **Copy the problem in a neat format.** If the solution required considerable effort, chances are that the work needed to arrive at the answer is scattered over several sheets of paper. By putting the work in an orderly format the information will

also be more ordered in your mind and more easily retained. This will also facilitate restructure of your personal "construct" and help in the solution of other problems.

Note the steps 1 to 3 are almost automatic and require little actual conscience thought. However, while performing these steps, the problem is being better defined and put into a format where the solution will become more evident. Step 4 is where the formal solution is generated. It is here that the problem conditions are applied to a known system of information so that a solution can be obtained. Step 5 can be typified as "cranking" out the answer. The solution is essentially in-hand before this step.

Step 6 provides the opportunity to evaluate the problem and see how it compares with your personal construct. If there is an inconsistency, something is wrong, either in the answer to the problem or your construct of the universe.

Step 7 is one of the most important. The human brain works in a wondrous fashion. Memory gained from speaking is different than memory gained from writing, which is different from memory gained from seeing, etc. Rewriting a problem that you have solved reinforces these various aspects of recollection and contributes to the net (or web) of understanding. Things are always able to be better understood when viewed or experienced from different aspects.

The three areas of learning in physics all contribute to understanding matter and its interactions. Most importantly, however, the understanding gained permits us deeper reflection upon our own place in the universe.

HOW TO STUDY CHEMISTRY

By
Donald G. Brannon

Donald G. Brannon, Ph.D.,
West Virginia University,
Professor of Chemistry,
WV Institute of Technology

Chemistry is the study of the physical and chemical properties of matter. Since matter is anything that has mass and occupies space, chemistry is a very broad subject and has a direct impact on most fields of study. The study of chemistry deserves a positive attitude and a willingness to work on the part of the student.

Faithful class attendance is a must even though it may not be required. Chemistry is a building process, one step at a time with each new step depending upon the previous step. Material discussed during an absence must be learned before the next class period. This usually requires several extra hours of study to accomplish and plays havoc with one's normal study schedule. However, attending class and not paying attention is a mental absence which has to be made up with appropriate study.

Reading and outlining the assignment for the next class period is recommended. This allows the student to better understand the material and to ask questions about anything that is not completely understood. However, neat and complete lecture notes are needed if the material is to be learned. Everything written on the board has to be noted along with the verbal explanations. Some students find it worthwhile to tape record the lecture (with consent of the instructor) and play it back when the notes are reviewed. The student should briefly read over the notes as soon as possible after the class. Most students find it very worthwhile to re-copy their chemistry notes that evening and note any questions they need to ask the instructor; do not be afraid to ask questions.

Approximately three hours of study time are needed for every hour of class. This should be spread out during the entire week (including weekends) and allows the student to learn the material and not just memorize it. Many chemistry concepts need time to be absorbed and are not conducive to cramming sessions. The periodic table is very helpful in remembering trends in properties and yields approximate electrons configurations directly.

Homework concerning the material covered in a class period should be done before the class meets again. A calculator is a must for working homework problems and taking exams. Many students find they learn more by doing homework in small groups. This does not mean copying homework, it must be an exchange of ideas. If a homework problem can not be solved in ten minutes, proceed to other problems and come back to it later. If it still can't be worked, ask your instructor.

In order to solve problems it is necessary to carefully read the problem and write down all the pertinent data and what is to be determined, all with correct units. If a chemical equation is involved, the equation has to be balanced. Often the units will indicate how to work the problem. For example, if density must be determined, the units of density is gms per ml or gms/ml. This means the mass of the sample in grams must be divided by its volume in mls to get the correct units.

If units do not lead to an immediate solution, the data should suggest an appropriate equation, if not, refer to the textbook and work through similar example problems. It usually boils down to coming up with one equation with one unknown. If two unknowns appear, a second equation relating the two unknowns has to be found.

Often a definition can be stated as an equation. If a problem asks for the Mass % As_2O_3 the definition of percent is part/whole x 100;

the part has to be gms of As2 O3 in a particular sample. This leads to the equation

$$\%AS2\ O3\ =\ \frac{gms\ AS2\ O3\ (part)}{gms\ sample\ (whole)}\ \times\ 100$$

The grams of sample would have to be given, but the gms of AS2 O3 must be found in order to solve the problem. This could be given directly or it may have to be found from the data. Expand the definition as needed until the equation has only one unknown.

HOW TO STUDY BIOLOGY

By
John M. Parks

John M. Parks, Ph.D.,
University of Oklahoma,
Professor of Biology,
WV Institute of Technology

　　Biology is the study of life, and therefore, is possibly the most interesting and exciting academic discipline. One's life is filled with biological observations derived from past and present experiences, and we are constantly curious about the many variations that we observe in life. Biology lectures and laboratory experiences will serve to explain, delineate, and add in a scientific manner to those observations of life.

In approaching the study of biology, the student should expect that the subject material will cover a very wide span of material ranging from the minute mechanics of a cell to the manner in which populations interact with each other. Biology contains a wide range of vocabulary that is derived not only from biological research of the past, but from chemistry, physics and math as well. In fact, biology may very well be defined as applied chemistry, physics and math. While the volume of terminology requires a great deal of memorization, the essence of mastering biology as a discipline comes with understanding and communicating the concepts that are inherent within that terminology.

As with other academic pursuits, a critical point in studying biology lies in using the observation and hypothesis sequence of logic. Most biology classes will contain a laboratory component which is designed to give students ample opportunity to integrate observations with lecture and reading materials.

Biology courses will include a central component which is the lecture or theory part of the course. This is the part of the course where an instructor will guide the student into a sequence of directed observations and hypotheses. It is very important for the student at this point to take very good classroom notes, and if the instructor permits, to ask questions during the lecture. Self-involvement can only aid the learning process. Most of the testing program will center around the lecture component of the course.

After each lecture the student should review those notes, update and clarify them, and if any questions or doubts remain after the review, then the student should contact the instructor soon in order to correct any doubts on those notes. Certainly, if the notes are unclear or confusing at the beginning of the course those notes should be rewritten with clarity after each lecture. Use of the textbook recommended for the course and library sources should be used to clarify lecture notes. With practice notetaking will quickly improve.

There will be a laboratory component to most biology courses. This component will usually be designed to support lecture theory and help the student to visualize and communicate lecture material. It is important for the student to correlate in his/her own mind lecture and laboratory materials, and, not to think of the lab portion as a separate mass of concepts and information. The laboratory experiences should teach the student about the observation-hypothesis sequence of logic, and, should teach the student about the use of scientific procedure and equipment.

The bulk of the laboratory study will require a degree of expertise in the following areas:

1. professional use of the microscope,
2. recognition of organisms or parts of organisms on prepared slides,
3. recognition of plant and animal specimens as well as anatomical parts of them, and,
4. design and completion of certain lab experiments.

Most biology courses do have laboratory exams that are practical in nature, thus, careful notes must be taken in labs as well. Generally, good performance on lab exams should be reflected by good performance on lecture exams.

Clearly, passing to excellent performance in a biology course requires good notetaking, an active involvement in laboratory activities, a distinct effort to integrate lab work with lecture theory, a willingness of the student to ask help from the instructor in and out of classroom, and, finally, a willingness on the part of the student to constantly review and clarify class notes.

* * * * * * *

HOW TO STUDY HISTORY

By
Stephen W. Brown
&
Otis K. Rice

Stephen W. Brown, Ph.D.,
West Virginia University,
Professor of History,
WV Institute of Technology

Otis K. Rice, Ph.D.,
University of Kentucky,
Professor of History,
WV Institute of Technology

History weaves the movements, events, and personalities of the past into a seamless whole, and only by careful study can the student begin to grasp its meaning and significance. At the same time that it provides insight into the past experience of man, it illuminates the problems, issues, and concerns of the present. The student who would understand history must adopt methods that insure a strong sense of chronology and its importance, appreciation of the relationships of movements and events to each other and to those of earlier and later times, the importance of cause and effect relationships, the ability to analyze data critically, and skill in synthesizing accumulating information.

For the college student, as well as for any other person interested in genuine understanding of history, the following study procedures have proved their effectiveness:

1. Begin study by reading an entire assignment or selection with the purpose of obtaining major ideas and broad concepts of

the ideas, forces, and events treated by the author of the text(s). As you read, attempt to relate the material at hand to subject matter previously covered and thus set the new information into a meaningful context.

2. Following the first reading, re-read the assignment, this time focusing on details of key movements, issues, and events and on men and women who had important roles in their development. Make notes of what appear to be points of special importance. In this manner, you will be reasonably well prepared for class lectures and discussions.

3. These readings, each with its own specific purpose, should enable you to take notes in class without undue strain. You should not need to record everything the professor says; instead, concentrate upon salient points and try to relate them to textual materials with which you are already familiar.

4. Before the day is over, and certainly while the lecture is fresh in mind, review your lecture notes and notations made during your reading of the text. This is the time to fill in missing data and to jot down questions you may need to ask the professor.

5. Your review of the lecture of the day should be accompanied by a review of the material from the previous lecture(s). This combination of careful reading, effective note-taking, and prompt and continuous review reinforces knowledge gained and each step promotes retention of essential information.

6. Since there has been an on-going reinforcement of knowledge and its significance, there should be no need for elaborate mnemonic devices and painful last-minute efforts to recover vital information for tests. If you have studied carefully, you will have accumulated a major body of knowledge, and the pre-test review will consist chiefly of activities that expedite recall of material already largely internalized.

7. Since the purposes of learning and understanding history do not end with passing a test, the serious student will encounter many ideas and events that invite further exploration. In furtherance of such interests you should examine bibliographies and suggested readings that appear in the textbook, consult

with your professor for recommendations, or examine the library card catalog for additional sources of information.

Even though you may use the most effective study procedures possible, a word of caution is necessary to you as a history student. If you desire truly to understand and appreciate the past, you must see it from the values and perspectives of the times. You can not select from the past only those aspects that appear to have relevance to our own times, for past eras had an integrity of their own and excessive concerns with presentism may distort history. When you can understand the past on its own terms, you will then indeed be better prepared to understand the times in which you live.

* * * * * * *

HOW TO STUDY PSYCHOLOGY

By
Rita Wicks-Nelson

**Rita Wicks-Nelson, Ph.D.,
New York State University at Stony Brook,
Professor of Psychology,
WV Institute of Technology**

Psychology is the study of behavior and mental processes. As a behavioral or social science, it began in the late 1800s. From the beginning it was interested in fascinating questions:

How does the mind work?

What are intelligence and emotion?

What causes humans to be loving, jealous, and aggressive?

In answering these questions, psychologists have divided themselves into specialty areas, such as developmental, personality, learning, and clinical psychology.

How can psychology best be studied? That depends partly on the specialty areas: some require practice in experimental methods and statistics, others require analyses of case studies. All specialties call for reading of texts and other materials. Study methods also depend on whether the course is introductory or advanced.

This discussion focuses on the introductory college courses, which survey the various specialty areas. Students are expected to acquire a basic understanding of the body of knowledge—facts, concepts, theories—that comprises psychology. Success in these courses rests on extracting information from readings and on memorizing and conceptualizing this information. The SQ3R method of study is particularly helpful to these endeavors.

The SQ3R Method

To use this technique, first *survey* the material to be learned: look at chapter introductions, outlines, and summaries in order to organize the topics. Then, taking a section at a time, *question* yourself about the material as you *read* it. Next, look away and *recite* what you have read, glancing back to see what you have forgotten. Finally, after working through all the sections, *review* the entire chapter. Repeat all the steps later. The SQ3R method appears simple, but it is effective because it facilitates basic mental functions: organization, active attention, practice, meaning, and comprehension.

Self-discipline

No study method can work, of course, unless students are motivated to use it. Even those usually motivated are sometimes distracted by other interests and concerns. Self-discipline is thus an important element of study. Such discipline is a learned skill. Psychologists have shown the following guidelines to be useful:

* Set particular times of the day for study and maintain this schedule.
* Select particular places for study—the library or a certain desk—and do not use them for other purposes.
* Set a goal for each study session and, if necessary, give yourself a reward for reaching each goal (for example, a TV break).
* Reward yourself continuously by thinking of accomplishments already achieved, no matter how small they seem.
* If needed, seek outside help before falling too far behind.

Pitfalls to Avoid

The study of introductory psychology can also be facilitated by avoiding certain common pitfalls. One of these is inaccurate expectations for introductory courses. Too often expectations are shaped by "pop" psychology presented in magazines or on television shows. Such courses distort the topics of psychology and describe it as "common sense" that can readily be grasped through superficial discussion. Psychology is accurately seen as a discipline that applies scientific methods to an array of topics.

Another pitfall to avoid is the excessive use of personal experiences to understand psychological phenomena. It is reasonable to draw on one's own experiences, but in excess this can interfere with learning by closing the mind to other possibilities. For example, when told that "children from upper-class homes are academically advantaged by their environments," students sometimes argue against the statement on the grounds that they come from middle-class homes but have good grades. Their experiences do not make the general statement false, but emphasis of these experiences seems to interfere with clear thinking.

Finally, it is important to avoid the common error of interpreting correlation as causation. Like other sciences, psychology attempts to understand cause-and-effect relationships; in fact, one of its main goals is to discover the causes of behavior. However, relationships are not necessarily causal. For instance, suppose that in seeking the causes of a childhood disorder, it is observed that parents of disturbed children treat them harshly; that is, a correlation (relationship) is found between the disorder and parental action. It is tempting to conclude that parental harshness caused the children's disturbance. This conclusion is unwarranted, though. Perhaps disturbed children are so difficult to manage that they cause parental harshness. Even this brief analysis shows that interpreting correlation as causation can result in misleading error.

The kinds of pitfalls just discussed are not unique to psychology. However, we may be especially vulnerable to them when the subject of study is ourselves.

* * * * * * *

HOW TO STUDY PHILOSOPHY

By
Paul C. Pappas

**Paul C. Pappas, Ph.D.,
West Virginia University,
Professor of History,
WV Institute of Technology**

The aim of this two semester course titled "Introduction to Philosophy" is to familiarize the student with western philosophers and their ideas from ancient times to the present. It attempts to prepare one to think, that is to synthesize and analyze ideas consistently, and to express himself precisely and concisely. Through a better understanding of man's ideological evolution, this course seeks to help students become tolerant and receptive to new theories and to view contemporary social and intellectual strife with a degree of objectivity. Finally, it encourages students to develop their own philosophy and to cope successfully with life's problems.

To acquire a good understanding of this course, the student must learn to define correctly the terms used in philosophy, such as dialectic, determinism, theism, materialism, etc. He/she must be able to define philosophy's aim and become acquainted with its fields, that is metaphysics (and its divisions), ethics, politics, esthetics and logic.

In preparation for an examination, one must keep in mind that there is no substitute for a sound knowledge of the subject matter discussed. It is imperative, therefore, that one reads the textbook assignment and readings before coming to class, that he/she takes good notes in class and participates as much as possible in the class discussions. Via text, class discussions and readings, the student must come to know the answers of various philosophers concerning life's essence and purpose, the freedom of man's will to choose, and man's ability to acquire accurate knowledge and to establish an ethical society conducive to happiness. He/she must become competent to explain how a major philosopher starting with a major premise deduced an organization of ideas, related and consistent, explaining the operations of the universe and man's purpose.

While taking an examination, a student must be able to recall quickly all pertinent information which he/she needs to use consistently to answer the questions. He/she must readily remember the differences and similarities in ideas among those philosophers which he/she is asked to discuss. In addition, the student must be able to express himself/herself well in writing. If one follows these instructions and makes a diligent effort, success can only follow.

* * * * * * *

HOW TO STUDY SOCIOLOGY

By
Ronald L. Johnson

**Ronald L. Johnson, Ph.D.,
University of Wisconsin,
Professor of Sociology,
WV Institute of Technology**

Sociology is based on a scientific approach to human interaction in society. Information learned in this course can be applied to a variety of situations in your life. Success as a student is based on careful study of the subject. Obtain a copy of the text as soon as possible. Scan it in a relaxed manner. Become familiar with the topic headings. Sample some of the subjects which seem to be most interesting.

The instructor generally provides a course outline during the first week of class. Learn the relative importance of the lecture as well the textbook. Many instructors develop their lectures from other material. Class attendance is important. In addition it is important to pay attention to the lectures. Take notes on the major concepts and other points emphasized in the lectures. Review the notes later on the day they were taken.

Time spent out of class in studying the course should be well distributed. The assigned topics should be read soon after they are given. A second reading should follow a few days later. At this time you should pay close attention to key concepts and their characteristics as well as major research findings. Bold-faced type, and italics are often used by authors to highlight these. In addition, well written paragraphs have topic sentences in them. These indicate the major point of the paragraph.

Underline important points or indicate them in the margin of the text, or on your own paper. During the few days prior to the test concentrate on the major points in the text and lecture notes.

It is important to be organized during the test. Budget your time wisely. Do not become involved in the questions on the early part of the test that you fail to complete the test by the end of the period. Furthermore read the instructions and the questions carefully.

Many instructors of sociology use essay questions. It might be helpful to outline your answer to an essay question. Focus on major concepts or properties related to the topic and organize your essay using correct English. Paragraphs, complete sentences, grammar, and spelling are generally important.

If your instructor makes out-of-class assignments, it is important to understand the instructions. Follow these carefully. Observe deadlines for turning in reports. Any difficulty in doing research, writing term papers, as well as other problems in the course, might well be resolved by contacting your instructor. Don't be afraid to use the instructor's office hours that have been created for your benefit.

* * * * * * *

HOW TO STUDY ECONOMICS

By
Mostafa Shaaban

Mostafa Shaaban, Ph.D.,
Indiana University,
Professor of Economics,
WV Institute of Technology

Economics is the study of the allocation of limited resources to best satisfy unlimited needs. For a nation, a business or an individual, there is a cost (opportunity cost) for every course of action. Nothing comes free. Economics concerns itself with minimizing opportunity cost or maximizing benefit from the same cost. Such cost could be labor, raw material or capital.

The study of economics involves the three main facets of learning:

1. Humanities where events are described in order that one may enrich his own life and learn from mistakes of time past.
2. Pure science where you seek explanations for what is happening. This part of economics is called economic analysis or economic theory. Theory to economics is like physics to engineering. You can not understand economic facts without understanding economic analysis in the same way you do not understand how computers function without understanding the physical theories behind building a computer.

3. Applied science where the theories are tested with varying degrees of success and failure.

In order to study economics successfully, you must always differentiate between the three different parts: descriptive, analytical and finally the possible application. The techniques for studying each part vary.

Descriptive economics

Descriptive economics is the easiest. In order to understand and appreciate our economic environment, facts and data are presented. Facts could be presented in words, numbers or graphically. Learning facts does not require more than being exposed to them. The question is to be able to categorize and analyze the facts in order to understand their implications or to be able to distill certain *principles*. I call economics "common sense made difficult" because while it is easy to amass and learn economic facts, it is often difficult to arrive at clear cut answers to economic problems.

Analytical economics

Analytical economics or principles of economics require more to study.

1. First, you must understand the *hypothesis* made in each situation. A hypothesis is a scientific statement, i.e., could be proven right or wrong. A statement like "New York is 5 miles south of Boston" is a scientific statement albeit wrong because it is verifiable. However, a statement like "it is unfair that millions are hungry while millions die of fatness" is not a scientific statement no matter how much people sympathize with the cause unless "fairness" is measurable like miles.

2. Second, you must guard against fallacy of composition. What is true in individual cases may not be true for the total. A business may thrive if workers could be persuaded to accept lower wages but, for the nation as a whole, a general decrease in wages can cause unemployment.

3. Third, you must watch for hidden or unstated assumptions. If we say that an increase in exports can help employment, we are assuming that all other things like investment, government spending, consumption spending and imports are at least not declining.

4. Fourth, you should be able to differentiate between positive science which examines *what is* and normative analysis which suggests *what ought to be*. Normative analysis invites value judgments and different beliefs. one should not get excited about normative analysis. In most economic books and articles, you will find argument for and against certain policy measures, each side is trying to present some analysis to prove his point. Study both arguments and base your preference on sound theoretical analysis in stead of "believing" a certain viewpoint without any logical support.

Applied economics

Applied economics, or what I call prescriptive economics, involves suggesting certain policy measures to solve certain economic problems. As stated above, this is where many will always disagree because of different background, political beliefs and the like. Such prescriptions are not dogmas or sacred texts. One could apply what he learned in economic theory to come up with different prescriptions. The real test for a certain policy measure is application. If it works, it is worth keeping.

While you are reading or listening to an instructor, you must try to answer for yourself two basic questions:

1. What variables is the book or the lecturer assuming to change and which variables will be treated as constants.

2. Why should the changing variables lead to the proposed conclusions. In other words, you should always look for the cause and effect to understand whether the information given you should be accepted or discarded on pure scientific basis with no room for emotional "beliefs".

Statistics, graphs and mathematics

Statistics, graphs, and mathematical equations are basic economic tools and should not scare you. They are different languages to explain the same thing. They have an advantage, however, over verbal explanation. They are clear, short and to the point. A very long table of numbers could be summarized in one equation, a graph or a few statistical easy-to-understand measures. In fact, serious economic analysis contains more of those and less words. It would be of great help to you if you try to make up your graphs and formulae to summarize what you read. This makes it much easier to study under the pressure of time.

Finally, in order to guarantee a good grade you can adopt the following habits:

1. Read the assignment before the lecture. If the chapter has a set of questions, answer the questions or at least read them.
2. Take good notes in the class room. Ask about what you did not understand either in the text or the lecture. There is no silly question.
3. The minute you have a chance, rewrite your notes enforced with what you learned from the book. This way you never forget any details as the fresher the notes the easier it is to read and decipher.

* * * * * * *

HOW TO STUDY MUSIC

By
Charles F. Martyn

**Charles F. Martyn, Mus.D.,
University of Michigan,
Professor of Music,
WV Institute of Technology**

Today's music student has an extremely diverse field of disciplines to study within the area of music. Many students in American schools begin in the performance area. They play in school bands, orchestras, sing in choruses, and a variety of smaller ensembles and entertainment type groups ranging from show choirs to jazz bands, brass ensembles, small Madrigal singing groups, string quartets, and in today's electronic world: synthesizer ensembles and pop-rock groups.

Their activities are only limited by the programs available to them at school and private study. An individual's study may extend from Music Education to theory, history, business, literature, electronic recording and musicology. The business of music today extends into the scientific area of acoustics. Academia expands the discipline into the philosophical field of aesthetics. The history of musical curriculum extends to antiquity and was an important facet with the ancient Greeks.

Music learning, besides being the demanding mental discipline that it is, extends principles of learning into the kinesthetic, the aural, and in the performance area of wind instruments, of course, the oral. Music, in fact, extends learning to the entire body; the hands, fingers, arms, legs, lungs, ears, and eyes, all starting with the brain. Total study is both a science and an art. Acoustics is a branch of Physics, yet the practical artistic application is in performance, theory and the basic science of mathematics.

The "how to" aspect depends on the student's specific interest. Let's look at one avenue briefly: performance. Possessing a performance degree myself, I am aware of the many hours of practice needed to fulfill artistic ambitions, heighten skills, examine literature, and in fact, perform the most demanding pieces of the repertoire.

A player in performance may select many avenues within that specialization such as the study of opera, orchestral literature, chamber music, and of course, solo repertoire. The standards are extremely high on a world class level. The competition is amongst the fiercest of any business climate, and the hours spent in mastery can scarcely be counted. The tension is very acute with high level graduate programs and a competitive environment prevails.

Practice would involve study of tonal materials, pedagogical materials such as etudes, orchestral literature, chamber music, symphonic repertoire and most significantly for the doctorate in performance, a major performance examination with concert, sonatas, and extended solo and ensemble works for my major instrument, the clarinet. The use of a metronome is a regular tool (a time keeping teaching machine) and is utilized by many students of the art. The metronome has been around in history for some 190 years, and is indispensable for disciplined, routine, and systematic practice.

Each specialization can also involve a performer into looking beyond their discipline and beyond the practice hours. As a clarinetist, I became involved in a craft of reed making. Learning that took some time, but enhanced the performance potentiality from the pragmatic frame of reference by enabling me to make reeds of extremely high quality with very consistent results. Musicologists practice the piano. Theorists may study electronics or computers. Composers may involve their discipline into various instruments, practice, mastering computers or recording equipment. Some invent new instruments or uses for older technologies.

Some performers are inclined to specialize in one area or another of the history of literature. Many soloists look to the baroque era or specialized ensembles in the Renaissance or avant garde contemporary schools of thinking, and in fact, branch out from that into areas such as composition or systematic musicology, ethno-musicology and the like. Jazz and improvisation have recently received much pedagogical study and many programs are extant in public schools, colleges and universities across the nation.

The study is severe and demanding, all the while frustrating, but enjoyable and rewarding. **The quest for excellence** can be a very demanding pursuit. The realization that I have come to ultimately in the advanced study of the art is that the day never arrives during a career where one can conclude, "that's it, that's perfection, there is no further to go." Serious students continue their study for a lifetime and learn to manage and organize their time throughout a career to continue individual and personal growth while extending their perspectives, views, knowledge, repertoire and interests.

Music is an international language and must be studied. It's several dimensions continue to expand and reflect modern society and the technology which is constantly evolving. Computers, electronics, and recording coupled with traditional mediums such as symphony, opera, chamber music, solo performance, bands, choruses, folk groups and popular music the world over, assure a marketplace and consumers with buyers and sellers fulfilling a basic need for human expression, communication and enrichment.

Chapter 11

HOW TO STUDY APPLIED SUBJECTS

"It is believed that any engineering course normally should serve two major objectives: First, it should lay down the fundamental principles followed in the engineering profession; and, second, it should indicate by problems or illustrations the manner in which these principles are applied to concrete situations"

Laurence P. Simpson,
Coauthor of "Law for Engineers and Architects"

TOPICS

1. Chemical Engineering
2. Civil Engineering
3. Electrical Engineering
4. Mechanical Engineering
5. Computer Science
6. Accounting
7. Physical Education

HOW TO STUDY CHEMICAL ENGINEERING

By
Shakuntala Ghare

**Shakuntala Ghare, Ph.D.,
Virginia Tech.,
(Former) Professor of Chemical Engineering,
WV Institute of Technology**

Chemical engineering students normally require to study be-tween 15 and 20 courses in chemical engineering. They also have about 15 courses in mathematics, general engineering, physics and electrical engineering. Chemical engineers study almost as much chemistry as a chemistry major. Besides all these courses they need about 10 courses in English, economics and humanities. The chemi-cal engineering discipline in many colleges requires more courses than any other discipline.

Technically an average student is supposed to finish all require-ments for a bachelor's degree in four years. However, several students find out that they can not maintain a better grade if they take a full load. I would strongly suggest any student entering the chemical engi-neering discipline to evaluate his/her capacity, economic situation and other factors and decide to take longer than four years to get a degree. A decision to be a student for five years should be taken as early as possible to facilitate arranging of courses. This is particularly impor-tant in small schools where some courses are taught only once every year, and courses are arranged sequentially with the previous course being a prerequisite.

General guidelines:

1. Attend all classes. Usually the person who conducts the classes is the one who gives tests and many times grades it or at least controls the grading. It is always helpful to see what that person has to say about a given topic. Many professors specifically give an idea about what can appear in a test. There are also several hints during lectures, which can give the student some idea about what to expect on a test.

2. Do all the assigned homework. Many times, particularly in chemical engineering courses, points received for home work constitute part of the final grade. Even if this is not the case, the practice of doing homework helps in the test.

3. If you do not understand any part of the lecture or any part of the homework, talk about it to the instructor. There are a few very important points to be observed when talking to a professor. If he/she gets an impression that you have no interest in the subject, but are only looking for a good grade, that person's enthusiasm in helping you might diminish a little. Show some interest in the subject, some desire to learn, and you can get the best help for your problem. Always try to meet the professor at his/her office during the office hours or by prior appointment.

Some special concerns

Chemical engineering is a discipline that depends equally on chemistry and engineering. The physical and chemical data is commonly given in SI units, while engineering data is available in British units. knowing where to find conversion units is extremely important. Spending too much time in finding them may deprive you of enough time to complete the test. Being familiar with both unit systems always helps.

Examinations in chemical engineering tend to be open book, because of the involved formulae. Reading the textbook and knowing exactly where to find the equations is important. Do not ever think you can read the book during examination time and find the requisite equation.

Most professors give partial credits for the problems even when the answer may be wrong, provided the problem is solved in a systematic manner. Try to solve all the problems, which helps in collecting partial credits.

Study the homework problems before the test carefully. These problems generally serve as guide posts for learning the subject.

* * * * * * *

HOW TO STUDY CIVIL ENGINEERING

By
Richard F. McCormick

Richard F. McCormick, Ph.D., P.E.,
Virginia Tech.,
Professor of Civil Engineering,
WV Institute of Technology

Engineering is a profession which involves the application of scientific knowledge to the solution of practical problems. Civil Engineers plan, design, and supervise the construction of many facilities that are essential to modern life as we know it. A current motto of the American Society of Civil Engineers is "CIVIL ENGINEERS

MAKE THE DIFFERENCE—They build the quality of life." Clean water, safe disposal of sewage and hazardous wastes, adequate highways and other transportation systems, safe buildings and bridges, pipelines, space facilities, and so on are all very important to modern life—these are the purview of the Civil Engineer.

The development of a Civil Engineer involves two stages. The first is the acquisition of scientific knowledge. The second entails learning how to apply this scientific knowledge to the solution of practical problems. The first two years of a civil engineering curriculum basically involves the study of math, physics, chemistry, and various courses in the humanistic social studies. The last two years of the program involve Civil Engineering courses which apply the concepts previously learned to specific problems in Civil Engineering.

Study habits that are successful for learning the concepts of math, physics, chemistry, and so on will also be valuable in studying Civil Engineering courses. Some habits are very important and should be cultured very carefully. Three of these valuable study habits are as follows:

1. **Attendance**—A good student always attends every lecture of every class. This characteristic is extremely important especially in basic foundation classes such as Statics and Dynamics. These courses are the type which continuously build on topics previously studied. Freshmen often are away from home for the first time, and no parent is there to get them out of bed for an 8 a.m. class. Rest assured that the professor will not call to awaken you. You must discipline yourself to attend every class.

2. **Note taking**—Most engineering instructors consider the things they write upon the board to be important. A good student takes notes in class. Especially important are example problems that are worked on the board. Test questions often are taken from example problems that the professor explains in class.

3. **Homework**—The only way to learn an engineering subject well is to work problems. Homework problems must be completed and submitted on time. Only students who conscientiously complete their homework assignments will succeed in

a Civil Engineering program. Since most engineering classes meet on alternating days, it would be wise to begin your homework in the evening of the day it is assigned. The day's lecture will still be fresh in your mind, and if you encounter difficulty, help can be obtained from the instructor several hours before the assignment is due.

In addition to these three valuable study habits, good students have other characteristics. They go to the instructor for help when they are having problems. Do not wait until an exam has been failed to seek help—go as soon and as often as you have trouble with a particular topic or homework assignment. It is also important to develop good personal habits as a Civil Engineering student. The importance of proper food, exercise, and sufficient rest, especially before exams, can not be stressed enough.

ASCE Student Chapter

Finally, the education of a Civil Engineer is not complete without participation in his/her professional society. The American Society of Civil Engineers (ASCE) has organized student chapters at each college and university offering a Civil Engineering program. The activities of the chapter are aimed at introducing each student to the profession. Field trips, outside speakers, social events, regional conference competition and concrete canoe races all help to round out the education of a civil engineer.

* * * * * * *

HOW TO STUDY ELECTRICAL ENGINEERING

By
Robert C. Gillespie

Robert C. Gillespie, Ph.D.,
West Virginia University,
President,
WV Institute of Technology

At first it may seem presumptuous to try to tell someone how to study any particular topic, much less electrical engineering. Furthermore, it has been some time since I have been in the position of studying electrical or any other engineering. What I believe to be of value to the reader, however, are some of the techniques I have used in the past to help students accept and understand various areas within the discipline.

Probably the useful thing a professor can do when teaching a new topic or one with particular difficulty is to relate the outcome to something the student might understand. One such concept is that of system description when studying control systems. Most students simply feel that most systems can not be described with a first or second order differential equation. How about imagining the intuitive speed time curve when putting the pedal-to-the-metal of the common automobile? What happens? Initially, there will be a large speed increase which will gradually, as time goes on, level out to a constant. Note that the rate of speed increase will be large at first and slow to zero with time. Sketch it. it looks like the classic exponential curve—a simple equation to describe such a system. Imagine all such common speed systems. They perform basically the same. Believe your professor when you are told that the system is described by a simple equation. Try to imagine the behavior of your system before you look at the equation. You will gain the faith and confidence you need to truly understand control systems.

How about the concept of transients? Is there really such a phenomena? Simply recall what happened to the lights the last time you plugged in your hair dryer. Did the light dim momentarily? Probably so. How about pulling the plug out of wall on your running vacuum cleaner in the dark? Be careful, but note the arc that is drawn. Transients and induced voltages are concepts that this or that related phenomena demonstrate.

One thing your television may show you is the degree of nonlinearity of the scanning waveforms. Have you ever noticed that sometimes your picture is smaller at the top than the bottom? Imagine that you are getting the scanning voltage from an exponential curve and you are into the part of the curve which is nonlinear. Notice how steep and how closely the lower part of the curve approximates a straight line.

Ask your professor for examples. They help.

Importance of Studying Math

Study your calculus very carefully. Listen and try to understand when your professor talks about rate of change of distance, of velocity, and of acceleration. Even though very early in your studies most of the problems were not of an electrical nature, there is usually an electrical equivalent. Study your math all of the time. It must be part of you.

Laboratory Experiments

Most laboratory experiments are designed to verify some principle taught in the classroom. Very rarely does the instructor make it necessary to make the connection. Make it yourself. What are you trying to show? Take advantage of the opportunity to fine tune your understanding of circuits in the lab. There is a particular benefit when the circuit does not perform as expected. You figure out why? Your understanding and your confidence will exponentially increase if you dig it out yourself.

Role of Hobby in Studying

Lastly, make some aspect of your studies more like a hobby. Subscribe to one of the popular electronic magazines and read it. Try to understand it. Become proficient with a PC. Try "ham" radio. Make it a hobby at least while you are in school. Above all, study, and ask questions.

HOW TO STUDY MECHANICAL ENGINEERING

By
G. Puttaiah

G. Puttaiah, Ph.D., P.E.,
Pennsylvania State University,
Professor of Mechanical Engineering,
WV Institute of Technology

Mechanical engineering is one of the most demanding curriculums on any college campus. Competition to do well is intense in this field because it attracts better students from among the college enrollers. You should be capable of and willing to put in long hours of intense effort, especially during the junior and senior years.

Learn to understand and master the basic concepts with a minimum of memorization. Fundamental concepts and ideas of different courses in mechanical engineering are extraordinarily interwoven and dependent on each other. Mere memorization is a sure way to develop a shallow background that will lean you down the path of failure. Well digested concepts can never be forgotten. Develop the habit of understanding and remembering ideas in the context of their importance and applications. For instance: concepts covered in Strength of Materials are so basic to mechanical design, manufacturing, and such other areas that if you understand and retain the concepts of the former, your performance should be good in the later.

Similarly, fundamental thermodynamic principles are the basic building blocks of heat and mass transfer, power plant engineering and such other energy related courses. Concepts covered in early mathematics courses such as Calculus, Differential Equations, etc., are extremely important for a better performance in Mechanical Engineering.

The following study-related practices on the part of the student have been known to be time-tested strategies for superior performance in Mechanical Engineering:

1. **Attendance:** Attend all classes irrespective of any temptation/excuse not to attend. It enables you to be on top of things; it substantially reduces the effort you need to exert to understand unfamiliar subject matter. More importantly it develops self-discipline which is an absolute necessity for success in all professions.

2. **Classroom Activities:** Take good notes on the material discussed by the professor. Take part in class discussions. An enquiring mind is a smart mind. Successful engineers always ask why?

3. **Homework:** Complete all homework and assignments to the best of your ability. They need not always be one hundred percent correct. Good work habits, self-discipline and deep understanding of concepts can come only from such exercise.

4. **Study Habits:** Keep up a steady pace of learning throughout the semester. Don't accumulate work. Make it a habit to clear all assignments when due. Good grades will follow without fail.

5. **Conference with Professors:** It has been generally observed that students do not meet with their professors as often as they should. College professors are required to maintain posted office hours and most of them will be happy to talk to their students during this time. Office visits can be extremely useful to you. You can get your doubts cleared away with the least amount of time spent; you can maximize your rate of learning. Knowing your professor personally helps to perform better in his/her tests. In addition it will develop self-confidence in you and improve your self-image.

6. **External Reading:** Develop the habit of reading some professional magazines such as MECHANICAL ENGINEER-ING, MACHINE DESIGN etc., and books related to the courses you are taking, which are not prescribed texts. It helps to broaden your knowledge of the subjects in mechanical engineering.

7. **Discussions with Your Classmates:** Exchanging ideas and opinions with your friends could be one of the most effective ways you could develop your personality. It not only helps with your class work but also broadens your outlook on many important current events.

* * * * * * *

HOW TO STUDY COMPUTER SCIENCE

By
Robert A. Marshburn

Robert A. Marshburn, M.S.,
American University,
Professor of Computer Management,
WV Institute of Technology

The computer disciplines of Computer Science and Computer Information Systems provide challenging course work. From basic computer literacy to the advanced programming and systems courses, you will be faced with learning many new concepts and a new vocabulary of technical terms. You will learn new languages as well as a new vocabulary, and you will be asked to apply the new languages to solve programming problems of ever-increasing complexity. Essentially, you the computer student must become a proficient problem-solver.

The rewards for successfully meeting the challenges of the computer disciplines are clear in today's job markets. Are you up to it? Examine your work habits and academic record before you decide to commit to the challenge. As a successful computer or computer information systems student, you must exhibit careful work habits. You must like to "get things right" by checking and re-checking your solutions. Especially with computer programming, you must pay attention to details—the computer is very "picky" about details!

Having reasonable quantitative skills is important. Although the actual mathematics level of your course may vary widely from course to course, you must be adept at algebraic manipulation and logical thinking. Above all, you must be a determined problem-solver who will not quit until the last "bug" or error is eliminated. "Beating the computer" by reaching a final solution should be your primary goal and joy!

If you are up to these challenges, how can you best tackle the course work ahead? What study methods are most useful for each type of computer course? For the introductory courses your first year, the primary objectives will be to develop a strong vocabulary of computer terminology and to gain a solid foundation of computer hardware and software concepts. You should look up any technical term in the textbook glossary or a technical dictionary whenever you encounter such terms in your textbook readings. If the term is still unclear, ask your instructor or tutor to define it in familiar terms.

Terminology and basic concepts will also be stressed in class lecture and discussion. In your class notes, be especially careful to note examples and definitions for later reference. Complex concepts will often be introduced through simple analogies in the textbook or class lecture; make sure you note the analogies and understand their significance. It is **not** generally wise to memorize definitions or basic concepts verbatim; try instead to "internalize" your own personal definition or analogy.

For computer programming courses, you must remember that you are faced with two distinct challenges:

1. to learn the syntax and techniques of a new language, and
2. to apply the language in constructing algorithms to solve specific problems.

The first challenge is best met by reading the textbook carefully for rules and examples as each new language element is discussed in class. It is best to read **before** class, so that class examples become a review and a chance to ask questions. The second challenge is more difficult. In order to successfully apply your newly learned language constructs, you must attempt to see logical patterns in each textbook and class example.

Learn and use structured programming methods from the start; remember that big problems can be cut down to size through modular structures which exhibit the **same** logical patterns you have seen in

class or the textbook. Use program planning tools such as the hierarchy diagram and flowcharts or pseudocode **before** attempting to develop program code. Desk-check your code or have a programming
partner "walkthrough" your code to spot errors or omissions.

Most of the non-programming courses in the computer disciplines will stress problem-solving, from simple capacity and timing
problems of basic hardware concepts to complex algorithms in the
area of operations research. It is essential to practice problems until
you feel comfortable with their solution methods; solve the required
problems, re-solve problems whose solutions are given, and at least
verbalize the solution set-up for still more problems. Most problems
on tests or quizzes will be similar to the assigned problems, so you
must look for similarities.

Before a test or quiz, review the problems you have solved and
think of the problem types or models. If the test or quiz is "open
book", **do not depend on the book** for your solutions; use the book
as a reference only.

* * * * * * *

HOW TO STUDY ACCOUNTING

By
Howard Nunley

Howard Nunley, M.S., C.P.A.,
University of Kentucky,
Professor of Accounting,
WV Institute of Technology

In order for the student to be successful in the study of accounting, it is necessary to develop a vocabulary of accounting terms. Accounting has often been called the language of business and you cannot communicate if you do not understand the language.

In addition to the vocabulary, it is essential that the student have a thorough understanding of three important concepts—the business entity, the matching process, and the cost principle.

The business entity concept assumes that the entity, or business unit, is separate and distinct from the owner(s). This concept can be expressed as an equation:

$$Properties = Claims$$

For every piece of property someone has a claim. In accounting, properties are called assets; some examples of assets are cash, accounts receivable, inventory, and building. Assets may be tangible or intangible.

Claims are divided into two classifications: claims of outsiders which we call liabilities and claims of the owner(s) which we call proprietorship, capital or net worth. Thus the equation can be expanded so that

$$\text{Assets} = \text{Liabilities} + \text{Proprietorship}$$

In the life of every entity are a series of happenings or events that need to be recorded. We refer to these events as transactions. Every transaction will affect the equation in some manner.

If we increase one side of the equation—something on the other side must increase. If one side decreases, something on the other side decreases. We must always maintain a balance in this equation.

In order to determine how profitable our entity has been, we must wait until the final liquidation of the entity. After all the assets are realized and all of the liabilities have been paid, then and only then will we know how profitable our entity has been. Obviously, we cannot wait until the final wind-up so we divide the life of the entity into annual fiscal years. The matching process attempts to offset the revenue with all of the cost and expense in connection with earning it.

Generally accepted accounting principles are based on the accrual method as opposed to the cash basis. Under the accrual method, we recognize revenue when we earn it, not when it is received, and we recognize expenses when they are incurred, not when they are paid. Under the cash basis, we recognize revenue when we receive payment and we recognize expenses when cash is disbursed. Whenever the financial statements contain receivables and payables you will know that the accrual method is being used.

The cost principle simply means that we record acquisitions at cost—whatever we paid for them. In other words, we cannot look at a financial statement and determine what the business is worth. For example, a building might be carried on the financial statement at $75,000. but its fair market value might be $200,000. As a general rule, accountants would write an asset down but would not carry it at an amount above cost.

If the student has an understanding of the concepts as outlined in this article, they will have taken the first step in the mastery of a difficult subject.

Anyone seeking a career in the business world would be well advised to include the study of accounting in their preparation.

* * * * * * *

HOW TO STUDY PHYSICAL EDUCATION

By
Elizabeth A. Miller

Elizabeth A. Miller, M.S.,
West Virginia University,
Professor of Physical Education,
WV Institute of Technology

How many times has a Physical Educator had to field the questions of "How can you study for a physical education test?" or "What can a professor ask on a square dance test, badminton test, or swimming test, etc.?"

This educator feels the student studying for the theory classes in physical education would not necessarily employ any different techniques than those used in studying for other disciplines such as history or literature. However, the activity classes in physical education are another concern. And that is the purpose of this particular portion of this book.

It is the belief of this writer that a student enrolled in a physical education activity class should employ certain study techniques to ensure himself/herself of a better understanding of the sport or activity which would ultimately lead to his/her desired behavioral outcome.

1. First, every student must come to the realization that physical education activity classes are not just *play* periods but actual learning sessions just as other academic disciplines. When he/she has programmed himself/herself into the correct mental state, then he/she can progress with speed to the next step.

2. Secondly, it is highly recommended that the student secure a brief understanding of the historical background of the particular sport in question. For example, become familiar with how the sport began, how it got its name, how it was originally played as compared to the modern day style. Denote the changes in rules, regulations, dress code, equipment, playing area, etc.

3. Thirdly, the student needs to familiarize himself/herself with the likenesses and differences of this sport's relationships to other sports he has already mastered or has a thorough concept of. For example, a football player who is enrolled in a physical education activity class of badminton, should be able to sense the likeness of endurance of running in both sports. The same would go for a variety of other sports.

4. Fourthly, the student should denote the values the various sports may possess (social, physical, psychological).

Once he/she has acquired the above standards he is then ready to complete the following five steps of his sequential study techniques:

1. Master the sport's vocabulary
2. Identify present equipment and playing area
3. Develop the basic playing skills and scoring techniques of the particular sport with regards to the rules and regulations of the game.
4. Conquer the basic strategies and playing situations.
5. Become an assertive participant and a competitive title contender by repeatedly practicing the skills to a respectable performance level.

The above five steps do not come with just first try. Therefore, the student must continuously avail himself/herself to as many of the visual aids as often as possible. These aids can be in the form of repeated requests of teacher demonstrations, repeated challenged matches with fellow classmates, repeated viewing of film strips or movies or any other visual aid as deemed necessary.

Whatever abilities one has as he/she enters a physical education activity class, this educator feels they will improve if the student follows the previously mentioned guidelines in studying. Perseverance and sincere hard work will be great contributors to the aspired goals of having attained a particular sports performance with enough satisfaction for a life-time of fun.

Techniques for Taking Tests, Report Writing, and Effective Speaking

Chapter 12

HOW TO PREPARE FOR AND TAKE QUIZZES, TESTS AND EXAMINATIONS

"You must concentrate upon and consecrate yourself wholly to each day, as though a fire were raging in your hair,"—instruction to a medieval samurai.

Taisen Deshimaru,
author of "The Zen Way To The Martial Arts."

TOPICS

1. Importance of Tests
2. Different Types of Tests
3. Test-taking, a Skill You Can Develop
4. How to Prepare for and Take Quizzes
5. How to Prepare for 1-Hour Tests
6. How to Prepare for Final Examinations
7. Specific Tips for Essay Tests
8. Specific Tips for Multiple-Choice Tests
9. Specific Tips for True-False Tests
10. Specific Tips for Problem-Oriented Tests
11. Other Forms of Tests
12. Strategies during and after Tests

IMPORTANCE OF TESTS

Right Attitude

Tests play an important role in your learning process. It is essential that you develop a positive attitude towards tests which will not only reduce anxiety about tests but will also help you enjoy the pleasures associated with learning. The real purpose of every test you take is the self-assessment of your understanding of the material covered in a particular course. However, in our system of education, an outside authority is usually required to assess a student's learning and progress, and in a college environment this role is generally assigned to the instructor. From your point of view as a student, however, it should be immaterial who the assessor is. What is important is whether you are really learning.

Unfortunately, grades are associated with your learning and since grades have a dominant factor in the modern competitive environment, the student tends to view the test with a feeling of psychological discomfort. It is not uncommon when this discomfort takes undue proportions in some students, manifesting in severe psychosomatic disturbances such as headaches, loss of sleep, diarrhea, loss of concentration and even total blackout during or before a test.

A certain degree of anxiety towards any test is a normal and natural human response. It is even beneficial to you in that it acts as a spark to your motivation to do well on a test—when you develop the right attitude towards tests. The secret of getting better grades has its roots in this psychological factor.

Self-Expression

Tests provide the opportunity for self-expression using the material learned, thus expanding the boundaries of knowledge of the student. This is all the more true in essay tests, problem-oriented tests, and in oral tests.

Beside indicating one's own progress tests have a potential to awaken the spirit of self-competition for better grades next time. It can also motivate the student to compete with others and friends in the class.

Wrong Major/lack of Prerequisites

Among many other things, poor scores on tests can indicate that a student may be in a wrong major or that he/she does not have an adequate background of prerequisite courses. Thus tests provide an opportunity for self correction. It is essential that the student sees his/her academic advisor and student counselor, if need be, when the test scores are consistently poor. Withdrawal from the course before the official withdrawal date for the quarter or semester will help to prevent damage to his/her academic standing.

Need for Extra-effort & Better Time Management

Tests can indicate that the effort put forth by the student was not adequate and that he/she needs to put in extra-effort on his/her own part or some extra tutoring in some cases.

Since only you know how much time and effort you put in preparing for the test, test scores can also indicate whether you need to reorganize your time budget.

Tests have a needling effect on the lazy and the indifferent (who are otherwise capable of putting up a better performance) forcing them to study regularly, reorganize their activities and rearrange their priorities.

Improvement of Test-taking Skill

Taking tests and more tests during your college years improves your test taking skills, which will be useful for you in your future career. Demonstration of continuous education in one's career is needed in today's competitive environment for professional and career advancement and one such index is through passing the appropriate examinations in one's field of interest or specialty.

Teaching Effectiveness

The test at the classroom level serves another very important function for the professor—it tells him/her how effective his/her teaching has been and whether improvements are needed in his/her communication techniques. A fair and open-minded professor is sensitive to the performance of his/her students in the tests and constantly seeks ways and means of improving his/her skill of teaching in as much as the student is trying to improve his/her skill of test taking.

DIFFERENT TYPES OF TESTS

It is important to realize that all tests are not the same and that there are different types. Because of their difference, your method of preparation should be such to suit the particular test. Any test you may take while in college or elsewhere will generally fall into one or other of the following classifications. This knowledge will help you greatly in getting ready for any test.

1. Written tests (Closed book/Open book)
2. Oral tests
3. Laboratory tests
4. Performance tests
5. Take-home tests
6. Quizzes
7. 1-hour tests
8. Examinations (2- or more hours)

Written Tests

Most tests you take in college, in general, will be with your notes and books closed. However , there are a few courses, particu-larly design-oriented which need the use of a handbook of tables or a large number of equations in the test. In such courses, the professor may give an open book test.

Oral Tests

Here the student is judged based on his oral presentation in the presence of one professor or a committee of professors. In general these are given in senior and graduate level courses.

Laboratory Tests

Courses which have a lab attached may partially or fully test the performance of the student in the lab. Most science and engineering courses have labs attached to them for the student to have hands-on experience.

Performance Tests

Tests in athletics, physical education, driving, swimming, music, etc., require the student to attain various levels of performance which will be determined by the professor.

Take-home Tests

These are given, if at all, mostly in graduate courses. The student is expected to play fair and not cheat.

Quizzes (10 or 15 minutes)

Quizzes are generally of a very short duration, such as 10 or 15 minutes. Not all professors give them, but some do. Quizzes may be announced or unannounced. They may be given at the beginning or at the end of a regular class meeting. They are intended to cover the material discussed during the previous class or any specific reading assignment given by the professor the class before.

1-hour Tests

Tests generally imply an hour long duration or precisely the duration of the regular class period. Most classes are of 50 minutes, and the test is designed to last that long. Tests usually cover the material presented since the previous test or from the beginning if it is the first test.

Examinations (Two or more hours)

Those of a longer duration generally from two to four hours are referred to as exams. They may cover the whole material of the course or a part of it as designated by the professor. When the whole course is covered, it is also called a comprehensive test.

In addition to the above classification, you may often come across the following terms:

1. Midterm tests
2. Final examinations

3. Objective tests
4. Subjective tests
5. Design tests
6. Entrance tests
7. Professional License tests.

Midterm Tests

In almost all undergraduate classes in colleges and universities, it is customary to report the student's progress through mid-semester/ mid-quarter grades called midterm grades. You should expect at least one midterm test during the first half of the semester, if not more.

Final Examinations

As the name indicates, these are given at the end of a semester or a quarter to wind up the course. Their weight towards the final grade will be much more than any other individual test, as announced by the professor at the beginning of the semester or quarter.

Objective Tests

Tests containing questions with single answers are generally referred to as objective tests. They include:
1. Multiple choice tests
2. True or false tests
3. Fill in the blank tests, and
4. Problem-oriented tests.

Subjective Tests

Tests with questions which may be answered in many different ways giving room for the student's ability for expression are generally called subjective tests. They include:
1. Essay tests, and
2. English theme tests.

Design Tests

In the areas of applied sciences, particularly in engineering, there are many tests on the designs of systems under study. There is no single answer in designs, but they are subjected to a set of design criteria. Many of these tests may need the use of design tables and charts. Hence, this type of test falls under a distinctly different category. In general they are open book tests.

Entrance Tests

All entrance examinations conducted for the primary purpose of selecting a few among many applicants, whether for jobs or college admissions, are called entrance or qualifying exams.

Professional License Tests

The primary purpose of these tests is to test the professional competence to permit the candidate to practice the profession for which he/she has been qualified academically and otherwise. The nature of these tests varies depending on the profession; for example, engineering professional tests tend to be design tests whereas medical professional tests tend to be multi-choice objective tests.

TEST TAKING, A SKILL YOU CAN DEVELOP

Based on your experience in the tests you took so far in high school and elsewhere, I am sure that you can recall many instances where a studious student who knew the material well was not necessarily the one who got the highest grade. Worse yet, some of the seemingly easy-going students who spent more time playing and less time studying probably got by with good grades. The message is loud and clear—test taking involves more than just studying the text book. It is a skill that needs to be developed, just like any other skill such as driving, swimming or hunting.

"Elevated Enthusiasm"—The Psychological Component

Since the outcome of any test is an uncertain event, it constitutes a stress in itself, and as such most students develop a mental block towards the test. When you aspire for good grades you should examine yourself and your attitude towards tests and defuse the mental block.

It is essential that you accept tests as inevitable mountains to climb on your way to reach your goal. In this positive acceptance lie the techniques of adaptation that will help you climb successfully. With this acceptance, reaffirm your faith in yourself that you can do well in any test and the determination that you should do well. This serves as the subconscious motive force in your subsequent test taking preparations. Look forward to the test as an opportunity for intensive learning and as a challenge for getting better grades. This triple process of self-motivation, self-faith, and self-challenge is expressed in one term as the state of **"elevated enthusiasm"**. It is this enthusiasm that provides the added energy needed for the strenuous and disciplined academic preparations that lie ahead for the test.

Anticipated Preparation—The Physical Component

A hunter goes hunting with anticipated preparation, but the preparations of a lion hunter and those of a deer hunter are different. In the same way a test-taker should align his/her preparations, academic and otherwise, for the type of test he/she is going to take. It is this ability to anticipate and prepare for a test that spells the difference between good and bad grades.

The techniques of preparation for the various types of tests are presented in the following sections.

HOW TO PREPARE FOR AND TAKE QUIZZES

Announced Quiz

Depending on the professor's whims and fancies, quizzes may be given once every week, every month, or as a predetermined number spread through the semester/quarter. Rare indeed is the professor who gives a quiz every class. It is important for you to determine the exact extent of the reading material that will be covered in the quiz. Then check whether you have all of them at your study table or at the library. Usually quizzes are used to test the assigned reading not discussed in class, or they may cover the material discussed in the class the previous day or week. The guidelines for preparation are as follows:

1. Read, and make your own summarized notes on the material to be tested.

2. Anticipate questions and prepare the answers for them.
3. The evening before and the morning of the quiz are critical. Review the material and your summary during this time.
4. Before going to sleep the day before the quiz make yourself a "mock-quiz" and reflect on it.
5. Remember that the duration of the quiz is only 10 or 15 minutes. Every minute counts during the quiz. Be relaxed but alert.
6. Before starting to answer the quiz, close your eyes for a few seconds and recall your review and summary to your mind. This will help you bring to instant focus what you are going to write.
7. Write legibly and steadily with a No.2 pencil or a pen.
8. Turn in your answer paper on time, but never before. If you happen to have a couple of extra-minutes, spend them reviewing what you have written.

Once you have turned your test in, accept your performance as your best at that point of time—even if you think that you have not done well. This self-acceptance will pave the way for continuous self-improvement in later quizzes and tests.

Unannounced Quiz

Not many college professors resort to surprise quizzes. Some even consider it unethical and unprofessional. The purpose of a quiz is only to test the understanding of a student after giving him/her a fair chance to be prepared. However, it is for the professor to decide. If you do run into a course with unannounced quizzes, the only added guideline you need is that you should study that subject systematically every evening before the class, anticipating a quiz next day on the material covered in the previous class.

HOW TO PREPARE FOR ONE-HOUR TESTS

One-hour tests are generally announced a week or 10 days or even earlier giving the student ample chance to study and prepare for the test. The preparation itself falls under 3 distinct categories:

1. Preliminary preparation,
2. Academic preparation, and
3. Ancillary preparation.

Preliminary Preparation

1. Prepare your study goals and a study plan from the day of announcement of the test. It is essential that you have clear-cut goals about your test and a workable plan to take you there. This will provide direction to your efforts.
2. Rearrange your priorities in time budgeting, giving importance to the preparation for the coming test.
3. Make provision for an hour or more **every day** exclusively for the coming test. It is the systematic and consistent effort on your part that will enhance the effectiveness of your preparation.
4. Pep up your **"elevated enthusiasm"**. Remind yourself everyday about your determination for self-excellence. Look forward to the test with the challenge of a mountain climber.

Academic Preparation

1. Know as much about the test as possible. It is the fear of the unknown that acts as a restraint in your efforts and prevents you from doing your best. Ask your professor and talk to your fellow students about the test at least once before the test.
2. Know about the exact territory to be covered. Revise your notes to make sure to have all the materials available for study.
3. Specifically apply SQ3R study technique to the textbook and classnotes every day.
4. Review all assignments. The reading and problem assignments assigned by the professor have more importance in his/her eyes than you may realize, particularly from the test point of view. In fact, they are learning aids for the subject matter discussed in class.
5. Review your periodically prepared summary sheets, and make a grand summary exclusively for this test. Be sure to review this every day till the day of the test.

6. If the subject matter is problem-oriented try to work out as many problems as possible; do not just read worked and example problems. Review your equation sheets and model problems, if any, pertaining to the course.

7. Go hunting for old test papers for this course, particularly those given by your professor in the previous semesters. Trying to answer old questions is an excellent way of preparing for the test. You don't have to feel guilty about it.

8. Prepare a set of anticipated questions and their answers based on **your** study and review. This puts you in command of the subject matter from your perspective. Often times, it may not be much different from that of your professor.

Ancillary Preparation

Though not as a part of the direct preparation the following ancillary steps can be taken to enhance the overall effectiveness of your preparation.

1. Periodically make appointments with your professor to clarify your doubts and ask questions regarding the test. Watch out for clues and hints from the professor's remarks and include them in your preparation.

2. Join a study group of your friends and take part in the discussions. Listen to their comments and explanations.

3. Keep your recreational activities to the minimum for the week preceding the test, giving yourself extra-time for preparation.

4. Pay attention to your general health. Eat well but wisely. Get enough sleep each day so that you can study at the top of your efficiency.

HOW TO PREPARE FOR FINAL EXAMINATIONS

The dates for the final examinations are generally set for the last week of the semester/quarter which is known as the examination week. Preparation for the final examination is not of an exclusively different kind. It is simply the extension of the preparations used for routine tests. However, there is a subtle difference. Unlike these during-semester tests the final examination can be comprehensive, covering the subject matter of the whole course, or at least substantially more material than one-hour tests. The duration of a final examination is also likely to be two or three hours.

It is imperative that you give yourself not less than three weeks preceding the final exam week for preparation. Make a suitable study schedule for these three weeks with appropriate budgeting of time for **all** of your exams.

Start preparing for the exams exactly on the same pattern as presented for the 1-hour tests in the preceding section which shall include the preliminary, academic and ancillary preparations. Keep in mind that your study schedule should give you adequate room for systematic and consistent preparation for each and every one of your final exams.

SPECIFIC TIPS FOR ESSAY TESTS

Many students feel uncomfortable with essay tests. There is no need to, if they know how to prepare for and take an essay test. It does require **recall** and **memory** on the part of the student and an ability to organize and express his/her ideas to create an essay satisfactory to the professor, all under the pressure of a test.

It also requires studying and understanding of the material and there is no room for guess work. Simple recognition of right answers as in some other forms of test will not do. Further, a reasonable command of writing with an adequate array of words and phrases is needed for creating a good essay, not to mention a knowledge of the rules of grammar and spelling.

For the above reasons, on the face of it, essay writing appears difficult. But, when you realize that ability to express in writing (as well as in speaking which is discussed in a later chapter in this book) is a skill that can be developed, you will find that appropriate and adequate preparation will help you face an essay test with confidence and ease.

There is another bright side to the essay test. Because few students write good essays, particularly in tests, your chances of getting good grades are high if you have developed the skill of good essay writing. Professors who give essay tests are quick to spot a pleasing essay and they tend to reward the student who can do so with a good grade.

Preparing for an Essay Test

The following 6 steps are basic to the effective preparation for an essay test:

1. Study the whole material designated for the test and try to understand it. Use the SQ3R technique which is the most suited for essay tests.

2. Prepare your own anticipated questions that are most likely to be asked in the test. Treat these questions as if they were from a real test and **practice** answering them in the literal sense by writing out the answers on a sheet of paper. Remember that this is the single most important step in your preparation for an essay test. Having written the answer, review it critically to see if you have made any factual mistakes, and check spelling, grammar, etc.

3. Make a list of key words and phrases, even idioms, pertinent to the essay material. Review this once a day or more often. Writing out this list will help you get a command of the expression needed for writing the essay.

4. Learn the precise meaning of the most often used directional keywords of an essay test such as:

analyze	evaluate
compare	examine
contrast	explain
criticize	interpret
define	justify
describe	outline
differentiate	state
discuss	trace

5. Learn to view the essay material from the professor's viewpoint. Pay attention to the pet opinions of the professor.

6. Before the test, learn from the professor his/her criteria for grading the essay, so that you can organize your

ideas and mould them to suit his/her criteria while taking the actual test.

Taking an Essay Test

Following specific hints will help you to take an essay test successfully:

1. On receiving the test, the first thing to do, of course, is to read the directions and determine the number of essays to write. Budget your time accordingly and start with the essay question for which you are well prepared.
2. Locate the directional keywords of the question such as analyze, criticize, discuss, etc., and make yourself poised to mobilize your thoughts in that direction.
3. Use the **"pearl-string"** technique to organize your thought. On a worksheet write all the ideas, phrases, and words related to the topic that pop up at random in your mind. Put a circle around each distinct idea. Each circled idea is a **"pearl"**.
4. Budget your time, keeping an eye on your watch. Recall your professor's viewpoint on this question and start writing picking the "pearls" in a suitable order. Pay attention to the opening sentence of your essay and start "stringing the pearls".
5. Use new paragraphs as evidence of your organization of thought. Use facts to support your arguments. Write short and simple sentences. Aim for clarity of expression and effectiveness of communication rather than creativity and style.
6. Keep track of your time budget without being pressured.
7. Write neatly. Neatness and a good handwriting are your best assets in an essay test. End the essay with a paragraph to forcibly present the central theme of what is asked for in the question. Always try to write more than less.
8. Spend a minute or two reviewing what you have written checking for spelling, grammar, punctuation, and other errors. This step is very important. You are in fact looking at

your own creation in the form of an essay, your "string of pearls"—as it will be seen and graded by your professor.

9. Finally a word of caution. Don't ever try to use scribbled writing wantonly to hide your weakness in spelling, etc. It is the surest way of getting poor grades.

SPECIFIC TIPS FOR MULTIPLE-CHOICE TESTS

Probably the most popular kind of test in education, business and industry is the multiple-choice test. Developing the skill to take multiple choice-tests successfully is among the most important things for you to do to improve your grades while in college and to take competitive exams later for your career and professional advancement.

In a multiple-choice test, you are given one main incomplete statement or a question called the **stem** and a set of several choices called the **options or alternatives**. You are asked to select one correct answer from those many options. The following example is typical of multiple-choice test questions:

Stem	Urban transportation is most efficient when
Options	1. It includes buses 2. It includes bicycles 3. It does not include passenger cars 4. It does not include commercial vehicles 5. It has a balanced integration of all the modes.

Despite the apparent simplicity of the format of the multiple-choice test questions, this kind of testing can be not only demanding but confusing. The form of test itself is such that the professor will be able to test you on a vast amount of material. The primary aim in multiple-choice testing is to test how thoroughly the student has understood the material rather than how much one has studied. Therefore, it is not enough just to study the material; you need to develop the skill of taking multiple-choice tests.

How to Prepare for a Multiple-Choice Test

Unlike an essay test, multiple-choice questions do not require any composition ability, organizational skills or even spelling skill. It does not mean that you can go to the test with no preparation. Since the multiple-choice questions are aimed at your understanding of the material, it is necessary for you to choose the right type of technique to study the material for comprehension.

Multiple-choice type of testing is adaptable for all the three major types of learning: information, manipulating information and problem solving. Depending on the nature of the course work and the whims of the professor multiple-choice questions can be used for the whole or part of the test. Find out from him/her all you can learn about the test and start preparing accordingly.

Remember that a multiple-choice test can cover not only a lot of ground but in greater detail than any other test. Hence, you must prepare for a multiple-choice test with an organized effort. Do not just rely on intuition and luck; use the following guide lines.

1. Study all the assigned material.
2. Use appropriate study techniques such as SQ3R for comprehension and understanding.
3. Predict questions on your own and answer them for practice.
4. Be systematic in your daily routines, following the study plan which you have prepared for yourself.

Taking a Multiple-Choice Test

1. On receiving the test read through it fully, placing a tick mark in the margin in front of the ones whose answers you know or that look familiar.
2. Start with a question you know. Read it carefully. Be sure that you fully understand the question before considering the options given for the answer.
3. Read the options, weighing and examining every word and phrase, and determine which answer best fits the stem.
4. If needed, choose your answer by the process of elimination.
5. Look for built-in hints or clues in the form of **strong, 100% words** (words that allow no exceptions; absolutes), and **weak**

words (words that allow for exceptions in varying degrees.)

Some strong words and phrases are:

all	none
always	without fail
everybody	without exception
never.	

Some weak words are:

generally	often	may
usually	sometimes	may be
most	probably	perhaps
many	essentially	

When strong and weak words are used to check for logical consistency between the option and the stem you can find the correct option more easily.

6. If you find two options that convey identical sense in a question both must be wrong.

7. When two answers are opposite in a question, eliminate one by reasoning.

8. When you don't know the best option to a question, go by your first impression.

9. When you are forced to guess eliminate absurd and silly options.

10. Do not leave any question unanswered; if logic fails guess an answer.

11. The option given in an unduly long sentence is likely to be wrong. Read it carefully before you decide.

12. Review your answers when you have finished the test. Do not change any of your answers unless you are 100% sure.

SPECIFIC TIPS FOR TRUE-FALSE TESTS

The form of testing through true-false questions is not as popular as the essay or multiple-choice tests. Many professors do not believe that true-false tests can effectively reflect the true learning of the student. True-false questions are in effect statements and the student is asked to show whether the statement is "true" or "false" by placing the word in front of the statement. A typical question is as follows:

> Write a "T" in the space if the answer is true and "F" if it is false.
>
> _____ 1. By definition, an elastic material is time-dependent in its response to an applied load.

Even if the student does not know the answer, he/she has a 50/50 chance to guess it correctly. For this reason some professors assign a penalty for a wrong guess, such as losing double the score for every wrong guess.

There are, however, some merits to the true-false method of testing. it can cover a lot of material and therefore is popular on final examinations. Some professors resort to it to provide a variety in the form of testing and give it as a part of the test, if not the whole test.

The strong point in favor of true-false tests lies in its ability to test the student's learning regarding the accuracy of facts and the relation between facts, events, and ideas.

How to Prepare for A True-False Test

1. Pay attention to factual information learning which requires organization, summarization and categorization of the facts learned.
2. Aim for learning facts and relationship.
3. Remembering the facts learned is crucial to taking the test; you will do well to set up concentrated study sessions two or three days before the test for effective recall.
4. Learn to analyze the keywords and phrases in the test which will be reflective of the nature of the statement given. In a way, they are indicators if you have learned to recognize them. These words are known as **qualifiers.** Words like always, never,etc., are absolute qualifiers, whereas words like usually, most of the time, etc., are relative qualifiers. The true or false nature of the statement of the question must be evaluated in terms of these qualifiers.

Taking a True-False Test

1. On receiving the test read through it once completely. Place a tick mark with a pencil on the margin in front of the questions you can correctly recognize immediately.
2. Start with the ones you have marked. Look for the qualifiers in the statement such as always, never, usually, most, frequently, normally, almost, etc. Based on your knowledge of the subject you can now analyze the statement in the light of the qualifiers to arrive at your answer.
3. Just place a T or F in the space provided as your answer. Do not try to interpret the statement or justify your choice.
4. If you recognize a part of the statement to be false, the whole statement is false.
5. If you don't know the answer to a question do not leave it blank. Guess using your first impression. You still have a 50/50 chance of being correct.

SPECIFIC TIPS FOR PROBLEM-ORIENTED TESTS

By virtue of the nature of the subject matter, courses in mathematics, physics, accounting, engineering, etc., generally require a different form of testing other than multiple-choice or true-false. The most meaningful form of testing for these subjects is to give a set of problems and the student is asked to solve them using mathematical and other skills learned before or during the course. The questions usually have a unique answer. However, design problems in engineering may have more than one correct answer which are subject to a certain criteria.

The learning in these subjects is concept-oriented rather than information-oriented, and accordingly the techniques of studying and preparation for the tests will be different. You should bear in mind that these subjects can not be learned just by reading. **Visualization** and **comprehension** should go together for understanding the material and for this reason studying these subjects will take more time than an information oriented subject.

How to Prepare for a Problem-Oriented Test

1. Be aware that there are two elements of importance in your preparation: (1) comprehension and understanding of the fundamentals of the problem, and (2) handling or using appropriate techniques to solve the problem.
2. Find out about the extent of the material that will be covered in the test. Employ those techniques of study such as visualization to promote the comprehension and understanding of the studied material.
3. Prepare a collection of model problems based on the professor's emphasis in the class lectures and review it once a day.
4. Prepare a set of equations that are fundamental for the material of the test and needed for problem solving. Review them for thoroughness.
5. Learn the art of thinking through sketches and free-body diagrams. These are powerful tools for solving problems which need a mental picture.
6. When the use of design tables is needed or when there are too many equations to remember, some professors declare a open book test; some allow a formula sheet written in your own hand-writing. In such a test a methodical preparation and organization of the allowed materials makes the difference.
7. Be very familiar with your calculator and all its functions. If possible carry a spare calculator to the test.

Taking a Problem-Oriented Test

1. Read through all the questions and start with the one you are most familiar with.
2. Make sure what data are given, and what exactly you are to find before you attempt to solve the problem.
3. Wherever possible, make use of a sketch or a free-body diagram to think clearly through the problem.
4. Check your arithmetic calculations **at every step** before you go further.
5. Keep an eye on your watch for time management. Problem solving may involve concentrated thinking and it is easily possible for you to lose track of valuable time.

6. When you have solved a problem, write your answer clearly as the very last step within the space on the work sheet for that problem. Make it look prominent by underlining, or placing a box around it or placing an arrow by the side of the answer.
7. Revise your work sheet after you have done all the problems. Go over the problems that you are doubtful about. Never leave the examination hall without revising all the problems.

OTHER FORMS OF TESTS

Three other forms of tests are also employed sometimes, other than the three we have discussed. They are: matching questions, short-answer and fill-in the blank questions. At the college level they are seldom given as complete tests. However, many professors use them to introduce variety in the questions and also to supplement the main form of testing in subject areas most suited for these forms.

Matching Tests

Matching is primarily based on the principle of association in educational psychology. It tests your familiarity with the concepts, facts, issues, personalities, events, etc. Matching questions in general are presented in two columns, a list of questions and a list of answers with the direction that the questions in one column be matched with answers in the other. Your task is to connect the right answer with the right question. Matching definitions and terms is also a popular form of matching in subjects where many terms are to be learned precisely for effective communication.

Taking a matching test is relatively easy since you have only to decide which member of the question list belongs to which member of the answer list. Start with the known ones and guess the unknowns.

Fill-in Tests

Fill-in tests aim at measuring your ability to recall facts or generate an answer to a problem which may be simple to compute. They do not aim at interpretation of facts or solving complex problems. For this reason they are very popular as minor questions in a test to supplement the main test. Your task is to write your answer in the space provided in the question, which is usually in the form of a statement.

Fill-in tests are very effective for subject matters dealing with facts, dates, events, names, concepts, and direct use of formulas. It serves as a good method for the teacher to check how well you have studied and how much attention you have paid in the class.

Two examples of fill-in questions are shown below:

1. _____ is the key to effective learning.
2. A freely falling body has an acceleration equal to _____ ft/sec/sec.

Taking a fill-in test requires organized learning, holding in memory and effective recall. And there is no room for guess work. For this reason preparing for a fill-in test must be done with all seriousness in a systematic manner as discussed earlier.

Short-Answer Tests

Short-answer tests are basically similar to the fill-in tests. The purpose of short-answer questions is primarily to test your recall of specific facts or other information and their manipulation. You are asked to write an answer which, unlike an essay test, can be just a word, a phrase, or a simple sentence at the most, or the answer to a simple problem which you are expected to solve arithmetically or otherwise. Explanations are not needed.

Following examples are typical of short-answer questions:

1. Who is a hypochondriac?
2. What is the time taken for a body to fall freely through a height of 32.2 ft?

Preparing for and taking a short-answer test is not any different from that of a fill-in test. You must remember that there is no room for guess work and that you must study all the material of the test thoroughly and in an organized manner before taking the test. Concentration, memory and recall are the key words to be associated with the learning and preparation for short answer tests.

STRATEGIES BEFORE, DURING, AND AFTER TESTS

No war was ever won by an army that had no fighting strategy for the battle it fought. No football match worthy of its name was ever won without a playing strategy. Strategies are systematic steps to follow with a clear-cut aim or goal in view, anticipating at the same time impediments and difficulties on the way. It is strategy that you must be aware of to take you successfully towards your goal to get better grades and graduate with distinction.

Strategy before a Test

1. Have a study plan and a well defined study goal from the day of announcement of a test. In case of a final exam have them ready and get started weeks ahead.
2. The key to learning is organization. Organize your study habits and study materials for systematic learning.
3. Budget your time as discussed before.
4. **The week before:**
   * Have a study plan and a well defined study goal from the day of announcement of any test. In case of a final exam have them ready and get started at least two weeks ahead.
   * Do not cram. Read to understand.
   * Be regular in going to bed every night to get regular sleep.
   * Minimize your extra-curricular activities. Avoid completely strenuous physical activities and exercises.
5. **The day before:**
   * Revise only your notes, summaries, model problems, and equations.
   * Do not keep studying the textbook and new material that you have not studied within the week.
   * Do not study late into the night.
   * Go to sleep early. As you lie on your bed close your eyes and recall the entire summary of the subject matter for the test. Visualize your sitting in the exam-

ination hall and taking the test. Look forward with
eager anticipation to the dawn of the morning.

6. **The hour before:**
    * Go over the summary sheet for the last time.
    * Arrive well ahead of time to the examination hall and
      be in your seat at least 5 minutes before the test be-
      gins.
    * Check your gear, pens, pencils, straight edge, calcu-
      lator, and eraser; place them on your table in a stable
      and handy position.
    * Close your notes and books and relax. Take three
      diaphragmatic deep breaths, breathing out slowly,
      which will help focus your mind and help you con-
      centrate on the test. Suggest to yourself that you will
      do well in this test. Look forward to receive the test.

Strategy during the Test

1. On getting the test, skim the questions for a minute or two.
   Do not get unduly anxious; remember that even those questions you know well may look unfamiliar and difficult under
   the stress of first exposure in the test.
2. Start answering the question that is most familiar to you.
3. Leave out the problem you don't know and move to the one
   you can handle.
4. Come back to these unanswered questions after you have
   done the known ones.
5. In problem-oriented tests, you may easily lose track of time
   working on a problem. Be time conscious and keep an eye on
   your watch. If you get stuck in a problem, do not keep working trying to figure out the solution. Move to the next problem which you can handle. Come back to the problem left in
   the middle after you have done the others.
6. Set aside the last 5 minutes for reviewing your test.
7. Write your answers clearly and legibly with clear demarca-
   tions between questions by drawing a line or providing extra
   line spaces.

Do not cheat—no matter how strong your temptations are. Cheating is cowardly and is the anti-thesis of learning. Besides, if you are caught the penalty for cheating on tests can be devastating, varying from temporary suspension to total dismissal from your college or university.

Strategy after the Test

Developing a proper attitude towards tests by recognizing their due place in your college life is essential to get the most out of your college education. Following are some salient pointers for attitude building:

1. It is natural that you will feel apprehensive as you come out of an examination, and you may think that you have not done well enough.
2. Do not enter into a post-mortem analysis of the test with another student just after the test. It does not serve any useful purpose.
3. Go home or to another activity with a positive feeling that you did every thing you could in preparing for and taking the test.
4. Look forward to the next test with the spirit of a mountain climber.
5. Be sure to be in class the day the professor returns the test. If he/she discusses the test, note your errors for future guidance and learning.
6. Do not argue with the professor for a small gain of points in front of the class. Meet him/her in his/her office and present your case. Politely bring to his/her notice any errors in grading. Remember that professors tend to be more favorably responsive to your encounter in their office rather than in the class room.
7. If you had a good score in the test, be happy and resolve to do even better next time. If you had a poor score try to learn from your mistakes and find out how you can improve your skill in preparing for and taking tests.

8. A test is only a crude measure or tool that attempts to evaluate your learning and knowledge of the subject matter. Do not entertain any self-pity or inferiority complex that you can not score high.

Remember that you have the potential to develop your skill at learning and take tests and graduate with distinction just like any body else has. It is only your self-effort through self-discipline that makes the difference.

Chapter 13

HOW TO WRITE ESSAYS, TERM PAPERS AND THESES

"Writing is both an art and a craft. In the novelist, the playwright, and the poet, the art is paramount to the craft. In the technical writer—because he has a specific task to do—craft is paramount."

Richard W. Smith,
author of "Technical Writing"

TOPICS

1. Writing as a Skill
2. The Process of Writing
3. Stumbling Blocks to Effective Writing
4. Differences between an Essay, Term paper, and a Thesis
5. How to write an Essay
6. How to Write a Term Paper
7. How to Write a Thesis

WRITING AS A SKILL

The greatest weakness in most college students today is the lack of skill to write and present a report or paper which is well organized, lucid, and readable. Writing is a creative activity of thought transfer which has as its primary purpose the communication of ideas from the writer to the reader. It is this power of communication that wields enormous influence in shaping and changing the views of others.

The old adage that the pen is mightier than the sword has proved itself time and again in the history of civilized societies. It is no wonder that every school or college that you attend places so much importance on your developing this skill of writing.

Writing as a skill can be improved and developed, just like any other skill, by diligent application, and consistent practice, and by learning the fundamental principles of the writing process itself.

THE PROCESS OF WRITING

The process of writing involves the following six distinctly different and sequential stages:

1. Selection of an idea or theme
2. Collection of supporting and related ideas
3. Organization of the collected ideas
4. Drafting or committing to paper
5. Revising
6. Finishing.

All ideas need a nucleus to start with which may be an idea or a theme. It is analogous to having an idea to build a structure—may be a house, a palace, or a multi-storied skyscraper. The second stage calls for collection of supporting and related ideas which are needed for the elaboration of the conception of the first stage. It is like visualizing the various functional components for the desired structure. Next is the organization of the collected ideas so that a clear and effective communication can be established. It is akin to making the architectural blue print of the structure envisaged.

The fourth stage involves the actual writing in which the organized ideas are spun into words without losing track of the central theme known as the first draft. This stage is equivalent to starting to build based on the blue print. The next stage is revising the first draft, adding, subtracting and rearranging the text to make it readable and communicative as desired which, in turn, is similar to architectural minor adjustments but not altering the core of the structure. The last stage of the writing process is to call quits and get the final report typed or printed and present the created product. It is, of course, equivalent to finishing and the formal opening of the built structure in its final form.

Though these six stages of writing are universal for all writing projects, there are subtle differences in their application to specific projects which are discussed in the following sections of this chapter.

STUMBLING BLOCKS TO EFFECTIVE WRITING

It is essential that you be aware of the five main stumbling blocks to effective writing so that you can safeguard yourself against them in your preparation before taking up a writing project. They are:

1. Lack of enthusiasm for the project undertaken.
2. Lack of an adequate vocabulary and a reasonable command of the language.
3. Lack of adequate familiarity with grammar, syntax, punctuation, and spelling.
4. Fear of criticism from professors and others.
5. Not recognizing the time factor as an element in the process of writing.

A lack of enthusiasm is indicative of a lack of motivation in the writing project, without which no worthy outcome can be expected. (It is possible for anyone to motivate himself/herself in almost any project through attitude modifications and changes in perspective. However, it is up to the individual. No one else can do it for him/her.)

The second major block to effective writing is a lack of command of the language and a deficient vocabulary. This can be overcome through systematic and continuous reading and learning, which will also improve one's familiarity with grammar, syntax, punctuation, and spelling, the third impediment.

The fourth writing block, namely, the fear of criticism from professors and others, is a normal human response at the psychological level and it can be overcome, at least minimized, through willingness to accept a self-image that is less than perfect. Again, it is up to the individual to bring about this self-acceptance through self-image building techniques discussed elsewhere in this book.

Another factor often overlooked in the creative process of writing is the need for the allocation of adequate time. Many don't realize that there lies an incubation period from the conception of an idea to its transliteration into words. A lack of adequate time often becomes a block to effective writing.

DIFFERENCES BETWEEN AN ESSAY, TERM PAPER AND THESIS

As you progress in your college years you will have, at many times, a need to complete a writing project, which may be an essay, term paper, or a thesis. To do a good job it is essential that you know the differences between them.

Essay

An essay is a short literary composition on a single subject, usually presenting the personal views of the author. It falls under the category of writing based on personal experience and is generally referred to as **informal writing**.

Essays are short in length and seldom continue more than four or five pages. The topic for the essay may be assigned by the professor, or you may have to choose one yourself. They require very little, if any, outside reading, and, for the most part your personal experience is the source of information. They are often written in class or on short notice. The primary purpose of essay writing is to gain the valuable experience of writing. Essay writing serves as a preparatory exercise for the more ambitious and formal term papers and theses which are yet to come.

Term Paper

A term paper is a student essay on a topic drawn from the subject matter covered during the college term. The topic is often assigned by the professor, or he/she may present a list of topics and the student will be asked to choose one. And, in some cases, the professor may ask the student to choose his/her own topic from the subject matter covered and get the professor's approval before starting writing. This is done primarily to help the student who might otherwise choose a topic that may be too far off tangent to the course or for which enough research material may not be available or accessible.

Term papers are classified as **formal writing** because they require the use of more than one source and go beyond the realm of personal experience or knowledge of the writer. Some professors specify a minimum number of sources that the student must consult and list in his/her term paper.

Usually the professor specifies a guide line for the length of the paper in terms of a number of words or type-written pages. While 10 to 15 pages are normal, it is not uncommon for professors to be flexible about the length of the term paper.

Unlike an essay, a term paper is generally specified in terms of a format as to how it should be written and presented. Because of the time needed for the research involved, a due date is specified for submission sufficiently ahead of time. Term papers are usually considered equivalent to one midterm test in point value as far as the course is concerned.

Thesis or Dissertation

A thesis, also called a dissertation, is a research report which is intended to advance an original point of view of the writer as a result of detailed research and investigation. The importance of the thesis lies in the fact that it is a prescribed requirement for advanced academic degrees, often times for the Master's and always for the Doctorate degrees.

A thesis can be purely theoretical, with a hypothesis originally formulated and proved through logical arguments, or it may be based on an original hypothesis proved through experiments. Because of this requirement of originality, working for a thesis becomes time consuming, and for this reason no time limit is generally imposed on thesis submission. However, from practical considerations of funding and other factors, it is in the student's best interest that he/she should try to complete the project of thesis writing in reasonable time.

Also, no limitations are imposed on the length of writing for the thesis, and there are no limitations on the number of sources to be consulted. However, because of the formal nature of the thesis, specified formats for the presentation of the written material are prescribed.

Another major difference lies in the manner in which a thesis is graded. Unlike a term paper it is not graded by a single professor. The student, now called the candidate for the degree, has to present copies of his/her thesis to a predetermined number of faculty members forming his/her examining committee, usually from three to five, sufficiently ahead of time of the date of examination. The candidate then makes an oral presentation of his/her thesis and defend himself/herself before this committee. The unanimous verdict of the committee is needed for the acceptance of the thesis.

The student has to have a faculty member to advise and guide him/her in the whole process of investigation and writing of the thesis, who is able to transmit his/her expertise and experience in that field of inquiry.

HOW TO WRITE AN ESSAY

We mentioned before that an essay is a work of informal writing which does not normally require much outside reading, besides the textbook and any other assigned reading materials.

Though no hard and fast rules can be given for writing an essay, the following step by step procedure will be useful for the novice writer:

1. Decide on the topic or title of your essay, if the professor has not assigned it.
2. Read the assigned material carefully and take notes as you read. Re-read a couple of times more to get a feel for the perspective of the author.

3. On a blank page in front of you put all the ideas you have noted down during your reading and arrange them as if you were constructing a map of ideas.

4. Close your eyes in contemplation and visualize the ideas on the paper in front of you by fusing them into a map in your mind.

5. Having visualized the map of ideas, now start writing using the topic as the core of your essay, this time from **your** perspective and using your own words and phrases.

6. Use new paragraphs to convey the change in ideas discussed in the previous paragraph.

7. Using your visualized map of ideas as your guide keep writing, elaborating on these ideas. As you gain experience in writing, you will find that you are capable of a certain degree of spontaneity of expression which will flow during a concentrated writing period.

8. After the writing is completed, read and revise, correcting the obvious mistakes of spelling, and syntax.

9. Do any cosmetic editing where needed, and have the essay typed or printed in its final form for submission.

10. Remember that a good essay is a product of creative writing and that it can not be done in haste. It requires time, effort, and imagination.

HOW TO WRITE A TERM PAPER

There are **six** basic steps that are essential for all term papers. As a matter of fact, these are the fundamentals for any writing project, which we have mentioned before under "The Process of Writing."

1. Choice of subject and topic
2. Research and collection of material
3. Organization of the material and outline
4. Writing based on the outline
5. Revising
6. Finishing.

Because obtaining good grades in your term paper is dependent on your thorough understanding and effective application of these procedures, they are discussed below in more detail.

Choice of Subject and Title

Rare indeed is the professor who assigns the subject area and the topic for the term paper to individual students. The choice is generally left to the student to give him/her the freedom of choice and an opportunity to learn to choose topics within the framework of the course outline and any criteria specified by the professor. Following are the four points to consider in selecting a topic for the term paper:

1. The subject matter must be interesting and appealing to you.
2. It should not kindle negative emotions such as anger, fear, or grief in you, obviously because of the bias that will restrict your rational thinking.
3. It should be narrow enough to be covered adequately and reasonably within the time allotted for the term paper.
4. Availability of and accessibility to related information using your college library and other sources at your disposal is an important consideration in the choice of the subject matter and topic.

You will be better off by discussing your subject and topic selection with your professor and getting his/her approval. Most professors will be happy to assist you in your choice. Once approved you can proceed with confidence to the next step of researching the topic.

Research and Collection of Material

At least five different sources must be located for in-depth reading related to the topic of the term paper. They can be text books, journals, newspapers in any form, reference books, encyclopedias, special reports and other similar sources. Read them with a paper and pencil on hand and write down the relevant material, noting the source and the author.

Reading the sources without taking any notes is acceptable for initial comprehension, but closing the source without any written notes is detrimental to the subsequent steps in report writing. It is better to collect more information than less, and to get as many view points as possible.

Organization of the Material and Outline

Once you have collected all the desirable material for the term paper, you are in a position to organize them and start writing. The most effective tool for this vital process is an **outline**. An outline may be a brief resumé of a particular topic or it can be a complete summary of the entire subject. It is a systematic arrangement of all the relevant items related to the topic, orderly arranged with main headings, sub-headings, and subordinate headings, if any.

The outline must not be confused with the contents listed in the front of books and reports. In a sense, the outline is the forerunner of the contents, which it finally evolves into. However, the outline is not a rigid structure. It serves only as a guide and as new ideas are encountered during the progress of your writing, they can be accommodated to extend or modify the outline.

There is no hard and fast rule as to how an outline must be written. Since the primary purpose of an outline is to organize the material collected from different sources and help you write a well-structured report highlighting the salient points through headings and subheadings, it is up to you to write your own outline before starting to write the report itself.

A typical outline for a term paper in a course in Transportation Engineering may look like the one below:

OUTLINE OF ROAD TRANSPORTATION
IN THE UNITED STATES OF AMERICA

Introduction:

Purpose of road transportation:

movement of people, materials, farm products, manufactured goods, defence, recreation, etc.

Sources of collected data.

History of transportation prior to roads

Advent of motor vehicles

Development of road system:

Federal, state, county, local and toll roads

Growth in urban areas:
    Urban arterial road network
    Hierarchy of the roads
Traffic on the roads:
    Type, pattern and volume;
    Future of road transportation
Conclusions (or Summary)

You can see from this outline how easy it is to start writing the paper using it as a guide. The researched and gathered material can now be separated and grouped for reevaluation. You are now ready to begin the actual writing.

Writing Based on the Outline

Remember that the purpose of your writing the paper is for it to be read and evaluated by your professor. He/she looks for clarity of expression and readability of the report, besides the quality of the contents of your paper. Style in writing is important but not essential. The following pointers can serve as guides for the effective writing of term papers:

1. Start with an introduction of the topic of your term paper. Begin the introduction with an attention-getting statement which will have a tone of provocativeness, curiosity, imagination, and the like.
2. Use simple words and short sentences.
3. Check every now and then to see whether what you have written is communicative of what you wish to say.
4. Make liberal use of illustrations, analogies, comparisons, contrasts, and examples. They render a sense of concreteness to otherwise abstract statements.
5. If it is a technical term paper, use only a few key equations and graphs in the main body of the paper. An equation or two in a page of words lends visual respectability to the page. Often it is a key factor in getting a better grade in the term paper.
6. Pay attention to paragraph arrangement. Start a new paragraph to introduce a change in the trend of expression or ideas. Avoid too short or too long paragraphs which tend to create a visual imbalance.

7. Follow the outline as your guide for the writing, section by section, making sure that continuity of expression runs through the sections.
8. End your report with your best effort in creative writing. The few sentences that you write in the concluding paragraph should be forceful and should conclude the topic of your term paper.
9. During the course of actual writing pay attention to spelling, grammar, and punctuation.

Revising

What you have written is the first draft of your report, which must be revised. It is better if you can wait for a day or two and then start revising. In this way, your mind will be clear on the topic of the term paper and you will be able to read it more objectively than by revising it immediately after writing.

Following are the points to watch and correct during revision:

1. Mistakes in spelling, grammar, and punctuation.
2. Capitalization and hyphenation.
3. Vague sentences; too long sentences.
4. Readability and continuity of expression.
5. Paragraphing. A series of relatively short paragraphs, with an occasional long one, is more pleasing visually than too many long paragraphs.

Still better it would be if you can find someone else to go over the manuscript of your first draft who can offer constructive criticism and point out mistakes. This will improve the quality of your report considerably.

Finishing

Once the revised draft is complete to your satisfaction, the final step is to get it ready for submission to your professor. Attention to the following points will ensure a favorable first impression on him/her:

1. Have the report typed in double space with a carbon copy for yourself, or have it computer printed with a copy for yourself.

2. Go over the typed copy and make sure that it does not contain any mistakes and that it incorporates all the revisions you had made on the first draft.

3. Follow the instructions of your professor for the format of the paper. Your report should contain a title page, a table of contents, footnotes, and a bibliography or references. Any material that you considered relevant to the main topic but not fit for the main body of the paper can be included as an appendix.

4. Be sure to place the report in an attractive cover to present a strong visual impact on the professor.

5. Last, but not least in importance, is that you should submit your final report **on time**. When you are aiming for better grades you should not ask for an extension of time for submission, which many professors may not give. Besides, even if he/she allows extra time, by asking for it you are likely to ruin your credibility.

HOW TO WRITE A THESIS

Since a thesis or dissertation is judged for its originality of approach and its contribution to widening the frontiers of knowledge in the subject area under investigation, no hard and fast rules can be given as to how to write a thesis. However, the mechanics of writing a readable thesis that presents the originality of the investigation and its results are undoubtedly important for its acceptance by the examining committee.

Writing for a thesis should aim at highlighting the following points:

1. The problem statement
2. Literature review
3. Formulation of a hypothesis
4. Methodology of investigation
5. Discussion of results and arguments
6. Conclusions
7. References.

The process of writing the first draft of the thesis is pretty much the same as we had described before for writing a term paper as far as the following are concerned:

1. Organization of the collected material into an effective outline,
2. Writing based on the outline,
3. Revising, and
4. Finishing.

Unlike a term paper, more revisions may be necessary to produce the final draft of the thesis. Photographs and figures may be needed in many cases depending on the subject area of investigation.

In general, it is a requirement that the thesis be presented in a bound form of prescribed format. It is similar to the form of a hardbound book. Near almost every college campus, printing establishments can be found that specialize in thesis binding. However, the final binding is usually deferred until all the corrections and modifications have been incorporated and the thesis has been totally accepted by all the members of the examining committee. You may contact your college or university library for more details and instructions about the format for your thesis requirements.

Chapter 14

HOW TO SPEAK YOUR WAY TO BETTER GRADES

"No matter how easily public speaking comes to some, as compared with others, it is not a natural talent; it must be (and can be) learned. And what one has learned another can learn."

Herman Holtz,
author of "The Business of Public Speaking"

TOPICS

1. The Importance of Speaking
2. Stage Fright
3. Oral Participation in the Classroom
4. Group Discussions
5. Panel Discussions
6. Round-Table Discussions
7. Committee Meetings
8. Debates
9. How to take an Oral Exam
10. How to Present a Seminar
11. The Art of Public Speaking

IMPORTANCE OF SPEAKING

Among the various means of communication from one person to another, or to a group, nothing is more powerful than speaking. It is not just what you say but also how you say it. Direct communication through speaking has the potential to kindle the emotions of the listener. Speeches can inspire, incite, and spur the listener to instant action; speeches can insult and induce eternal enmity; speeches can also bring hope, love, and kindness. Lasting love and friendship among people would be a myth without the gentleness of the words exchanged.

Speaking implies listening. Speaking without listening is a mechanical process and has no contribution in interpersonal relationship. To be a good speaker it is essential to develop the art of effective listening. Besides, listening is an important tool of learning. Modern school and college systems rely heavily on this method of teaching in the formal classroom settings where the teacher talks and the student is expected to listen and clarify his/her doubts through questioning.

There is another side to speaking in the classroom for the college student. At one time or other during your college years, you will be required to stand before the class and speak or take part orally in a group discussion or present a seminar. This may be a partial or full requirement in getting a grade for that course. Of course, to get a better grade you have to do a good job of the speaking situation to the professor's satisfaction. Effective speech is communication at its best. It is an acquired skill based on knowledge and practice—similar to the skill of writing.

STAGE FRIGHT

The uncomfortable feelings of anxiety which a speaker in a formal speaking assignment in front of an audience experiences is commonly known as stage fright. If you think you suffer from this malady, you are not alone. Even experienced speakers feel it sometime or other. Psychologists confirm that stage fright is an universal phenomenon and is not much different from any anxiety or fear provoking situations.

The symptoms of stage fright are manifest in varying degrees with different people. A trembling voice, shaky hands and knees, and perspiration to varying degrees are generally the external symptoms, whereas an unpleasant feeling at the pit of the stomach is the accompanying internal counterpart.

Stage fright is a normal human reaction which you can learn to handle. In most cases it lasts only for about the first five minutes until the speaker settles down to his topic of speech. The following tips will help to get you started and gradually overcome stage fright in subsequent speaking assignments.

1. Face the audience and scan the whole assembly once.
2. Start your talk with a general statement, such as, that you are thankful for the opportunity, etc.
3. Have your talk well organized the day before and write some notes on a handy index card. Keep this card in your hand. Remember that this card is your psychological prop.
4. Begin after glancing at the card.
5. Make eye contact with your audience. The more contacts you make, the quicker you will be relieved of the initial anxiety, and you will be able to concentrate on the topic more fully.
6. A thorough preparation of the subject matter of the talk is a prerequisite in overcoming stage fright. Such preparation helps to boost your self-confidence when you become aware that you know something more than your audience.

ORAL PARTICIPATION IN THE CLASSROOM

Even though in the normal classroom environment the professor takes center stage almost all of the time, there are ample opportunities for you to express yourself orally. Many professors start the day's lecture and end it with "any questions?" giving a chance of few minutes for the students to ask about something that was not clear to them or to comment on something relevant to the course. Since the question is thrown to the open class, most students shy away from speaking. You can take advantage of this rare opportunity by coming to the class with prepared questions and speak out at the appropriate time. This is a valuable first step in developing your skill for group communication.

In some courses, once or twice a semester, each student is assigned a period of time, usually about 10 minutes, for a formal oral presentation on a preassigned topic, or a book review, or on the term paper which the student himself/herself has written.

There are some courses, particularly in the areas of speech, management, leadership, etc., in which the student will be required to take part in group discussions, panel discussions, and debates. No doubt, these are good opportunities for preparing oneself for future speaking situations that may be encountered in professional life.

GROUP DISCUSSIONS

To get the most out of your college life, it is not enough that you go through the academic program, pass the courses and graduate. There are so many opportunities on college campuses today for a willing student to get adequately prepared for a career or profession, and to move to leadership positions in the future. Success in the future is largely dependent on effective interpersonal relationships and on the ability to communicate in groups such as the family, community, clubs, councils, committees, boards, church groups, professional meetings etc. By taking an active part in various campus activities and serving as a member in committees of interest to you, you will learn the art of group discussion along with the skills needed to communicate in groups.

Group discussions in general can be grouped into informal and formal types. Informal forms of discussion do not require a leader, and the exchange of ideas is effected through direct expression of thoughts without sticking to any organized procedure. The so-called "social hour" preceding organized meetings, the meeting of a family over the dining table, discussions with your friends in the college cafeteria and in your dormitory lounge are a few examples of the informal type. Besides being a good listener, it is important that you develop the art of speaking with your peers in a polite and non-emotional manner. Being able to discuss issues without becoming emotional and overly argumentative is an unmistakable sign of maturity.

When group discussions are conducted in a formal manner, a leader is needed to conduct and guide the proceedings. Among the many forms of formal group discussions, the panel, round-table, and committee meetings are important for a college student to be aware of.

PANEL DISCUSSIONS

A panel discussion generally consists of three to six panel members, a leader called the chairperson, and the audience. The purpose of the panel discussion is to present various view points of a problem or topic selected for discussion, with a common focus towards possible solutions, or to bring greater awareness of the problem to the audience.

The panel members will be the main speakers, and are given the topic ahead of time for thorough preparation. Each panel member highlights different aspects of the topic of discussion. The chairperson conducts the proceedings and sets an orderly pace so that each member is given a fair share of time and opportunity. He/she prevents any arguments among the panel members and allows audience participation at the appropriate time. It is also the chairperson's duty to finally summarize briefly the main contributions brought out by the panel discussion and adjourn the meeting.

By taking part in panel discussions as a volunteer on the panel, you will learn the art of discussion and public speaking better than by reading any book.

ROUND-TABLE DISCUSSIONS

In contrast to a panel discussion, a round-table discussion is less formal in nature. All the members of the group directly take part. The leader or chairperson seats himself/herself at the head table, and the other tables are arranged to form a circular, oval, or even a square loop. Up to 30 persons can be accommodated in round-table type of discussions.

A topic for the discussion is given beforehand so that all members can come well prepared. The chairperson starts the discussion by presenting the facts of the topic and opens the floor for discussion. Various members speak up from time to time as thoughts occur to them. There is no strict order or form of procedure to adhere to, other than maintaining a "one at a time" rule. The professor generally acts as the chairperson so that he/she may point out errors, direct the discussion, and stimulate the members to think along new lines. In the end, the chairperson sums up the discussion and presents those facts and conclusions on which there is a general agreement among the members of the group.

In any one of your courses if you get a chance to participate in a round-table discussion, you should make the most of it. In fact, this is the most satisfactory type of all group discussions. The chief advantage is that it permits a thorough exchange of opinion and leads easily to group decision and action, a vital ingredient in democratic institutions.

COMMITTEE MEETINGS

While being in college you will have many opportunities to serve as a member of various committees, depending on your interest and the extent of your involvement in extra-curricular activities. Almost all committee meetings function as the round-table type, with a chairperson for the committee who calls the meeting to order and conducts the business.

You may not realize the importance of serving on committees at this time in your college career, but it is well worth remembering that it is a big plus for you when you apply for jobs later on. Besides your grades, your activities during your college years, such as serving on many committees, speak more eloquently about your personality than any other single factor. Even if you did not speak out much in those committee meetings, being a participant in the decision making process through group discussion during the college years adds a vital dimension to your experience that contributes to success in your future life.

DEBATES

Debate is an orderly oral controversy on an issue that has opposing sides. It may be informal or formal. Informal debating is not governed by set rules as is formal debating. It is freer and more flexible and does not call for a decision about the outcome of the debate. On the other hand, formal debating is a matched speaking contest between two teams or two persons, such as the Presidential candidates, which must follow definite rules in presenting their arguments and refuting the opposition. One or more judges are appointed to evaluate and pass judgment on the debate.

Formal or informal debate upholds the right for free speech, one of the cornerstones of a democratic society. It also implies that the debaters should respect the opinions of each other even though they may be in total disagreement, and present their respective arguments persuasively and with proper reasoning.

Some specific points to keep in mind for the debaters are:

1. Your aim in the debate is to win listeners to your side.
2. Always be courteous to your opponents.
3. Have a well thought out plan for the logical arrangement of the material you want to present.
4. Prove that your ideas or plans are both possible and necessary.
5. Try to appeal to the intellect of the listeners through sound reasoning, and to their feelings through human-related stories, anecdotes, and personal references.
6. Use facts, examples, statistics, and quotations as your evidence.
7. You should avoid the following :
    * Antagonizing the listeners
    * Use of offensive statements
    * Straying away from the main theme of the debate.

Be sportsman-like in listening to the verdict of the judges; should you lose, accept your defeat with dignity and a smile and be quick to congratulate your opponent.

HOW TO TAKE AN ORAL EXAM

It is not often that you run into the situation of taking an oral exam. An oral test is sometimes administered by the professor as a make-up for a test that you missed, or in place of a test in which you had an unusually low grade. It is not a right on the part of the student; it is for the professor to decide. The important point here is for you to note that such an avenue may be available to you should there be a need.

Also, in some courses there may be a partial requirement to take an oral examination, such as in some laboratory courses, and in the presentation of a thesis for the master's or doctoral degrees.

In a make-up type of oral exam you meet with your professor in his/her office. He/she will ask you a series of questions and you are to answer them orally. Oral tests are usually of short duration from about 10 minutes to half an hour.

Preparing for the Oral Test

Following points will help in the preparation for an oral test:

1. Ask the professor for the subject area covered in the oral test.
2. Read all the materials assigned for reading.
3. Try to get a copy of old test questions, oral or written, given by the same professor on previous occasions and prepare answers for them.
4. Set your own oral questions as if you were giving the test and write all the answers.
5. Standing in front of a mirror read aloud all your questions and answers repeatedly until your voice comes out naturally and clearly.
6. Now, close your eyes, visualize yourself sitting in front of your professor in his office; you ask questions and answer them yourself so that you can hear them audibly and clearly. This visualization will help to minimize the anxiety of facing the professor and answering his/her questions.

Taking the Oral Test

1. Arrive at the professor's office five minutes early. This will give you time to compose yourself.
2. Sit in the chair shown by the professor only after he/she bids you to sit.
3. Be at ease and be attentive to the questions. Reflect on the question for a couple of seconds and speak your answer loud and clear.
4. At the end, thank your professor for his/her time and trouble taken to give the test, and leave without any reference to the test taken.

HOW TO PRESENT A SEMINAR

What is a Seminar?

There is a lot of confusion regarding the use of the word "seminar". In the last two decades there has been a marked increase in the need for specialized knowledge in all professions, and in the public and private lives of people. One of the most effective means of serving this need has been labeled a "seminar", in today's usage of the word, meaning a conference for the dissemination of specialized knowledge to a selected group of people.

However, the word "seminar' has been traditionally used to designate a small group of advanced students in a college or graduate school engaged in original research or study under the guidance of a professor who meets regularly with them for reports and discussions. It could also mean a course of study so pursued or a scheduled meeting of such a group.

Public Seminars

These are open to the public. They may be free or for a nominal fee. They are announced through the public news media so that interested persons can attend them. Usually the topics of the seminar are in some areas of interest to the participant such as health, stress management, electronic word processing, etc. Mostly they are of the self-improvement and self-help type. They may last anywhere from two to eight hours in general.

There will be one or more speakers or leaders who have expert knowledge of the topic of the seminar. Besides lectures, they may give handouts and other related materials to supplement the lectures.

Professional Seminars

Unlike public seminars these are open only to special groups of people who are members of an association, or a professional organization, or employees of the sponsoring organization. Topics are necessarily of a specialized nature, which calls for a basic knowledge of the participant in that field or subject area. Usually they are arranged in small groups of not more than about thirty people for effective learning.

There will be one or more "presenters" of the seminar who are specialists or experts in the subject area. Formal lectures with visual aids and supplementary handouts, even books, and question and answer sessions at the end constitute professional seminars. Some of them may also include a workshop session for practical hands-on training.

College Seminars

Of course, college seminars are drastically different in that the participant's performance is evaluated and graded by the professor. Seminar courses are usually offered only for the senior undergraduate and graduate students. The primary aim of the college seminar course is to learn the art and technique of presenting seminars.

Since passing the course with a good grade is your aim, you should know precisely how the seminar course is conducted and what is expected of you. Practices vary from college to college and from professor to professor. However, the principles are the same. Obviously the best thing to do is to have it spelled out by your professor.

In general each student is assigned a topic for research within his/her major area by the professor, or you may be allowed to choose one of your own. As your research proceeds, you must meet him/her periodically, such as once in 2 weeks or once a month, and appraise him/her of your progress. The professor may provide you with necessary guidance for further progress.

By the end of the semester, you end your research with a written report and orally present your study to the whole class in a formal manner, giving them a chance to ask questions. Your professor takes the role of a judge to evaluate your "presentation", and he/she will also act as the grader for your report. Based on the dual outcome, he/she decides on the final grade for the course.

Seminar Presentation

Your "presentation" is primarily a speaking assignment with your peers as the audience. The focus is on your ability in oral communication. Remember that you have one big advantage, that is, you know at this time more about the topic of your presentation than any one else in the audience; use this knowledge to prop up your self-confidence.

The following pointers will be of help for an effective seminar presentation:

1. Dress well, and in good taste, fit for a formal conference.
2. Have lecture aids prepared in the form of slides, overheads or even wall charts. They will be a tremendous help in directing the gaze of your audience from you to the visual aids shown. They will also help you to stay on your topic.
3. Talk loudly and clearly so that a person sitting in the last row will have no problem in hearing you.
4. Do not mumble. Do not eat the last words of your sentences.
5. As you talk, face your audience directly, establishing eye contacts with as many as possible. Never fix your gaze on one person.
6. Be time conscious. Have your speech rehearsed in your room the day before so that you will have a better estimate of the time needed for your presentation.
7. Wind up your speech with a well-rounded summary of your research and your own conclusions.
8. End your presentation about 3 minutes before time with a "thank you", and open the floor for questions.
9. Be brief and to the point in answering questions. If you don't know the answer, be bold to say so.

The Report

Turn in your seminar report to the professor on time, in the format he/she specified. The guidelines for report writing are the same as presented in the previous chapter of this book.

THE ART OF PUBLIC SPEAKING

As you progress in your college life you may have many opportunities for speaking before a general audience, if you are willing to do so. Public speaking falls under a totally different category known as "persuasive speaking". Persuasion is the conscious attempt to modify the thought and action of the listeners so that they are won over to the views of the speaker. Persuasive speaking is a subject by itself on which many volumes have been written. For a detailed reading you are recommended to go to your library. A brief summary is given below.

Public speaking has two major components which the speaker should be aware of: 1. matter, and 2. delivery.

Matter

1. Speak only when you have something worthwhile to say, which you are convinced is true.
2. Prepare thoroughly; you should have mastery over the subject matter of your speech to gain the respect of the listener.
3. Be clear in getting your ideas across to the audience. The listener should not feel confused. The organization of your ideas in the presentation is the key.
4. Stick to your subject.
5. Be fair. State any opposing viewpoint as well as its proponent could present it, and then give your reasons against it.
6. Be brief. Since the concentration of the listener can not be held too long over any idea that you are trying to get across, it is important that you present it forcefully but briefly.

Delivery

For the subject matter of your speech to have the desired impact on the listeners, it is essential that you deliver the speech effectively. The rules of effective delivery are:

1. Dress well. Pay attention to fitness and color.
2. Speak slowly and clearly so that every word of what you say seeps through the listeners' comprehension. Remember that speech is an intellectual performance.
3. Keep your emotions under complete control. The management of emotions is a sign of maturity and it is expected of the speaker. You may be excited over the ideas you are presenting, but you should not become overly emotional.
4. Be sensitive to the mood of the audience and be adaptive. This adaptive spirit means your goodwill toward those whose beliefs, attitudes, and experiences your speech would affect.
5. Control your voice and be articulate.
6. Establish eye-contacts with your audience, constantly, but

gradually, shifting your gaze, throwing a balanced look over
the whole group.

7. Use your language well. It should not be ambiguous; rather,
   it must be concrete and specific.

8. Do not throw personal attacks or insults, and do not condemn
   outright the opinion of another speaker. Remember that he/
   she has as much right to his/her opinion as you have to yours.

9. Be time conscious and close your speech on time with a smile
   on your face.

Contributory Factors in Learning

Chapter **15**

PERSONAL, ACADEMIC, AND CAREER COUNSELING

"Counseling can make or break the student's academic career. If it is done early and done properly it can really help the student succeed."

Prof. Phil Wankat,
Head of Department of Freshman Engineering,
Purdue University

TOPICS

1. Who Needs Counseling?
2. Counseling—The Invisible Mental Reinforcer
3. Personal Counseling
4. Academic Counseling
5. Career Counseling
6. A Counselor's View Point
7. Typical Concerns or Questions

WHO NEEDS COUNSELING?

Modern college education is a complex process. It is almost impossible for a freshman entering a college or university to know precisely what to do all the way to earn the degree which he/she desires. Many academic courses need prerequisites, and a certain sequence of courses has to be followed to build a base for understanding the subject matter. A proper load of courses needs to be maintained for optimum learning on the part of the student. Too heavy a load can push the student to poor grades, and too light a load will prolong his/her stay in college for a longer period of time, which is both unwarranted and expensive.

Being away from home, particularly for the freshman, brings its own problems of learning to live by oneself and adjusting to the rigors of the outside world. Personal time management and financial management are difficult for many. There will be problems to be handled arising from social and recreational pursuits such as dating, dormitory living, alcohol, and drugs.

For many, who can not receive much monetary support from home, financial problems will be looming constantly over the horizon. The student can not be expected to know all the sources and avenues of financial aid available to him/her.

Returning and elderly students who were away from college life for a few or many years often find themselves in deep waters in the first semester, academically speaking, and may need assistance to find their feet for the successful pursuit of their objective of graduating with a degree.

Career! After all, modern college education is a training ground for a job, career, or a profession for many. Where the jobs are, what to do to get one, when and how to prepare, how to write a resumé, how to take an interview when called for, how to keep the job when one is offered, are but a few questions to which the college student should know the answers, if he/she wants to optimize his/her job potential in the career world.

From all these, you will note that literally every college student will need counseling of one sort or another at one time or other during his/her college years. To know when and where to go for help is as important as getting it. For this reason students entering a college or a university are introduced to an orientation program. The orientation program is generally designed for students to become familiar not only with the buildings, classrooms and the administration of the institution, but also with the various sources of help and counseling available to them as a part of their college education.

COUNSELING—THE INVISIBLE MENTAL REINFORCER

What exactly is counseling? Counseling in its simplest form is the giving of advice or guidance by a knowledgeable person to a seeker. The giver is referred to as the counselor and the receiver as the counselee. Counseling also means a consultation and discussion on a specific issue of interest to the counselee.

Counseling, in fact, is a form of learning for the counselee on specific matters affecting his/her personal life on the emotional side for which there may not be a universal or objective solution. The knowledge and experience of the counselor are the key elements with which he/she tries to evaluate the specific problem of the individual student, with reference to the latter's personality, environment, and history of events leading to the problem. It is a complex process though it appears simple.

All the college student's problems can be grouped into two categories: 1. personal, and 2. non-personal. Personal problems are peculiar or unique to each individual, and as such they need to be tackled on a one to one basis between a counselor and the student. These problems affect him/her emotionally preventing him/her from concentrating on the studies. He/she can not handle them simply because he/she does not know how to respond for a lack of worldly experience and wisdom. This is the time he/she needs the help of a student counselor.

Non-personal problems are related to academic, financial, career, and other matters which are not as critical as personal problems. However, it is important for you to know that specially trained counselors are available for you to go to, should there be a need. You should not hesitate to go to them to discuss your situation and seek their advice and guidance. Contact the office of the Dean of Students of your college for assistance.

Counseling acts as an invisible mental reinforcer. It strengthens your mind and helps you see things from a better perspective with the aid of the counselor. Remember that the counselor's sole purpose is to help you; he/she is non-judgmental on your values. Your faith in your counselor, as well as yourself, is essential for your choosing a right course of action. Also remember that unlike a physical problem no medicine is involved in counseling other than the counselor's words. The solution to your problem lies in your paying attention to his/her words and trying to follow them with faith in practice.

PERSONAL COUNSELING

Personal counseling generally revolves around providing guidance in attitude and behavior modifications to cope with problems which are of a personal nature. Problems of the following nature are dealt with by the personal counselor:

All types of stress and their management,
Time management,
Dating problems,
Pregnancy counseling, and
Alcohol and drug-related problems.

Listening to the student's problems, the counselor tries to suggest the best possible course of action for the student to follow.

In addition to individual counseling, the counseling office also offers developmental workshops and seminars on topics common to most students, such as stress management, time management, assertiveness, study skills, sexual assault, eating disorders, etc.

ACADEMIC COUNSELING

Freshman Advisor

Almost all colleges and universities have freshman advisors for each major academic area of the institution, such as business, engineering, liberal arts, etc. The freshman advisor offers counseling in academic matters, and helps the student get started in the respective major with a proper choice of courses in line with the student's academic profile. He/she meets with the advisee individually a few times the first semester to iron out any difficulties the student might have.

Departmental or Academic advisor

Once you have decided on a major the chairperson of that department will assign a faculty member to be your academic advisor. In that capacity his/her function is to advise you on the right courses you should be taking semester by semester so that you can meet the graduation requirements with the least possible difficulties. He/she will also advise you on withdrawal from courses when you may have difficulties in them. You will need his/her approval both for registering courses at the beginning of each semester and for withdrawal from any course during the semester.

It is important that you discuss your mid-semester grades with him/her as soon as the grades are received to monitor your academic progress and achievement. By following the advice of your academic advisor you will be able to graduate in your chosen major without loss of time.

CAREER COUNSELING

Very seldom is a college education pursued for the sake of academic pleasures. For many it is a path to a meaningful career to which the best part of a person's adult life will be devoted. Wrong career choices can not only prevent a person from using his/her full potential, but also become a source of perennial stress and unhappiness. On the other hand, a career properly chosen to suit the personality, sense of values, skills and ambitions of the person can make living interesting, stimulating, and challenging.

In order to help the college student make the right choice of a career while he/she is still in college, almost all colleges and universities provide a wide variety of assistance programs for students to become aware of the various avenues and sources for potential employment, and to help them conduct a successful job search.

The career counselor is a professionally trained person whose services are free of charge for college students. The Office of Career Services offers them help in all phases of career development through an integrated career program. This office provides an up-to-date and realistic bridge between college and the world of work. In order to take advantage of the opportunities offered by this office, you should acquaint yourself with its services as early as possible, preferably in the first year.

A COUNSELOR'S VIEW POINT

By Hattie Nunley

**Hattie Nunley, M.A.,
West Virginia University,
School Counselor (Retired),
Valley High School, Montgomery, WV.**

The counseling office is an integral part of every school. It is here that students can take a "course" in themselves. They can benefit from skilled, professionally-trained counselors who have the time and facilities necessary to establish an effective counseling relationship. In this relationship, they may discuss concerns ranging from those related to educational or career decisions to those very personal in nature. They can learn to think objectively about themselves and they can learn ways of understanding themselves and others. For this self-study, they can choose group counseling, individual counseling, or a combination of the two.

There is no magic in the process of counseling. It requires work on the part of the counselor and the counselee; and, its effectiveness depends upon the effort put forth by the counselee and the goals he/she establishes. Counseling is not simply a matter of getting the counselor's solution to an immediate problem. There are times when advice is appropriate; but, hopefully, the end result of counseling will be that the student learns to make independent decisions and becomes a more mature person.

Counselors work with students in personal-social, educational and career counseling. These functions are interrelated and can be successfully dealt with individually or in groups.

Personal counseling is the heart of a counseling program. It is here that students can share in confidence their innermost concerns and feelings with a counselor who is nonjudgmental, who demonstrates respect for the worth, dignity, and quality of their human rights, who can empathize with them, and who is a caring person. With the counselor's help, students can clarify their thoughts and actions, develop a better understanding of themselves and those with whom they have close relationships, and deal with immediate problems.

Often it is difficult for students to determine what their problem is. Through counseling, they can learn to identify their problem and the options for solving the problem, evaluate these options, and choose the one that seems to be the most appropriate. Working through this problem-solving situation can help the student learn methods of dealing independently with future problems.

Educational counseling can be invaluable to students who have trouble establishing their educational goals. By helping them relate their ability, aptitude, achievement, test scores, work and life experiences to their ambitions, the counselor can assist students in choosing classes or programs which help them reach the goals they have set.

Choosing a career is one of the most important decisions made during life. Obviously, the more students know about themselves and the more they know about careers, the more likely they are to find a job in which they can be happy. In career counseling, students can locate the occupations which seem to be the most compatible with their values, interests, ability, and aptitudes. This, of course, will provide them the greatest chance for success.

The continual changes in society bring new challenges and concerns to students of all ages. Dealing with these challenges and concerns can be much easier with the help of a counselor.

TYPICAL CONCERNS OR QUESTIONS

Following are some of the typical concerns or questions of the adolescent male and female students of the modern times:

* I don't have confidence in myself.
* I get nervous and up tight before tests.
* I feel left out.
* I need to improve my study skills.
* My parents are too strict!
* No one cares about me.
* I can't decide on a career.
* I hate school!
* How can I make better grades?
* My girlfriend and I broke up and I'm really upset.
* I'm always depressed.
* I want to go to college, but my parents don't think I can make it.
* I just can't go on.
* My parents are always fighting.
* Someone I love drinks too much. How can I help him?
* My parents think I should make all A's.
* I'm under too much pressure.
* How do I come across to other people?
* My parents are getting a divorce.
* I act before I think!
* I don't want to use drugs, but I won't have any friends if I don't.

These concerns expressed by the students to the counselor undoubtedly reflect the spectrum of problems and difficulties inherent in the society we live in. The problems will always be there; what is important is how to cope with them. It is here that the counselor's words make the difference. His/her advice can help the student look at the problem from the right perspective, face the problem boldly, and do something constructive to overcome the seemingly disturbing and ominous nature of the problem. The counselor's advice is nothing else but a reflection of his/her experience, training, and wisdom, and it can be considered as an appropriate prescription for the problem on hand. The counselor's greatest reward, of course, is the satisfaction he/she gets in seeing a student tide over the problem and grow more mature and confident than before from that experience.

Chapter **16**

EFFECTIVE USE OF YOUR COLLEGE LIBRARY FOR BETTER GRADES

By

Virginia Atwater, M.L.S.

"This importance of the library increases as the freshman becomes an upperclassman and finally a graduate."

J. A. Rickard,
author of "A Student's Guide to Better Grades"

TOPICS

1. The College Library
2. The Catalog Section: To Look for a Book
3. "PER", "MF", "PAM", "DOC", & "ERIC"
4. Reference Books and Books on Reserve
5. Importance of Index
6. Periodicals, Magazines, and Newspapers
7. Computerized Indexes: InfoTrac, etc.
8. Researching for a Term Paper
9. Interlibrary Loan
10. Develop the "Library Habit"

Virginia Atwater, M.L.S.,
University of Missouri,
Ex-Staff Librarian,
West Virginia Institute of Technology

THE COLLEGE LIBRARY

Your college library can seem frightening until you know your way around. Once you are comfortable, you will find that it can improve your life in ways far beyond its use for school work.

As a new student you will probably go to the library because teachers assign research papers, daily readings, or questions that need looking up. At some colleges you may have to decide which library to go to. Large universities have a Main Library and Departmental Branch Libraries for different subjects. Mid-size university libraries assign different rooms to different subjects. Small colleges just divide subjects by putting them in separate sections of the bookshelves, which librarians call stacks.

All libraries have people, signs, and how-to pamphlets to help you find things. Besides books and journals, they may contain many facilities for your use. Computer terminals, typewriters, copiers, reference dictionaries, conference rooms, study cubicles, microfilm-microfiche reader-printers, lounges, etc., are commonly found in most college libraries.

THE CATALOG SECTION: TO LOOK FOR A BOOK

It is best to start at the **catalog** when you look for a book. Catalogs, or lists of books and other things in the collection, are usually in central places. Expect to find either a "**Card Catalog**" (with lots of drawers) or a "**Book Catalog**" or a "**Computerized Catalog**". Spend some time studying the directions on how to use this particular finding guide.

You can locate books by looking up the subject, title or author. Whether you type these into a computer and read the screen, or search for them alphabetically in cards, you will find BIBLIOGRAPHIC INFORMATION—useful details about the book. These include author, title, date of publication, subjects and **call number.**

The library may use the **Dewey** or **the Library of Congress System** of numbering to identify the books. For either one you simply copy the letter/number combination. You will find the book of the shelf by matching this combination the way it is given in the catalog

with those on the **spine** (backbone) of the book. Books on the same subjects stand together on the shelves.

"PER", "MF", "PAM", "DOC" AND "ERIC"

When you read the catalog card or computer screen notice whether the item described is actually a bound book. You may see "PER" for a periodical, such as a magazine or journal. "MF" means microform, "PAM" can mean pamphlet and "DOC" a government document. If you don't watch for this, you may feel frustrated when the "book" you want is on a card of microfiche.

"ERIC" is the abbreviation for Educational Resources Information Center. ERIC is put out by the Federal Government of the United States of America on a continuous basis. It is a cornucopia of articles on current thinking and research on all aspects of education, which are properly indexed. They are available in abstract forms and microfiche, and also through computerized database.

REFERENCE BOOKS AND BOOKS ON RESERVE

Some notes in the catalog indicate special locations for library materials. REFERENCE BOOKS are usually set apart. You can not check books out when they are marked with "R" for reference. The "Vertical File" (VF) is a special place where libraries keep pamphlets or clippings in boxes. A local history room, a rare book collection or a government document area each will have its own abbreviation.

Suppose you read that the book is ON RESERVE. That means a professor asked to have it moved from the general collection because he/she is assigning it for his/her whole class to read. It stays in the RESERVE room or area and circulates out to students for only an hour or two at a time, though sometime overnight. Professors also leave photocopied articles on reserve. You should quickly read or copy these since the whole class will have to share.

To find things in the various areas of the library you can use the library's printed guidebook or look for signs or ask a librarian. Library professionals are trained to answer questions. The modern librarian is user-friendly.

IMPORTANCE OF INDEXES

If you ask a librarian for help in research for a paper or a special project, she/he will show you REFERENCE books to start with, possibly encyclopedias. Encyclopedias give a broad description of the basic facts about your topic. Then you might plan to use books from the main collection to get a closer look into details.

However, if you want to write about a subject taken from a recent news item, periodicals would be the place to check. The most important stop, before you pick up any magazine, is the **index table**.

The large periodical indexes are almost always best because they cover not just one but hundreds of different magazines. New issues of each index come out every month or oftener. Most list only magazines but a few also include books, pamphlets, conference papers, reports and government documents.

Following are some of the important indexes you should be aware of:

READERS GUIDE (it indexes easy to read magazines)
THE BUSINESS PERIODICAL INDEX
INDEX TO APPLIED SCIENCE AND TECHNOLOGY
EDUCATION INDEX
SOCIAL SCIENCE INDEX
PUBLIC AFFAIRS AND INFORMATION INDEX (PAIS)

You will also find abstract services (THE ENGINEERING INDEX, for example) that add short paragraphs about the contents of each article.

Most printed indexes are alphabetical by subject. They mention each article's author (if known), the title, an abbreviation of the name of the periodical where it is found, the volume, date and page number. If there are lots of articles on your subject, I suggest that you photocopy the whole index page and save a lot of writing.

PERIODICALS, MAGAZINES AND NEWSPAPERS

Look for the list of periodicals the library subscribes to. Depending on its size and budget, the library will take most, but possibly not all, the journals mentioned in the index. The library's periodicals list may be in the main catalog, alphabetized along with the books. Some libraries allow you to take the periodicals off the shelves yourself. Others have you fill out slips to give the library assistants who bring them to you.

Microfilm and Microfiche

Back issues of magazines are usually bound by year in hard covers and look like books. Some come out in microfilm or microfiche and you must use reader/printers located within the area to read them. A diagram, near or on the printer, will show you how to load the microfilm and operate that particular machine. Or ask a staff member since they may prefer to do it, anyway. For magazines in hard copy, bound or unbound issues can be photocopied.

Most libraries subscribe to several important metropolitan newspapers and also local papers. There are printed indexes for many of the leading papers. The following are among them:

THE NEW YORK TIMES
THE WALL STREET JOURNAL
THE WASHINGTON POST
THE CHRISTIAN SCIENCE MONITOR
THE LOS ANGELES TIMES.

Microfilmed back issues of these papers and indexes may go back 20 years or more—even to the beginning of their publication.

COMPUTERIZED INDEXES

In most modern libraries computerized indexes are being used along with printed indexes. You will find some of these databases familiar, since they cover the same ground as the Readers Guide and others. You will be glad to find that they are easier and faster to use.

InfoTrac II

InfoTrac II from Information Access Company is an automated reference system that provides computer-aided retrieval of bibliographic references stored on a compact disc. The InfoTrac II system is designed specifically for public access. You do not need a manual or special training to use the system. Each search step is self-explanatory and the color-coded function keys on the keyboard allow users to retrieve, display and print article references.

This database includes coverage of the MAGAZINE INDEX (over 400 popular and general interest publications) as well as index citations to NEW YORK TIMES. The database is stored on a compact disc which is updated, cumulated and delivered monthly. It is an ideal resource for research on current affairs, people, business, home and leisure activities, arts and entertainment, companies, products, etc. You can also search for consumer reports and graded reviews of books, movies, restaurants, etc. Many technical subject databases are now on CD-ROM and used in libraries for student searching.

Wilson Disc

Wilson disc is another electronic database of general indexes using CD-ROM technology.

Online Databases

A large variety of databases have long been available online in systems such as DIALOG or BRS. On these services you are connected directly with the central information centers giving hundreds of database choices in every kind of specialty.

Frequent updating makes most online databases more useful than information found on "canned" CD-ROM disks. They update some information sources weekly, daily, or even continuously whenever news occurs. You will find more abstracts and many full-text articles online.

RESEARCHING FOR A TERM PAPER

More and more emphasis is placed on being able to research and write a term paper on a topic in many college courses. The research part of the project will invariably need the use of the library. In some cases you may need to ask the reference librarian for help. The following hints will help you to do a good job of your research:

1. Pick a topic that will interest you whenever you have a choice and get your professor's approval before you start working. You will enjoy the long, hard work that goes into a term paper more if you care about the subject and do not find it boring.

2. Try to find information in your own library. Go for interlibrary loans only as a last resort. You will save time, money , and frustration.

3. Check to see what material is available before you settle on a topic. The tools you use to do your search depend upon your subject. Reference books such as encyclopedias, manuals, dictionaries or handbooks usually are used first to establish basic facts.

4. Books from the general collection give in-depth studies of your subject. Be sure to note the publication dates of any books you use so that you do not have to waste time on outdated information and outmoded technologies unless you seek them.

5. Be sure to list properly all the reference material you had consulted for the Reference section of your report.

6. Write your report based on the information you have collected pertinent to your topic in the format prescribed by your professor.

INTERLIBRARY LOAN (ILL)

You can order books and articles that your college library does not have from another library. This is called the **Interlibrary Loan** service. It is carried out through a computer search to locate another library that will send a book or copy of an article. But then you have to wait for fourth class mail delivery, which may sometimes take as long as two or three weeks.

To seek an interlibrary loan, you must talk to your library personnel in the Interlibrary Loan Department. Fill in the ILL request form giving complete bibliographic information: author, title, pub-

lisher, date of publication for books; and author, title of article, journal title, volume number, page number, and publication date for journal articles.

You must allow at least two weeks for completion of ILL requests. The loan period is determined by the lending library. It is generally from 2 to 3 weeks. You must assume all costs connected with ILL transactions related to your request.

DEVELOP THE "LIBRARY HABIT"

The library may be easy to forget when it is not needed for your next assignment. But you may miss out on many opportunities for getting better grades unless you include it in your study plans.

To get the most out of your college library, make it a habit of using it as often as you can. Some helpful hints are:

1. Familiarize yourself with all the sections, equipments and personnel of the library.
2. Browse through the stacks of books and journals, in general, as a hobby.

3. Do not hesitate to ask for the assistance of the library personnel when you need help. You will not only save time but can profit from their expertise, academically speaking.

4. Remember that if a church, temple, mosque, or a synagogue is a source of spiritual inspiration, a college library is a source of intellectual inspiration and academic excellence. It is the user, in either case, who profits most.

Chapter **17**

SERVICES AND FACILITIES AVAILABLE TO THE COLLEGE STUDENT

"The degree of diversity in a college's student body is frequently a good indicator of its intellectual atmosphere."

The Insider's Guide to the Colleges, 1989.
Compiled and Edited by
The staff of Yale Daily News

TOPICS

1. Tutorial Services
2. Appointments with Faculty Members
3. Recreational Facilities
4. Student Employment
5. Cooperative Education Program
6. The Student Government Association
7. Student Organizations
8. U.S. Army ROTC
9. Foreign Students Advisor
10. Career and Placement Services

The objective of this chapter is to draw your attention to the various services, facilities, and opportunities that exist in your college campus, which you can take advantage of for academic, personal, and career improvement. It is important that you be well-informed of all these facilities because they are primarily designed to help you in every possible way and assist you to develop to your full potential.

Some of these facilities are created to provide opportunities for student employment, whereas some others are designed for the development of leadership qualities of the participants. Some are for pure physical relaxation, and some are for the development of non-academic potentials and hobbies. We have already presented the various counseling programs available to you in a previous chapter, which you can make full use of for your academic and career planning.

TUTORIAL SERVICES

If You Need Tutoring

Almost all colleges offer Student Support Services of one kind or another, whose primary goal is to provide to students an extension of academic help on an individual basis. They generally include unlimited free tutoring, and academic counseling. Tutoring services should be sought as soon as difficulties arise. Do **not** wait until the last minute!

Following are five symptoms indicative of your need to seek tutorial help in any of the courses you are taking:

1. When you have difficulty in understanding the textbook after the topic is discussed in the class by the professor.
2. When you are not able to follow the professor as he/she lectures.
3. When you are unable to do the home-work assignments or when you have difficulty in problem-solving because of a gap in your understanding.
4. When your basic problem-solving skills are not adequate.
5. When you are not able to concentrate on your study due to emotional or other problems.

If you think you need assistance, do not hesitate to make an appointment with the coordinator of the tutorial services, which are generally administered through the office of the Dean of Students. The coordinator is a specially trained person who will be able to spot your problem and suggest or provide the appropriate remedy. The key to success, of course, is **your** willingness to put in the extra effort needed to improve yourself academically for the sake of better grades.

If You Want to be a Tutor

On the other hand, if you are a good student and enjoy "teaching" other students, tutoring offers a unique opportunity for you to develop your skills and earn some extra-money. You should contact the office of the Student Support Services and register yourself as a potential tutor. Tutors are students carefully screened and selected for their superior academic standing, ability to communicate, reliability and, above all, for their desire to help fellow students.

APPOINTMENTS WITH FACULTY MEMBERS

Every professor who teaches a course in a college makes room for meeting with his/her students to answer questions and discuss matters related to the course taught. Some have an open door policy which permits students walk into his/her office whenever the door is open. Some professors post available office hours for discussion at their door; others see students "by appointment only."

No matter how busy a professor seems to be, he/she likes to meet with his /her students, and seldom will refuse to spend some time with students to answer questions and clarify doubts. You should take advantage of this opportunity of meeting with every one of your professors on one pretext or another. Take with you genuine questions and doubts **after** going over the notes you took during the lectures.

The benefits are two-fold. You not only get your doubts cleared then and there, but also get acquainted with the professor and his/her approach to the subject he/she teaches. This is an important factor in preparing yourself for the tests in that subject. But, it is up to you to take the extra-effort of tracking down your professor for as many appointments as possible.

RECREATIONAL FACILITIES

The following recreational facilities are generally available in almost all colleges and universities. Some of them may need your student identity card for their use.

Swimming pool	Track field
Tennis courts	Body building gadgets
Table tennis	Weight lifting gear
Pool tables	Mechanical exercisers
Basketball court	Piano rooms
Football field	Week-end movies

It is important that you take time off from your study schedule for recreation of some kind for physical and mental relaxation. Many of these facilities are generally housed in the gymnasium and physical education buildings, and in student centers.

STUDENT EMPLOYMENT

There are several opportunities for part-time employment for college students right at their own campus. They are generally administered through the Office of Work-Study.

Federal College Work-Study Program

In an attempt to help students meet the cost of college education, the 1965 Education Amendments made provisions for College Work-Study Programs. Work-Study expands employment opportunity for **needy** students and provides needed services for the employer at a minimum cost. You should file an application with the Financial Aid Office to determine eligibility. Funds are generally distributed on a first come basis.

Recipients of the College Work Study program may work a maximum of 20 hours per week during full-time enrollment periods or a maximum of 40 hours per week during non-enrollment periods such as breaks, holidays, and summer providing there is evidence of intent to enroll the following semester.

The rate of pay per hour is determined by the amount of paid work experience, with lowest rate being equal to Federal minimum wage.

The Director of Work-Study generally has the sole responsibility for job placement, once notified of available positions by the varied departments of the institution.

Institutional Employment for Students

There is another student employment program similar to Federal Work-Study, except it is not based on need and wages are paid entirely by the employer. Positions are generally posted for 5 days for the employer in the Financial Aid Office. Once applications are screened by the Director of Work-Study, the employer determines who will be hired.

COOPERATIVE EDUCATION PROGRAM

One of the educational programs that is getting more and more popular in colleges and universities across the Nation is the Cooperative Education Program. In the year 1987 alone over 200,000 students attended colleges and universities nation-wide under the Co-op program. They earned over one billion dollars in wages and paid over 130 million dollars in federal taxes while still being registered as continuing students in their respective colleges and universities!

Co-op education is a voluntary program of alternating semesters and summer terms of full-time study **on** campus and full-time work **off** campus in Government, business, and industry. The Co-op concept in designed to give practical as well as theoretical training in the student's chosen field over a five-year period (three years for associate degree).

Several advantages result from this integration of academic and career experience. The work experience helps the student determine whether he/she wishes to pursue his/her chosen academic major early in his/her college career. On the other hand, the early exposure to his/her chosen field also helps him/her academically by adding new dimensions of understanding to his/her academic studies. Earnings, while a side benefit, are generally enough to assist the Co-op student in financing his/her education. Also, higher average starting salaries are usually offered to graduating Co-op students by virtue of their cumulative documented practical experience prior to graduation.

Typically, a Co-op student is placed in a job following completion of his/her freshman year in May. After the summer work, the student returns to school for the fall semester, and returns to the same employer for work during the spring semester. This year-round alternating pattern continues until the senior year, which is spent on campus. The plan is for most students to work for the same employer all five work semesters (three for associate degree), thus allowing him/her to assume increasing responsibilities, more challenging work, and usually, more pay each time. As a full-time employee of his/her company during his/her work semesters, the Co-op student is expected to meet the same standards as other employees. The employers, in general, are very considerate in providing compatible work assignments to Co-op students.

Initially a student must have a cumulative grade point average of 2.2 or better. To continue the program, he/she must be a full-time student and remain off probation. Freshman students may apply any time after completing the first semester, and may be placed in a job upon the completion of the freshman year.

If you think that the Co-op program suits your interest and need, you should contact the office of Cooperative Education in your college for further information to explore the opportunities that await you.

THE STUDENT GOVERNMENT ASSOCIATION (SGA)

All the colleges and universities have a forum for students to involve themselves in the decision making process on matters that directly concern them. Such a forum is formed through an election process in which the college students directly participate to elect their own representatives to serve as Senators in the forum, popularly known as the Student Government Association (SGA). The objective of this organization is to use the rights and capabilities of the students to govern themselves, within the reasonable and proper limits established by the administration of the college or university.

The SGA functions through a Senate consisting of district Senators elected from and by members of each student district or group. The executive branch consists of the President, Vice-President, and Cabinet of the Student Government Association.

The SGA provides a unique opportunity for the college student to develop his/her leadership skills. All full-time students with good academic standing are eligible to stand for election to the SGA. It is an opportunity you should not overlook while you are pursuing a college degree.

STUDENT ORGANIZATIONS AND CHAPTERS

To further its educational objectives and programs, every college or university extends recognition to a wide variety of student organizations and chapters. They include fraternities, sororities, various departmental, professional and special interest groups.

Contact the Student Activities Office for all the available student organizations and chapters on your campus. Depending on your interest you can join one or more of these groups and actively participate in their activities for personal development and relaxation.

U S ARMY R O T C

Army ROTC (Reserve Officers' Training Corps) is a college program which combines college courses in military science with summer training sessions to turn students into officers. Upon successful completion of the program and graduation, cadets are awarded a commission as a second lieutenant in either the U.S.Army, the Army National Guard or the U.S.Army Reserve.

Army ROTC offers two different programs to all qualified college and university students. The traditional 4-year program gives students the opportunity to take ROTC courses in each of their four years of college. The 2-year program is available for community and junior college students as well as any other students who did not take

ROTC during their first two years of college. Both of these programs are offered at more than 1,000 colleges and universities throughout the United States.

The program is directed by the U.S.Army ROTC Cadet Command, located at Fort Monroe, Virginia. Cadet Command is responsible for the administration and operation of the Army ROTC at the college and university level nationwide. Its mission is "to commission the future officer leadership of the U.S.Army."

ROTC provides the Army with more than 70 percent of its officers; and today, ROTC trained men and women are offering indispensable leadership in a wide variety of assignments around the world.

The Advantages of Army ROTC

* ROTC enhances a student's education by providing unique leadership and management training, along with practical experience.
* It helps a student develop many of the qualities basic to success in the Army, or in a civilian career.
* ROTC gives students a valuable opportunity to build for the

future by enabling them to earn a college degree and an officer's commission at the same time.

* ROTC helps provide the Army with capable, college-educated officers.

ROTC graduates will find that their background and experience in ROTC and the Army can be a valuable asset if they decide to pursue a civilian career. The practical experience they gain by leading people, managing money and equipment, and making things happen, can place them far ahead of other college graduates in competing for jobs leading to top management positions. Employers value these leadership qualities and prefer them in the people they hire.

Army ROTC Scholarships/Financial Assistance

Army ROTC scholarships are offered for two, three and four years and are awarded on merit to the most outstanding students who apply. Each scholarship pays for college tuition and educational fees which are required of all students, and provides a fixed amount for textbooks, supplies and equipment. Each scholarship also includes an allowance of up to $1,000 for every year the scholarship is in effect. The total value of a scholarship will depend on the cost of the tuition and other educational expenses at the college or university attended.

Students who receive a scholarship will be required to attain an undergraduate degree in the field in which the scholarship was awarded.

Non-scholarship cadets in the Advanced Course also receive an allowance of up to $1,000 for each of the two years, as well as pay for attending the six-week Advanced Camp. Students attending the Basic Camp of the 2-Year Program also receive pay for this camp.

Contact the office of Army ROTC in your college or university to learn more about the ROTC Program.

FOREIGN STUDENTS ADVISOR

Almost all colleges and universities that admit international students have a Foreign Student Advisor's Office. The Foreign Student Advisor provides assistance to these students in matters arising out of visa problems, and he/she acts as a liaison between them and the Department of Immigration and Naturalization of the United States. International students are required to stay as full-time students while they are in this country unless they have obtained prior permission for employment.

International students must be in touch with the Foreign Student Advisor in the college where they are enrolled and seek his/her advice and assistance on matters that could affect their legal status, as well as any other specific problems.

CAREER AND PLACEMENT SERVICES

The office of the Career Counselor provides assistance in all matters related to career choice and finding jobs in government, business and industry. Some of the services generally provided by this office are:

* Career Advising—Individual help is provided.
* Career Library—Information on a variety of jobs can be researched.
* Career Seminars—Offered on a variety of topics related to deciding on a career or hunting for a job.
* Videotape Library—Information is available on videotape about jobs, employers, and job campaign skills.
* Career Day—Employers representing all major areas of the world of work come to campus to act as resource persons. Students have an opportunity to get information in an informal setting.
* Employer Seminars
* Graduate and Professional School Information
* Employer Resource Files
* Jobs—Positions open for full time employment are in the career library filed according to types of jobs. The listings are constantly updated.
* On-Campus Recruiting—Employers come to campus to interview seniors for future employment. Students can receive feedback on their interview to help improve their interview skills.

* Credential Referrals—Many employers ask for referrals of students' credentials for consideration for a job opening. Your registration with this office ensures having a credential file.

Chapter 18

GUIDE TO FINANCIAL ASSISTANCE: STUDENT LOANS, GRANTS, & WORK-STUDY

"Education is a remarkably important investment in yourself and our country, so go for it! The money is there, all it takes is discovering how to find it."

Lana J. Chandler
& Michael D. Boggs,
authors of "The Student Loan Handbook"

TOPICS

1. Financial Planning for College Education
2. Major Sources of Financial Assistance
3. Eligibility Criteria
4. Financial Need
5. The Stafford Loan (GSL) program
6. The Parent Loan (PLUS) Program
7. The Supplemental Loan (SLS) Program
8. Perkins Loans
9. College Work-Study
10. Pell Grants
11. Supplemental Educational Opportunity Grants (SEOG)

FINANCIAL PLANNING FOR COLLEGE EDUCATION

If You Are the Parent

As a parent you will agree with me when I say that the greatest investment you can make is in educating your children to the highest level possible. Education brings identity and meaning to our lives and opens the door for a wide choice of careers for gainful employment. However, education, particularly at the college level, is getting more and more expensive. Not all parents have adequate financial resources to send their children to the colleges of their choice. Yet, they can still succeed in their goal through well-conceived financial planning.

The key, of course, is to plan well ahead, and to include the educational needs of the children in financial planning, along with other family needs such as home, investments, retirement, etc.

The other alternative is to obtain a loan for the purpose of children's education at the time of need. The "financial need" related to loans is discussed in a subsequent section of this chapter.

If You Are the College Student

As a college student you may not always be fortunate to have your financial needs taken care of completely by your parents or guardian throughout your college life. You must be prepared to bear or share the financial burden. Where can you turn to? What kinds of financial assistance are available to college students, in what forms, and how to get them are some of the questions discussed in this chapter.

The financial aid available to you, when you are qualified, comes basically in three different forms: namely loans, grants, and work-study. Loans are repayable money, grants are outright free money and work-study is money in exchange of your labor in preassigned employment within the campus. There are other aids like scholarships which are available in some circumstances.

Remember that having your financial problems under control is an important contributory factor in getting good grades in college. Also, a knowledge of the available loans and grants will ensure that you don't miss them when you are qualified.

MAJOR SOURCES OF FINANCIAL ASSISTANCE

You will be surprised at the wide variety of sources and organizations that are interested in assisting college students in their financial need. You need to learn about as many sources of aid as you can so that you don't miss out on any of them. The following steps will be of help:

1. Contact the **Financial Aid Administrator** at each college you are interested in. He/she can tell you what Federal and other aid programs are available there, and about how much the total cost of attending will be. If you are in high school, also talk to your **guidance counselor**. He/she can tell you about financial aid in general and where to look for help.

2. Your **public library** has information on state and private sources of aid.

3. Many **companies**, as well as labor unions, have programs to help pay the cost of post-secondary education for employees or members (or for their children).

4. Check with **foundations,** religious organizations, fraternities or sororities, and town or city clubs. Include community organizations, civil groups, and service clubs such as the American Legion, YMCA, 4-H Clubs, Kiwanis, Jaycees, Chamber of Commerce, the Girl or Boy Scouts, Rotary Clubs, and Lions Clubs.

5. National Merit **Scholarships** and Scholarships from the National Honor Society are available to students with high grades who qualify.

6. Don't overlook aid from **organizations** connected with your field of interest (for example, the American Medical Association or the American Bar Association). These organizations are listed in the U.S.Department of Labor's Occupational Outlook Handbook and can also be found in various directories of associations available at your public library.

7. If you are a veteran, **veteran's benefits** may be available. Check with your local Veterans' Administration Office.

8. Ask the **state educational agency** in your home state for information about state aid—including aid from a program

jointly funded by individual states and the U.S.Department of Education.

Each state has its own name for this program, as well as its own award levels, eligibility criteria, and application procedures. At the Federal level, this program is called the State Student Incentive Grant Program. For the address and telephone number of your state agency, contact the financial aid administrator of your college.

Federal Aid Programs

The following Federal aid programs are available to eligible college students in more than 8000 colleges, universities, vocational schools, technical schools, or hospital schools of nursing that take part in U.S.Department of Education financial aid programs:

1. Stafford Loans (formerly Guaranteed Student Loans: GSL)
2. Parent Loans (PLUS)
3. Supplemental Loans for Students (SLS)
4. Perkins Loans
5. College Work-Study (CWS)
6. Supplemental Education Opportunity Grants (SEOG)
7. Pell Grants.

These are discussed in detail later in this chapter.

ELIGIBILITY CRITERIA

Eligibility criteria may vary with each of the different aid programs. Check with the financial aid administrator of your college for the program you wish to apply for.

In general, you are eligible for **Federal aid** if you meet the following requirements:

1. You must be enrolled at least **half-time** as a regular student in an eligible program.
2. You must be a U.S.citizen or an eligible non-citizen.
3. You must show that you have financial need.
4. You must be making satisfactory progress in your course of study.
5. You must not be in default on any of the Federal loans.

6. You must not owe a refund on any of the Federal grants.
7. You must have a high school diploma, a GED, or have the ability to benefit.

FINANCIAL NEED

Most Federal student aid is awarded on the basis of financial need. Need is the difference between your **Cost of Education** (educational expenses such as tuition, fees, room, board, books, supplies, and other related expenses) and an amount you and your family are expected to contribute toward your education which is called **Family Contribution.**

The amount left over after subtracting the expected Family Contribution from your cost of education is considered your financial need. It is important to note that the financial aid administrator in some instances can adjust an individual Family Contribution—up or down—or can adjust the Cost of Education if he/she believes the family's financial circumstances warrant it.

Handicapped Student

If you are a handicapped student, your educational expenses may be higher and your need therefore greater—because of costs associated with the handicap. To make sure that these extra-expenses are recognized, the financial aid administrator at your college will work with a representative from your State vocational rehabilitation agency. They will coordinate resources so that your Department of Education and vocational rehabilitation aid will go as far as possible toward meeting your expenses.

THE STAFFORD LOAN (GSL) PROGRAM

What is a Stafford Loan (GSL)?

A Stafford Loan is a low interest loan made to you by a lender such as a bank, credit union, or savings and loan association, to help you pay for your education after high school. These loans are insured by the **guarantee agency** in your State and reinsured by the Federal Government.

The Interest Rate

Currently the interest rate is 8 percent for the first four years of repayment and 10 percent after that. An attractive feature of the GSL is that you are granted a six-month grace period, interest free, after you graduate, leave school, or drop below half-time before payments must begin. That gives you reasonable time to find a job and adjust to life outside of college.

How Much Can You Borrow?

Depending on your need, you may borrow up to—

* $2,625 a year, if you are a first-or second-year undergraduate student.
* $4,000 a year, if you have completed 2 years of study and have achieved third-year status.
* $7,500 a year, if you are a graduate student.

The total Stafford and GSL debt you can have outstanding is $17,250. The total for graduate or professional study is $54,750, including any GSL's made at the undergraduate level.

How to Apply for a GSL

1. Get a GSL application form from a lender, a college, or your State guarantee agency.
2. Fill out your part of the application.
3. Submit the application to the college you plan to attend to complete the part, certifying your enrollment, your cost of education, your academic standing, any other financial aid you will receive, and **your financial need**.
   Note: Before you can receive a GSL, your college must first determine your eligibility for a Pell Grant, if you are an undergraduate and your school participates in the Pell Grant Program. If you are eligible, the amount of your Pell Grant will be considered in determining your financial aid package, so that you won't be over-awarded.
4. When the college's portion of the application is completed, you or your college submits it to the GSL lender you have

chosen. If the lender agrees to make the loan and gets the approval of the guarantee agency, the lender will send the loan amount to the college in one or more payments. In general, for longer periods of enrollment, the loan will be divided into 2 or more instalments.

When to Apply

You should begin looking for a lender as soon as you are accepted by your college. After you submit your application to a lender and the lender agrees to make the loan, it usually takes 4 to 6 weeks to get your loan approved by the guarantee agency; so give yourself as much time as possible to complete the loan application process.

When to Pay Back Your GSL

Loan payments begin from 6 months to 12 months after you graduate, leave school, or drop below half-time status depending on the interest rate of your loan. The lender must usually allow you at least 5 years to repay the loan, and may allow up to 10 years.

How Much to Pay Back

The amount of each payment depends upon the size of your debt and the length of your repayment period, but you will usually have to pay at least $50 per month or $600 per year. You should ask your lender what your monthly payments will be before you take out the loan.

What if You Don't Pay

If you don't pay back your loan, you may go into default. If you do, the guarantee agency or the Federal Government can sue you to collect the loan, and you may be required to repay the entire amount immediately. Credit bureaus will be notified of your default, and this may affect your future credit rating. Also, the Internal Revenue Service may withhold your income tax refund and apply it toward your loan.

If your loan is in default, you can not get additional Federal student aid until you make satisfactory arrangement to repay your loan, and you won't be eligible for deferment of the defaulted loan.

Can Your GSL Be Cancelled?

Only if you become totally and permanently disabled, or if you die. However, if you serve as an enlisted person in certain selected specialties of the U.S.Army, the Army Reserves, or the Army National Guard, the Department of Defense, will as an enlistment incentive, repay a portion of your GSL. If you think you may qualify, contact your recruiting officer.

Know Your Lender

If you have any questions about the terms of your GSL, repayment obligations, deferment, or cancellation, check with your lender. Remember, only your lender can grant deferment or cancellation, or make decisions concerning your loan.

THE PARENT LOAN (PLUS) PROGRAM

PLUS, an acronym for Parent Loans for Undergraduate Students, is limited to the parents of dependent students attending participating schools. A "parent" is defined as the natural or adoptive parent or the legal guardian. PLUS loans provide additional funds for educational expenses and, like GSL's, are made by a lender such as a bank, credit union, or savings and loan association.

Interest Rate

Before July 1, 1987, interest rates on PLUS loans ranged from 9 to 14 percent, depending on when the loan was made. The interest rate for each loan is shown on the promissory note, signed by the borrower when the loan was made.

PLUS loans distributed on or after July 1, 1987 will have a **variable** interest rate, adjusted in June of each year. For the 1989–90 award year the interest rate is 12.00 percent.

Eligibility Requirements

To be eligible a borrower must:

1. Be a United States citizen or permanent resident.
2. Be free from default on a previous PLUS loan.
3. Be free from debt on a Pell or other Grants at the college being attended by the dependent student.
4. Have the lender's approval for the extension of credit.
5. Be the parent of an eligible dependent student.

The dependent student for whom the parent is borrowing must meet all the eligibility criteria (as outlined in that section) for financial aid.

Financial Need

Unlike the Stafford Loan, financial need is **not** a criteria. A PLUS borrower does not have to demonstrate financial need. However, like all borrowers, they may have to undergo a credit analysis.

How Much Can a Parent Borrow?

PLUS enables parents to borrow up to $4,000 per year, to a total of $20,000, for each child who is enrolled at least half-time and is a dependent student.

Repayment

Usually, PLUS borrowers must begin repaying principal and interest within 60 days after the loan is disbursed, unless a deferment applies. Deferments do not apply to interest, although a lender may permit the interest to accumulate until the deferment ends.

Contact the financial aid administrator of your college or your state guarantee agency for application forms and full details.

THE SUPPLEMENTAL LOANS FOR STUDENTS (SLS) PROGRAM

SLS loans provide additional funds for educational expenses and, like GSL's, are made by a lender such as a bank, credit union, or savings and loan association.

Interest Rate

SLS loans distributed on or after July 1, 1987 will have a **variable** interest rate, adjusted each year. For the 1989–90 award year, the interest rate was 12.00 percent.

Eligibility Requirements

Generally, to be eligible for this loan, the student must meet the eligibility criteria for financial aid (except financial need) and be "independent" under federal criteria. You are considered automatically independent if you:

1. Are over age 24.
2. Are a veteran of the U.S. Armed Forces.
3. Are a ward of the court, or both parents are dead and you don't have an adoptive or legal guardian.
4. Have legal dependents other than a spouse.

If you don't meet the above criteria, additional information is required to determine your dependency status. In exceptional circumstances, the financial aid administrator may allow undergraduate dependent students to apply for a SLS.

Financial Need

SLS borrowers do **not** have to show need, although like all borrowers, they may have to undergo a credit analysis. Also, your eligibility for a Stafford Loan and Pell Grant must be determined.

How Much Can You Borrow?

Under SLS, graduate students and independent undergraduates may borrow up to $4,000 per year to a total of $20,000. This amount is in addition to the Stafford Loan limits. A student may not borrow more than the cost of education minus any other financial aid received.

Repayment

SLS borrowers must begin repaying interest within 60 days after the loan is disbursed, unless the lender agrees to let the interest accumulate until deferment ends.

SLS borrowers get the same deferments as Stafford Loan borrowers. However, under SLS, the deferments apply only to principal. There are no grace periods for SLS Loans.

For loan application form and more details about specific repayment and deferment conditions, contact your financial aid administrator, your lender, or the guarantee agency in your State.

THE PERKINS LOAN

The National Direct Student Loan has been renamed the Perkins Loan as a memorial to Carl D. Perkins, the late chairman of the House Education and Labor Committee, for his support of public education and for his particular concern for a program of direct Federal loans to students.

The Perkins Loan is a **campus-based** program. Though it is funded by the federal government and the institution, it is administered by school personnel. Participating schools receive money for the program from the federal government and match the required amount. The college's financial aid administrator then distributes such funds to those applicants who meet eligibility requirements.

Interest Rate

The Perkins Loan is a low-interest loan, currently 5 percent.

These loans are for both undergraduate and graduate students and are made through the college's financial aid office. Check with your financial aid administrator to find out if your college or university takes part in the Perkins Loan Program.

Eligibility Requirements

To be eligible for a Perkins Loan, you must meet all the eligibility criteria (as outlined in that section) for financial aid.

How Much Can You Borrow?

The Perkins Loan amount awarded is based on the availability of funds earmarked for Perkins Loans at the college you are attending, the amount of any other financial aid you are receiving, and your financial need.

You may borrow up to:

* * $4,500 if you are enrolled in a vocational program, or if you have completed less than 2 years of a program leading to a bachelor's degree.
* * $9,000 if you are an undergraduate student who has already completed 2 years of study toward a bachelor's degree and has achieved third year status.
* * $18,000 for graduate or professional study. This total includes any amount borrowed under Perkins and other Student Loans for undergraduate study.

How to Apply

Each college sets its own deadlines. They are usually early in each calendar year, so apply as soon as possible. Find out what the deadlines are by checking with the financial aid administrator at your college.

Repayment

A Perkins Loan is a loan, so naturally it must be repaid. Repayment starts 6 months after you graduate, leave school, or drop below half-time status. The only exception is if a deferment is granted.

Up to 10 years may be allowed for repayment. The amount of each payment depends upon the size of your debt and the length of your repayment period, but you must pay at least $30 per month. In special cases—for example, if you are unemployed or ill for a long period of time—your college may allow you to make payments that are less than $30 per month or may extend your repayment period.

COLLEGE WORK-STUDY (CWS)

The College Work-Study Program provides jobs for undergraduate and graduate students who need financial aid. CWS gives you a chance to earn money to help pay your educational expenses. CWS is neither a loan nor a grant program. It provides students with jobs in order to earn money for college expenses. Both on-campus and off-campus jobs are supported by this Federally subsidized program.

The Federal government allocates money to each participating college for the CWS program. This money and the required institutional matching amount (currently 25%) is then awarded to all qualified applicants on a funds-available basis.

How Much Can You Earn?

Your pay will be at least the current Federal minimum wage, but it may also be related to the type of work you do and its difficulty.

Your total CWS award depends on your financial need, the amount of money your college has for this program, and the amount of aid you get from other programs.

Eligibility Requirements

Eligibility requirements are the same as for the other need-based Federal loan programs.

Find out what the deadlines for application are by checking with the financial administrator of your college.

How Are CWS Students Paid?

If you are an undergraduate, you will be paid by the hour. If you are a graduate student, you may be paid by the hour or you may receive a salary. No CWS student may be paid by commission or fee. Your college will pay you at least once a month.

On-Campus and Off-Campus Jobs

CWS jobs are both on-campus and off-campus. If you work on campus, you will work for your college. If you work off-campus, your job will usually involve work that is in the public interest, and your employer will usually be a private or public non-profit organization, or a local, State, or Federal agency. However, some colleges may have agreements with private sector employers for CWS jobs.

Remember, your college sets your work schedule. In arranging a job and assigning work hours, your class schedule, your health, and your academic progress will be taken into account. Therefore, it will not be possible for you to work as many hours as you would like to.

Part-Time Students

It may be possible for part-time college students also to get a CWS job. A college may use part of its CWS funds for part-time students, and even in some cases, for less than half-time students. To find out if your college does this, contact the financial aid administrator of your college.

PELL GRANTS

What is a Pell Grant?

Pell Grants are awards funded by the Federal government to help **undergraduates** pay for their education after high school. For many students, these grants provide a "foundation" of financial aid, to which aid from other Federal and non-Federal sources may be added. Unlike loans, grants don't have to be paid back.

Duration of a Pell Grant

Your Pell Grant eligibility will usually be limited to 5 full years of undergraduate study, not counting remedial course work. You can receive a Pell Grant for up to one full year of remedial courses.

You may receive a Pell Grant for a 6th full year of undergraduate study if you are enrolled in a program that requires more than 4 years to complete a bachelor's degree, and if the sixth year is necessary to complete the degree.

How Much Money Can You Get?

For the 1989–90 academic year, the maximum Pell Grant awarded to a student is $2,300. The amount of available money depends on how much funding Congress gives the program. Nearly $4 billion was distributed during the 1987–88 academic year. This will give you an idea of the immensity of this popular program.

Pell Grants generally range from $250 to $2,300, or 60 percent of the college's attendance costs, whichever is less. This wide variation is due to the methodology employed by the Pell Grant award which includes family income, number of dependents, and assets as the criteria.

In determining the amount of an award, the SAI, cost of attendance, and enrollment status are considered.

Eligibility Requirements—Student Aid Index (SAI)

A standard formula is used by the U.S.Department of Education to determine eligibility. Congress revises and approves this formula every year. This formula produces a **Student Aid Index** number. Called the Pell Grant Methodology, it establishes both eligibility and amount of the grant through the SAI number.

You may want to obtain a calculation guidebook which provides a line-by-line example of the Pell needs analysis, as well as sample forms which you may use to calculate your own SAI. For a free copy write to:

> Formula Book
> Department L-10
> Pueblo, Colorado 81009–0015.

Student Aid Report (SAR)

If you fill out the Federal application, you will receive a Student Aid Report (SAR) 4 to 6 weeks after you send in your application. The SAR contains the information you gave on your application and will contain numbers that tell you about your eligibility for Federal student aid—the Student Aid Index (SAI) number, and a Family Contribution (FC) number, which determines your eligibility for the campus-based and Stafford Loan Programs.

How to Apply for a Pell Grant

1. Complete the Federal form (Application for Federal Student Aid) or one of the non-Federal forms provided by the Financial Aid Administrator of your college.
2. Have it forwarded to the Federal processing center. (After processing, this center mails the Student Aid Report to the student's home address. The SAR comes in 3 parts if you are eligible for a Pell Grant. If you are not eligible for a Pell Grant, the report will consist of 2 parts).

3. File the SAR with the Financial Aid Administrator. He/she will use the Student Aid Index (SAI) number to determine the actual amount of your grant.

SUPPLEMENTAL EDUCATIONAL OPPORTUNITY GRANTS (SEOG)

What is SEOG?

A Supplemental Educational Opportunity Grant (SEOG) is an award to help you pay for your education after high school. It is for **undergraduate** students with exceptional financial need (with priority given to Pell Grant recipients), and it does not have to be paid back.

How Much Can You Get?

You can get up to $4,000 a year. It depends on the following:
1. Financial need,
2. Availability of funds earmarked for SEOGs at the college you are attending, and
3. The amount of any other financial aid you are receiving.

SEOG is a federally funded campus-based program. Participating colleges receive money for the program from the federal government, and then the college's financial aid administrator awards it to qualified applicants on a funds available basis.

Eligibility Requirements

SEOG is a grant program based on your financial need. The eligibility requirements are same as for other financial aid.

When to Apply?

Different colleges set different deadlines. They are usually early in each calendar year, so apply as soon as possible. Find out what the deadlines are by checking with the financial aid administrator at your college.

Difference between Pell Grant and SEOG

The Department of Education of the Federal Government of the United States of America guarantees that each participating college will receive enough money to pay the Pell Grants of its students. An SEOG is different. Each college receives a set amount of money for SEOG's, and when that money is gone, there are no more SEOG awards for that year. That is why it is important to meet the college's financial aid application deadlines.

Chapter **19**

THE COLLEGE STUDENT'S RIGHTS, RESPONSIBILITIES, ETHICS, AND MORALS

". . . and we discover what a man's moral principles are mainly by seeing how he in fact conducts himself."

P. H. Nowell-Smith,
author of "Ethics"

TOPICS

GENERAL RIGHTS AND RESPONSIBILITIES

The rights of an individual places responsibility upon others to respect those rights. The college student, in his/her status as a member of the academic community, has both rights and responsibilities. Within that community, **the student's most essential right is the right to learn.** The college has the responsibility to provide for the student those privileges, opportunities, and protection which best promote the learning process in all its aspects.

The student, for his/her part, has responsibilities to other members of the academic community, the most important of which is **to refrain from interference with the rights of others.** These are equally essential to the purposes and processes of the institution.

Students are citizens of several communities—city, county, state, and nation as well as the college. Certain types of misconduct may subject a student to the concurrent jurisdiction of, and the imposition of a sanction by, both the college and civil authorities. Each institution has their own judicial system providing the basic framework which will help further the educational aims of the institution and at the same time provide opportunity for the full development of students, academically and otherwise. You should contact the Office of Student Affairs of your college or university for complete information on the judicial system of your campus.

Freedom of Expression and Assembly

The student enjoys the essential freedoms of scholarship and inquiry central to all institutions of higher learning. In exercising these freedoms the student has certain rights and responsibilities, including:

1. To have access to campus resources and facilities.
2. To espouse causes.
3. To inquire, discuss, listen to, and evaluate.
4. To listen to any person through the invitation of organizations recognized by the institution.
5. To have a free and independent student press which adheres to the canons of responsible journalism.
6. To not violate the rights of others in matters of expressions and assembly.

7. To abide by policies, rules, and regulations of the institution and federal, state, and local statues and ordinances pertaining to freedom of expression and assembly.

Freedom of Association

Students may organize whatever associations they deem desirable, and are entitled to affiliate with any group or organization for which they meet membership qualifications. However, institutional recognition of student organizations shall be limited to those whose purposes comport with the educational mission of the institution.

Right to Privacy

The college student is entitled to the same safe-guards of the rights and freedoms of citizenship as are afforded those outside the academic community, including the following:

1. Privileged communication on a one-to-one relationship with faculty, administrators, counselors, and other institutional functionaries.
2. Respect for personality, including freedom from unreasonable and unauthorized searches of student living quarters.
3. Confidentiality of academic and disciplinary records.
4. Legitimate evaluations made from student records.

Responsibilities of Citizenship

The college student is expected, as are all citizens, to respect and abide by local ordinances and State and Federal statutes, both on and off the campus. As a member of the educational community, the student is expected to abide by the institution's code of student conduct which clarifies those behavioral standards considered essential to its educational mission.

Disciplinary Proceedings

Disciplinary proceedings for students accused of committing offenses must be consistent with such constitutional provisions guaranteeing due process of law as are applicable to them.

In all the disciplinary proceedings, **the student shall be considered innocent until proven guilty** of any charge.

ACADEMIC RIGHTS AND RESPONSIBILITIES

A student by voluntarily accepting admission to the institution or enrolling in a class or course of study offered by the institution, accepts the academic requirements and criteria of the institution. It is the student's responsibility to fulfill course work and degree or certificate requirements and to know and meet criteria for satisfactory academic progress and completion of the program.

Concomitant with the academic standards and responsibilities established by the institution, each student has the following academic rights:

1. The student shall be graded or have his/her performance evaluated solely upon performance in the course work as measured against academic standards. The student shall not be evaluated prejudicially, capriciously, or arbitrarily. The student shall not be graded nor shall his/her performance be evaluated on the basis of his/her race, color, creed, sex or national origin.

2. Each student shall have the right to have any academic penalty, defined by his/her institution, reviewed.

3. Each student shall have access to a copy of the college or university catalog or program brochure in which current academic program requirements are described (e.g., required courses, total credit requirements, time in residence requirements, special program requirements, minimum grade point average, probation standards, professional standards, etc.).

4. Students have the right to receive from the instructor written descriptions of content and requirements for any course in which they are enrolled (e.g., attendance expectations, special requirements, laboratory requirements including time, field trips and costs, grading standards and procedures, professional standards, etc.).

5. The instructor of each course is responsible for assigning grades to students enrolled in the course, consistent with the academic rights of the students.

ACADEMIC REQUIREMENTS

The institution shall define and promulgate the academic requirements for the following:

1. Admission to the institution.
2. Admission to limited enrollment programs.
3. Admission to professional and graduate degree programs (where offered).
4. The criteria for maintenance of satisfactory academic progress.
5. Successful completion of the program.
6. The award of a degree or certification.
7. Student honesty and originality of expression.
8. Graduation.

Normally, students may finish a program of study according to the requirements under which they were admitted to the program. However, requirements are subject to change at any time, with reasonable notice provided to the students.

ACADEMIC PENALTIES

A student who fails to meet the academic requirements or standards, including those for academic honesty as defined by the institution, may be subject to one or more of the following penalties:

1. A lower grade or failure of the course or exclusion from further participation in the class (including laboratories or clinical experiences), all of which may be imposed by the instructor.
2. Academic probation as determined and defined by the institution.
3. Academic suspension as determined and defined by the institution.
4. Academic dismissal.

Academic dismissal is defined as termination of student status, including any right or privilege to receive some benefit or recognition or certification. A student may be academically dismissed from a limited enrollment program and remain eligible to enroll in courses in other programs at the institution, or a student may be academically dismissed from the institution and not remain eligible to enroll in other courses or programs at the institution.

ACADEMIC APPEALS

Each institution has established policies and procedures by which a student may appeal or challenge any academic penalties imposed by a faculty member or by the institution.

These policies and procedures relating to appeals of academic penalties shall be governed by due process and shall include, as a minimum:

1. Written notice to the student (1) of his/her failure to meet or maintain an academic standard, (2) of the methods, if any, by which the student may correct the failure, and (3) of the penalty which may be imposed.
2. An opportunity for the student to meet with the faculty member(s) or other individual(s) who have judged his/her performance to be deficient, to discuss with these faculty member(s) or other individual(s) the information forming the basis of the judgement or opinion of his/her performance.
3. To have an advisor of his/her choice from the institution to accompany him/her in all such meetings.
4. An opportunity for the student to appeal the decision or judgement of faculty members through the established institutional appeals procedure within a certain number of calendar days (usually 30 days) after written notice of the decision or judgement.
5. An opportunity for the student to appeal to the President of the institution or his/her designee within a certain number of calendar days (usually 30 days) after the receipt of written notice of the decision or judgement.

The Final Decision

The decision of the President of the institution or his/her designee regarding an academic appeal is final.

REQUIRED ETHICAL CONDUCT

All college and university students are subject to, and are required to comply with, observe, and obey the following:

1. The laws of the United States of America.
2. The laws of the state where the institution is located.
3. Local city, county and municipal ordinances.
4. The policies, rules, and regulations of the college or university and its governing body.
5. The directions and orders of the officers, faculty and staff of the institution who are charged with the administration of institutional affairs on campus.

PROHIBITED CONDUCT

Disorderly Nature

Any and all students who behave in a disorderly or unlawful manner, such as the actions listed below, but not limited to those listed, in or about institutional property or facilities, are subject to institutional disciplinary action which may result in probation, suspension, or expulsion, whether or not there is prosecution for such violations in local, State, or Federal courts:

1. Fights.
2. Assaults or battery.
3. Public disturbances.
4. Unlawful assembly.
5. The violation of any municipal, State and Federal law, or the rules and regulations of the governing body or the institution.

Theft or Damage of Property

No student shall misuse, steal, damage, or destroy any institutional property or facilities or the property of any member of the institutional community.

Students involved in any such prohibited actions or conduct shall be subject to institutional disciplinary action which may result in probation, suspension, or expulsion, whether or not there is prosecution for such actions or conduct in local, State or Federal courts.

Disruption

No student shall, individually or by joining with one or more other persons, do any of the following:

1. Disrupt or interfere with institutional activity, program, meeting, or operation.
2. Interfere with the rights of any member of the institutional community.
3. Injure or threaten to injure, or coerce by bodily harm or restraint or threats thereof or any other means, any member of the institutional community or persons lawfully on the institution's campus, property, or facilities.
4. Seize, hold, commandeer, or damage any property or facilities of the institution, or threaten to do so, or refuse to depart from any property or facilities of the institution upon direction, pursuant to policies, rules, and regulations of the institution, by an institutional officer, faculty or staff member, or any other person authorized by the President of the institution.

Students involved in any such action or activities shall be subject to institutional disciplinary action which may result in probation, suspension, or expulsion, whether or not there is prosecution for such actions in local, State, or Federal courts.

Hazing

Hazing in any form is prohibited. Hazing includes any action which subjects a member of a student organization to a pledge or initiate activities which are personally demeaning or involve a substantial risk of physical injury. This includes both rites of initiation and informal activities.

All colleges and universities have some form of institutional policies that provide that students involved in hazing activities are subject to institutional disciplinary action.

Discrimination

No student shall, individually or by joining with one or more other persons, promote or demand action on their part or any other member of the institutional community that would constitute unlawful discrimination on the basis of race, sex, color, political affiliation, handicap, or age.

Students involved in any such action or activities shall be subject to institutional disciplinary action which may result in probation, suspension, or expulsion.

Sexual Harassment

Sexual harassment is defined as unwelcome sexual advances, such as requests for favors and other verbal or physical contact of a sexual nature, which adversely affect the work, learning, or living environment.

No member of the college community may sexually harass another. Sexual harassment is a violation of Title VII of the 1964 Civil Rights Act as Amended (Section 1604.11 of EEOC's regulation on sexual discrimination of 1980) and Title IX of the Education Amendments of 1972.

ACADEMIC DISHONESTY

Honesty among the members of any social group is required for the smooth functioning of the group. In college, new experiences, social awareness, and the academic life with its freedoms, frequently put individual honesty to test. Without honesty, both individual and institutional goals are meaningless. Academic dishonesty defeats the very purpose of being in college, that is to learn.

Academic dishonesty includes any deceitful act committed to affect any student's scholastic standing. All parties knowingly associated with the act are guilty of dishonesty whether or not they directly benefit from the act.

Acts of academic dishonesty include the following:

1. Plagiarism of an item submitted for a grade such as an answer on an exam or quiz, a laboratory report, a submitted

paper, experimental data, a computer program, or home-work.
2. Falsifying experimental data.
3. Using work accomplished by another person.
4. Assisting another person to cheat.
5. Falsifying records.
6. Improperly accessing computer stored information.

You should be aware at all times that academic dishonesty is the negation of true learning through honest means. It is against all moral and ethical principles. Besides, the penalty for engaging in it could be very serious and devastating. It could lead to suspension or expulsion from the college or university.

DISCIPLINARY ACTIONS AND SANCTIONS

Filing Charges Against Students

Students, faculty, administrators, or other members of the academic community may file charges against any student for conduct or activities in violation of the Code of the institution. A written complaint must be filed in the Office of the Dean of Students.

The Dean of Student Services or the Dean's designee will investigate the charges to determine if a violation of the Code of the institution has occurred and what further action should be taken. The Dean, or the Dean's designee, upon completion of preliminary review, may :

1. Dismiss the charges, or
2. Take administrative disciplinary action, not to include expulsion or suspension, or
3. Make referral to the appropriate judicial body.

If the violation could result in the student's suspension or expulsion, the Dean of Student Services will present the case before the Student Faculty Discipline committee. This committee has the power to recommend to the President of the institution any of the following sanctions against the student if found guilty of violation of the Code.

1. Official Warning

This action indicates that the student's behavior does not meet the College's expectations and conveys the expectation that they behave more appropriately in the future.

2. Disciplinary Probation

This action is intended to serve as notice to students that their violations are considered serious. The student is given a period of time specified by the judicial body to prove that he/she can become a responsible and positive member of the college community. Probation may include one or more of the following:

Social probation
Surrender of student activity card
Dismissal from College Housing
Self-improvement
Restitution
Work sanction.

3. Suspension

This action involves exclusion from all institutional activities for a definite stated period of time up to one academic year. Conditions of resumption of activities, if any, may also be imposed.

4. Expulsion

This action involves termination of all student status, including any remaining right or privilege to receive some benefit or recognition or certification. Conditions for readmission, if any, may be stated in the order.

Organizational Sanctions

Following are a few of the sanctions which may be imposed in cases of student organization offenses:

1. Denial of use of College facilities.

2. Denial of recognition of the group as an organization.
3. Forfeiture of right to representation in other organizations (Interfraternity Council, Student Government, intramural, etc.).
4. Forfeiture of right to representation in the Student Handbook or other publications.
5. Denial of privilege of some or all social or organizational activities for a definite period.

GRIEVANCE RESOLUTION

Grievance is a formal expression from a student expressing a circumstance which he/she feels resulted in unjust or injurious treatment from a functioning unit of the institution including the various administrative areas, departments and offices within the institution.

A written grievance must be filed with the Office of the Dean of Students. A step by step procedure of grievance resolution is outlined in the student handbooks of all institutions, which includes referral to a grievance committee. If you feel that you have been wronged in any manner that may constitute a grievance, it is better first to go to the Dean of Students for a formal discussion on the matter to seek his/her guidance before filing a written grievance.

MORAL BEHAVIOR AND THE COLLEGE STUDENT

Nobody has a right to impose morals on the college student, who is an adult, and who can decide for himself/herself the question of right or wrong. Yet, you, as a college student, must realize the distinction between legality and morality in your activities. It is imperative that your behavior under all circumstances fall within the realm of the law for your own advantage in the long run. No employer wants to hire a student with a criminal record, even if the violations committed were done ignorantly in "fun". Also, you will find it hard to live with yourself if you unintentionally hurt other people in an illegal act that is committed under the pressure of your peers. Be sensitive to the feelings of others and try to think about the consequences of your actions.

The Question of Right or Wrong

While being within legal bounds there may still be many situations where you may be confronted with a question of right or wrong, a moral dilemma. If your conscience seems clouded then talk to a trusted friend, advisor or counselor to help you see the situation more clearly.

Chapter **20**

WHAT EVERY COLLEGE STUDENT SHOULD KNOW ABOUT PROFESSORS

"The professor is concerned not only with the student's acquisition of facts and the development of his capacity to distinguish between what is and what is not a fact, but also with instructing the student in the ways in which he can discover the essential and reliable facts concerning the subject that is being taught."

Fred B. Millett,
author of "Professor"

TOPICS

1. The Professorial Spectrum
2. Professors Are Human
3. Professorial Expectations of Their Students
4. How Professors Decide on Grades
5. Rapport with Professors
6. How to Get the Most from Your Professors

THE PROFESSORIAL SPECTRUM

Though a college student is not normally concerned about the professors of his/her college or university outside of the classroom, it is important to know more about them and their approach to their chosen profession. The academic world of colleges and universities is divided, in general, into the following two categories from a functional point of view:

1. Faculty, and
2. Administration.

The members of the faculty assume the duties of teaching and research and are assigned the responsibility of assigning grades to the students who sign up for the courses they teach. Just as in any other profession, there exists a hierarchy of levels indicating the relative ranking of the faculty. The most common are:

Assistant Instructor,
Instructor,
Assistant Professor,
Associate Professor,
Professor.

Generally, academic qualifications and experience are the key factors in the appointment to these designations.

Besides these, there are adjunct professors and professors emeritus. The former are usually employed part-time to supplement the full-time teaching faculty or to teach specially offered courses. Professor emeritus is a designation conferred upon professors on their retirement from active faculty duties to recognize their distinguished and meritorious service to the college or university.

The other part of the academic institution is the rank and file of the administrators and the supporting staff. For the sake of efficient functioning, almost all higher educational institutions are headed by a single executive called the President of the institution. It is customary to appoint persons with extensive academic and administrative background to this top position.

Like in any other institution, the President generally appoints his/her top administrative aides in the designations of Vice-Presidents,

Directors, and Deans for the various departments, to suit the mission and functions of the institution. Again, it is customary to appoint persons with high academic and administrative backgrounds to these positions.

PROFESSORS ARE HUMAN

As a college student, you don't often have control over the choice of your courses and the professors who teach them. However, professors do make a difference in your grades, because the grading process in colleges and universities is not totally mechanistic and uniform. Along with the student's demonstration on learning, the professor's bias does play a role in the final grades. Professors are human, and, as such, they do carry with them certain attitudes and expectations, which could be entirely different even for professors teaching the same course.

Besides, the so-called "academic freedom" that is considered a fundamental right of professors permits them a reasonable degree of latitude in the way the subject is taught, and in the methods used to assign grades for the course work.

Being human, different professors' interactions with their students are quite different. Some are pleasant to deal with and some are not; some are helpful and some are not; some are sensitive and sympathetic to your feelings and some are totally insensitive and even apathetic. By being aware of the simple fact that no two professors are alike, you can formulate your own approach to each one as far as your dealings with them are concerned.

PROFESSORIAL EXPECTATIONS OF THEIR STUDENTS

Though, at this point in time, you may not fully realize the value of your being able to attend college and strive for academic excellence, you must at least recognize it as an opportunity for the development of your personality, intellectual and otherwise. Whether your professor expresses it or not, certain subtle expectations are inherent in his/her attitude towards his/her chosen profession, namely to teach students who sign up for his/her classes. The professor's bias is generally built around them. It will be helpful for you to be aware of the following subtle expectations of professors in general when you take courses from them.

Attendance

Most professors expect that you attend their classes regularly, and that if you are unable to attend you have a valid reason. They may not pay much attention to legitimate absences, but when a student becomes noticeably absent from classes on a continued basis without consent, the professor begins to form an opinion which can be detrimental to the student's interest.

Attentiveness

Since professors play the active role in the classroom setting, talking, writing on the board and presenting issues and topics, they expect the students to be listening to them, taking notes, and taking an active part in the process though playing a passive role. Nothing can be more annoying to a professor than seeing you sitting idly, totally uninterested in what is going on in the classroom, and paying no heed to what he/she is talking about.

Home Assignments

Professors expect their students to take home assignments seriously, which may be reading from the textbook, journals, etc., or problem solving, or report writing. They expect you to submit the completed assignments not only on time but also neatly executed.

Tests

Professors do expect their students to come well prepared for tests and to be honest in taking them. Lack of preparation easily shows up in the test score. Attempts at academic dishonesty on tests and reports are not difficult to detect for the professor. The repercussions of academic dishonesty can be devastating to the student when caught.

Professors do feel happy at the good performance of a student who has done well in the test, demonstrating his/her learning and mastery of the subject. They also feel satisfaction when grading a well-researched and written report or term-paper.

Office Visits

Most professors like their students to come to their offices with questions and doubts for clarification during their office hours. This gives them an opportunity to get to know at least some of the interested students in their classes. No professor wants to teach a class for the whole semester without knowing anyone in the class.

HOW DO PROFESSORS DECIDE ON GRADES?

Most professors let the students know at the beginning of the semester their policy for assigning final grades, such as assigning a certain percentage of points for each of mid-semester tests, reports, home-assignments, final examination, etc., from the cumulative points for the whole course. Some allow partial credits in problem-solving tests and some don't. Again, it is the professor who decides on the number of tests, reports, etc., for the course. Some use statistical analysis in fixing the final grades, whereas many use the conventional arbitrary cutoff points such a letter grade of A for the semester cumulative average points of 90 and above, B for 80 to 89, C for 70 to 79, D for 60 to 69, and an F for points below 60.

The professor's bias play a decisive role in borderline situations, such as in the case of a student with a cumulative point average of 79%, which normally would be interpreted as a C grade. But if the professor's subjective evaluation of the student's progress during the semester is positive, he/she may place the student in the B grade. To do this, the professor would need to know more about the student than just the test scores. It is here that a good rapport with the professor comes to his/her rescue, if the student has established a positive impression on him/her during the course of the semester by good attendance, assignments, personal office contacts, etc.

Of course, there are some professors who simply take an impersonal view of the whole process and don't consider factors other than the numerical average of test scores. Many don't hesitate to assign a lower grade to borderline cases. There is nothing that you can do if you happen to be in such a situation besides accepting the outcome as a result of the grading system. However, most professors do tend to be sympathetic towards genuine interest and hard work.

RAPPORT WITH PROFESSORS

There are many reasons why you should build a good rapport with as many of your professors as possible. Foremost among them is to increase your knowledge of the subject taught by the professor. By establishing good relations with him/her, you will be able to get your doubts cleared during brief office visits, which could save you a lot of time. Your rapport with the professor will be possible, of course, only when you are sincere in your approach, and you meet his/her subtle expectations.

The second most important reason is that through a good rapport with the professor, you will be able to get academic, as well as personal, counseling from him/her, if and when you need it.

Getting to know a professor can boost your self-image psychologically, particularly if you are in the early years of your college life. Nothing can be of a greater support for you than to know that you can turn to an understanding professor for help.

In the later years of your college life, your rapport with your professors can help you both for career counseling as well as for making career contacts through their vast experience.

It is all the more important for graduate students to have good rapport with their major professors and advisors not only for counseling in their research and investigations, but also for finding the right job in specialty areas in government or industry.

Another important reason that you may not be aware of now is that after graduation all college students will need a few reference persons who can vouch for their honesty and ethical conduct, not only when seeking jobs, but also when traveling or moving from place to place during career relocations. Professors, of course, are the most respected reference persons for employers and others.

HOW TO GET THE MOST FROM YOUR PROFESSORS

The following guidelines will be of help to you to get the most from your professors:

1. Take the time and effort to meet with every one of your professors in his/her office from the very beginning of the semester. Take with you genuine questions and doubts for answers and clarification after going over his/her classroom lecture material and home assignments.
2. Be regular in your attendance; submit your assignments and reports on time. Remember that sincerity can not be faked.
3. Of course, not all professors will be compatible to your personality; keep your contacts to the minimum with abrasive professors.
4. The professor is a busy person. Be time conscious while you are in his/her office. Let your queries be specific and written beforehand to optimize your meeting time with him/her.
5. Before every test make it a point to meet with him/her in his/her office to ascertain the subject area to be covered in the test. You may get clues regarding the relative importance of the topics in the test.
6. If you plan to list him/her as a reference person in your job applications, ask for his/her permission to do so.
7. After receiving the final grade, no matter what the grade is, meet him/her and express your thanks and gratitude for his/her help and support all the way through the semester in your learning process.
8. A genuine respect for the professor will enhance your rapport with him/her. Respect is a feeling of deferential regard or honor, which creates a congenial climate for accessibility to the professor.

PART 2

CAREER EXCELLENCE

The Twilight Zone

Chapter **21**

CAREER DEVELOPMENT AND THE RIGHT JOB

"Engage yourself in obligatory work; for action is superior to inaction".

The Bhagavad Gita

TOPICS

1. What Do You Want to Be ?
2. Where Do You Want to Work ?
3. How Are You Going to Get that First Job ?
4. Attributes of the Right Job
5. Anatomy of Your Job personality
6. Understanding Organizations
7. Targeting a Career

WHAT DO YOU WANT TO BE ?

Apart from imparting knowledge in many fields that you chose to study, college education also prepares you for an occupation so that you can be a productive member of society. Through gainful employment you not only earn money but also have opportunities to encounter the challenges of a career. Of course, the first thing that you have to decide for yourself is: what do you want to be.

A realistic self-assessment of the following 5 factors is the key to resolving this question:

1. Innate likes and dislikes
2. Interests
3. Aptitudes
4. Attitudes
5. Values.

Basically, they reflect your so-called "personality". Your successful career lies in those areas and activities which are not in conflict with these five factors.

It is important that you see yourself identified with the career area you propose to pursue. It is this identification that paves the way for a meaningful career; on the other hand, the lack of it can become a potential source of stress in your job performance, and prevent you from becoming successful at your profession or career.

WHERE DO YOU WANT TO WORK ?

The next question you have to resolve is about the geographic location of your place of work. Nearness to one's family, recreational areas, cultural activities, religious affiliations, opportunities for continuing education, etc., are some of the important deciding factors depending on your interests, needs and values.

Job location need not be confined to the national boundary. Many large corporations, even small ones, are multi-national, having their business activities spread out to many other countries. If you are interested in taking a job in a particular country of interest to you, you should prepare yourself accordingly while you are in college.

HOW ARE YOU GOING TO GET THAT FIRST JOB ?

The answer to this question is not easy. Some get their first job easily, whereas for others it may be a highly frustrating experience. The search for the right job is a complex process that needs to be understood and followed to become successful. It is **not** just accepting "any job" that happens to come along first on your way, but matching it against your values, interests, attitudes, skills and abilities.

It also requires negotiating to your best advantage and to the mutual benefits of both you and your employer. Successful job-search strategy is discussed later in this book.

THE RIGHT JOB

The job that you think is "right" for you should have the following five attributes. It should be:
1. Emotionally satisfying
2. Intellectually stimulating
3. Potentially challenging
4. Financially satisfactory
5. Not unduly stressful.

If a job is not emotionally satisfying it can become a source of stress very soon. It may lead to conflicts and dullness in life. If the job is intellectually stimulating and challenging, it amounts to an open invitation for you to meet the challenges of the job. Such a job can give you the opportunity to put your best foot forward and demonstrate your skills, abilities and leadership qualities.

Needless to say, the right job must be financially satisfactory both in salary and fringe benefits. Since you will be spending the best part of the day on your job, it is imperative that it should not wear you out physically. Staying physically relaxed on the job is conducive for greater efficiency and increased output on the job.

ANATOMY OF YOUR JOB PERSONALITY

It is important for you to be aware of the way you are looked upon by a potential employer when you are considered for a job. For all practical purposes you may consider yourself as the following four different personalities rolled into one:

1. The visual self
2. The functional self
3. The adaptive self
4. The technical self.

The Visual Self

This is what you are as seen and heard by other people. The seven elements of importance consisting the visual self are:

1. **Your Face.** The first impression that others have of you is through your face. Interviewers tend to look at your face first at the time of job interviews, and hence, the first impression they get based on your facial expressions is crucial in their evaluation process. It is not the beauty or handsomeness of physical features that we refer to here; it is the facial expression that is capable of conveying such qualities as intelligence, enthusiasm, friendliness, etc. A smiling face is indicative of the ability to relate to other people in interpersonal relations.

2. **Figure.** Relatively speaking, a trim or an average figure has a greater impact than a skinny or over-weight figure.

3. **Dress.** Interviewers note your dress much more keenly than you think. Your dress is an expression of your taste and outlook. Well-fitting clothes chosen conservatively are desirable.

4. **Grooming.** Grooming is index of one's trimness of appearance. It includes hair, make-up, clean fingernails, polished shoes and overall cleanliness.

5. **Posture.** Good posture is indicative of self-confidence, personal pride, health and vigor.

6. **Speech.** The tone, timbre, and accent of your voice is indicative of your level of education, cultural, and even geographic background. The tone also can reflect the emotional state of the person.

   The articulateness with which you express yourself is of interest to the employer, since it is reflective of your self-

confidence as well as your degree of proficiency in English
and communication.

7. **Enthusiasm.** Enthusiasm is a positive feeling that radiates
   from a person. It is unmistakably noticeable and it can not be
   faked. It is contagious and can make other people feel good.
   Enthusiasm is reflective of self-confidence and a whole-
   hearted faith in what one is saying. It enhances the impact of
   the visual-self on others.

The Functional Self

The functional self is reflective of the talents that can be developed through formal as well as informal learning. The functional
skills are essential for advancement in any career and are directly
useful for the following tasks in organizations:

Time management
Communication
Administration
Motivating people
Training personnel
Promotion of events, etc.

It should be noted that functional skills are those skills that enable an individual to function successfully in any career environment.

The Adaptive Self

The adaptive self can be described as constitutive of personal
characteristics. Some of these traits that can be of significant value in
the place of work are:

Being artistic	Independence
Compassion	Organizing ability
Conscientiousness	Persuasiveness
Enthusiasm	Reliability
Flexibility	Thoroughness.

These qualities are very important from the employer's point of
view because he/she can assess how well you will fit into a specific
work environment.

The Technical Self

The technical self is that aspect of yourself which reflects your special training, experience and expertise. They are essential to the performance of a particular job. Skills in this category include:

Accounting
Computer programming
Drafting
Language skills
Medical skills
Various engineering
Electronics, etc.

UNDERSTANDING ORGANIZATIONS

There are four basic work environments each with a wide range of jobs. They are:

1. Government, Federal/State
2. Health care
3. Education
4. Business/Industry.

Two other major areas are human service agencies and non-profit organizations.

Regardless of which environment you choose, you have to be aware of the fact that there is a basic structure in all organizations. The structure has two major sub-divisions:

Corporate, and
Operations.

Corporate staff generally includes all those in managerial positions. All organizations have their own organizational chart which shows the various positions in their hierarchy. By studying this chart you will be able to examine various job possibilities.

TARGETING A CAREER

Job Objective/ Career Goals

The job search process works best when it is structured around well-defined career goals and personal goals. The goals serve as the focal point and prevent you from drifting aimlessly in the job hunting process. Goals also provide direction for your career and help locate the right entry level job that is most suited to your job objective and talents.

The following steps will lead you to target your career ambitions:

1. Prepare your goals based on your needs, values, interests, etc., as discussed earlier such as:
   (a). immediate goals
   (b). short range goals
   (c). long range goals.
2. Check the goals for their feasibility. They must be:
   (a). realistic
   (b). achievable
   (c). well-defined.

Discuss them with your career counselor and others for their suggestions and modifications.

3. Carry out library and field research to gather information that will help figure out how your needs and goals match the needs of the market place.
4. Isolate the occupations and industries (or Government Agencies or Companies, etc.) that you would like to work for. They are now your targets for further exploration.

Chapter **22**

THE ALL-IMPORTANT RESUME AND COVER LETTER

"You can compose a resume which will make you stand out head and shoulders above all other applicants with similar qualifications. And employers want you to do it. How?"

Benedetto Greco,
author of "How to get the job that is right for you".

TOPICS

1. Why a Resume Is Necessary
2. Characteristics of a Good Resume
3. Components of a Good Resume
4. Format of a Good Resume
5. Resume Appearance
6. What a Resume Should Not Include
7. A Sample Resume
8. Design of the Cover Letter
9. 5 Tips for Designing the Cover Letter
10. A Sample Cover Letter.

WHY A RESUME IS NECESSARY

A resume is an evaluation of yourself by yourself. Its primary purpose is to serve as a tool in helping you secure an employment interview. Known variously as a personal data sheet, a personal profile, or a record of qualifications, the resume is a summary of your qualifications for the job you seek, and hence, it is a distinctive advertising brochure. To serve its purpose it must convince a prospective employer that you are an outstanding candidate, who has something of value to contribute to the growth of the organization, and that it will be well worth his/her time to grant you a personal interview.

To lure the employer to consider you as a prospective candidate put yourself in his/her position and see what are the factors you would consider from a person who has applied for the job. Of course, your major interest in a candidate would be when he/she has qualifications to perform the job duties advertised. It is important for you to realize this fact because it contains the secret of what to highlight in writing your resume for a particular job.

Therefore, you can see that a resume is not intended to be a categorical and overall summary of your qualifications and experiences, but rather a document highlighting your ability and experience matching the employer's job description.

CHARACTERISTICS OF A GOOD RESUME

Effective resumes should have the following characteristics:
1. Impressive looking
2. Well-organized
3. Easily readable
4. Key information at once visible
5. Qualifications and experience highlighted
6. Includes past accomplishments
7. Includes a well-defined career objective
8. Proper length—not too long, nor too short (Generally speaking, one page is appropriate for entry level positions).

COMPONENTS OF A GOOD RESUME

Though the headings chosen will depend on the material, the following listing constitutes all the essential elements needed for an effective presentation.

1. Identifying information.

Necessary data will be:
1. Full name.
2. Address.
3. Telephone number including area code.

Information such as: height, weight, age, sex, race, religion, national origin, ancestry, and place of birth can be omitted unless such information is relevant to the selection criteria.

2. Career objective (Job objective)

Your career or job objective is of critical importance and should include the job position desired by you such as store manager, junior engineer, marketing research analyst, computer programmer, etc.

Company-type, such as small, medium, large or the type of corporations preferred, such as local, national, international, etc., should be included.

The preferred industry, such as banking, farming, insurance, government, construction, public accounting, etc., should be included if relevant.

3. Education

One of your strongest selling points, of course, is your college education. Your employer will be interested in knowing:
1. What did you study?
2. What special skills have you developed?
3. How are these skills applicable to the job in question?

Focus on your subject major, special courses taken, specific assignments, term papers, research projects, and other information relevant to your career objective as well as to the job duties listed by the employer.

4. Work experience

If you have any work experience particularly related to the job in question that can be an asset for you. The employer would like to know:

1. In what capacity did you work?
2. What were your responsibilities?
3. What was the evaluation of your performance by your former employer?
4. How does your previous experience apply to the job in question?

Your resume should emphasize those job assignments which most effectively qualify you for the job objective. Highlight the responsibilities you were assigned and how well you carried them out. If you received recognition or promotion as a result of your successful performance, list them under this section.

If you have any part-time or summer work experience, don't overlook it. Make a note of it briefly even if it is not related to the job objective.

5. Honors and extracurricular activities

You may not think much of your extracurricular activities, but the prospective employers do. They review this section of your resume to get an indication of your outside interests, social awareness, desire to get involved, and leadership capabilities. You should also include activities such as professional chapter involvement, hobbies, club memberships, campaigns, awards, honors, and other personal interests.

In a sense, extracurricular activities speak more clearly about a person's attitudes and potentials than the grade report. Willingness to take responsibilities is something the employer is interested in, and it is easily demonstrated when you have involved yourself actively in campus organizations. Your concern for social issues and social awareness is demonstrated when you have participated in the activities of social organizations, church groups, or community projects. Any citation or recognition you received may be used to indicate your leadership capabilities.

6. Professional affiliations

If you have any professional experience, it is strengthened when you have professional affiliations. Your membership in the student chapter of professional organizations may also be included.

7. Skills

Be sure to mention any additional information illustrating your qualifications and special skills such as proficiency in a foreign language, organizing a fund-raising campaign for a church project, etc.

FORMAT A GOOD RESUME

Basically there are only two types of acceptable format. They are:

1. The chronological format
2. The functional format.

The chronological format lists the positions held in chronological sequence, starting with the most recent and working back to the individual's first professional assignment. This is the most popular and widely used resume format.

The functional format, on the other hand, highlights the candidate's background and accomplishments under broad functional categories such as engineering design, cost accounting, market research, finance, sales management, etc. Selected major accomplishments are then listed under these key functional headings in a descending order of importance, based upon their relevance to the current job search.

RESUME APPEARANCE

Pay special attention to the resume's appearance. A neat and well-organized resume makes a favorable first impression on the employer. According to **Ben Greco** "your resume should be distinctive,

tive, impressive, and professional". The following suggestions are well worth adhering to:

1. Use a high quality bond paper, white or buff in color.
2. Carefully proofread and check spelling, grammar and punctuation errors.
3. Get your resume typed or typeset professionally.
4. Make sure that your final copy is neat, well-spaced, and easy to read.

Have the final printing done by a professional printer using high quality equipment.

WHAT A RESUME SHOULD NOT INCLUDE

Be sure not to include the following:

1. Information about your high school. It is irrelevant.
2. Noticeable corrections, either typed, hand-written, or pasted. Sloppiness of the resume is indicative of mediocrity in job performance.
3. Personal information.

A SAMPLE RESUME

A resume sample is shown opposite. Books are available in your library in which you can examine many sample resumes suited for various jobs. It will be to your advantage to go through them before you start writing your own.

DESIGN OF THE COVER LETTER

A cover letter should accompany the resumes you mail out. This gives you an opportunity to personalize your information to a particular employer. The cover letter should be in business form and not more than one page in length; it is usually set up in three paragraphs as follows:

First Paragraph. State the reason for the letter, name the specific position or type of work for which you are applying, and indicate the source from which you learned of the opening (college placement center, news media, employment service, friend, etc.).

Second Paragraph. Refer the reader to the enclosed resume which summarizes your qualifications, training, and experience. Indicate why you are interested in the position, the company, its products or services, and what you can offer to the company. Explain how your

MARK R. MORGAN

P.O. Box 70 Old Main
Montgomery, WV 25136
(304) 442-3801

CAREER OBJECTIVE	Civil engineering position with an emphasis on computer applications.
EDUCATION	B.S., Civil Engineering, West Virginia Institute of Technology, Montgomery, WV May 1989
	A.S., Pre-engineering, Shepherd College, Shepherdstown, WV, May 1988.
	100% college expenses earned.
EXTRACURRICULAR ACTIVITIES	ASCE - member 1987-1989 attended national, regional, local conferences SIGMA PHI EPSILON FRATERNITY - 1986-1989 chaplain, 1988-1989

WORK EXPERIENCE

Computer Software Design	*Entrepreneur*, Montgomery, WV, Fall 1987 - present. •collaboration with Tech Faculty to develop marketable computer software for soil stress analysis and on a systems utilities package for personal computers.
Playground Designer	*Parks and Recreation Division*, Montgomery, WV, January - August 1988. •designed and assisted in construction of city playground.
Unitizer	*General Motors Corporation*, Martinsburg, WV, Summers 1985, 1986. •material handling and production line set-ups. •material tabulation in plant inventory. •production line assembly.
Management Trainee	*Weis Markets Corporation*, Martinsburg, WV August 1985 - May 1986, August 1982 - June 1985. •staff training, 2-5 persons. •ordered store merchandise. •created window and other displays. •customer relations. •interior design and setup for new stores.
SPECIAL SKILLS	AutoCAD design system. Computer languages: BASIC, Turbo BASIC, Turbo Pascal. Multiple hardware systems.
REFERENCES	Available upon request.

academic college background makes you a qualified person for the position. Do not repeat the information given in the resume, but rather highlight the aspects of your work experience and specific achievements that are of interest to this employer.

Third Paragraph. In the closing paragraph of your letter, have a statement or question which will encourage a response from the employer for a possible interview.

5 TIPS FOR DESIGNING A COVER LETTER

1. Type each letter individually on good quality white paper—8$^1/_2$ x 11 inch size in business form.
2. Address your letter to a specific person by name and title whenever possible.
3. Do not repeat the information given in your resume.
4. Indicate some familiarity with your potential employer's organization. Slant it toward what you can offer the employer, not what you think he/she should be offering you.
5. Let your letter reflect your personality. Use simple, direct language, and spell, punctuate, and paragraph correctly. Avoid constant use of the word "I".

AN EXAMPLE COVER LETTER

An example cover letter is shown below. You should consult your library for other samples to suit different employment situations.

A sample cover letter

P.O. Box 70 Old Main
Montgomery, WV 25136
January 23, 1989

Mr. George Clason
Director of Corporate Employment
Universal Design & Construction Co.
Charleston, WV 25304

Dear Mr. Clason:

In the College Career Services office I read your advertisement of an opening for a Junior Design Engineer in the Pavements Division of your corporation.

While my civil engineering studies have given me a solid academic preparation for an engineering position, I believe that many of my other experiences have helped me to round out my background for a company like Universal. As you can see from my enclosed resume, my work with the Parks and Recreation Division of the city of Montgomery, WV provided me with experience in pavements related projects. In addition, my senior design project at Tech on the design of highway and airport pavements has given me an in-depth experience of the engineering problems involved. These experiences have no doubt influenced the direction my career is taking and my particular interest in a company such as Universal both for the contribution I might make and the opportunities that it offers.

As I feel that I can demonstrate that I am a strong candidate for the Junior Design Engineer position, I would welcome the opportunity to do so. During the Easter break, I will be in the Charleston area and will be available for an interview. If you have a particular application form you would like filled in now, I would be happy to do so. I look forward to your affirmative reply.

Sincerely yours,

(signature)
Mark R. Morgan

Chapter **23**

JOB SEARCH STRATEGY

"Most people are not aware of the special techniques needed to conduct a job search. They equate ability to sell themselves with ability in their jobs. Nothing could be less valid".

Burdette E. Bostwick,
author of "Finding the Job You've Always Wanted"

TOPICS

1. Resources on Campus
2. Resources off Campus
3. Direct Contact
4. Mailing Broadcast Letters
5. Networking and the Hidden Job Market

RESOURCES ON CAMPUS

Job search is most effective when you approach the searching activity in a systematic manner. It should make use of all available resources on campus and off campus. You should collect all pertinent information and organize it for effective usage.

1. Campus Recruiting Programs

These are generally arranged through the career and placement office of your college or university. On most campuses, a **"career day"** is earmarked to help college students become more aware of current employment opportunities in the government, corporate world and other areas.

2. Job Listings

Many local employers interested in recruiting college students list their job openings with the career and placement office. They are properly displayed and advertised by this office to attract the attention of interested students. By going through these ads you also gain valuable information about the job market trend and about potential employers in the area of your career interest.

3. Alumni Office

This office is a place of contact for you to get the names and addresses of alumni working professionals in the area of your interest. You can use these contacts for further exploration of your career development and job search.

4. College Faculty and Administrators

Many professors maintain professional contacts through consulting work outside the college. College administrators also have wide contacts, especially through fund-raising and other projects. Talk to them about your job search and your area of interest to get possible leads.

5. Campus Organizations

Some of the campus organizations are professionally oriented. Others are student chapters of professional associations. They often sponsor career and industry related activities including on-the-spot visits. Be on the lookout and participate in their events to further expand your knowledge and make contacts useful for your job search.

RESOURCES OFF CAMPUS

1. Newspaper Ads

The want ads in the classified section of Sunday newspapers are ideal to get a good overview of the job market trend, including:

1. The type of jobs in current demand,
2. The type of companies that are hiring, and
3. The desired qualifications and salary range for the type of job in which you are interested.

2. Trade Journals and Company Newsletters

Scan the "Job Opening" section of these journals and newsletters to see whether you find one that matches your interest.

3. Professional and Trade Associations

Many of these associations provide valuable information on careers. Almost all of them have regular meetings for their local members. It will be to your advantage to attend one of their meetings and make contacts.

DIRECT CONTACT

Though this method of job search appears aggressive, it can be effectively utilized when you have a specific interest in a company or organization. Simply identify the companies you would like to work for in the area of your career interest, and mail them your resume and a specially designed cover letter. This method works best if you have already had introductions to the section or department head of the company or agency in which you have expressed interest.

MAILING BROADCAST LETTERS

What is a broadcast letter? The broadcast letter, as the name correctly indicates, carries out the function of broadcasting your desire to find a job in your field of specialization; it is specially designed to catch the attention of top company executives, rather than the personnel department. It is different from the resume, which you still may need.

Burdette Bostwick, author of "Finding the Job You've Always Wanted" feels that "broadcasting is one of the quickest and most effective ways of finding a position". However, you must have the patience and perseverance to mail large numbers of broadcast letters.

The broadcast letter technique is very effective when:

* You have special talents and experience which may be of special appeal to a company.
* The company has been looking for someone with your abilities.
* Your expertise can contribute to the company's growth or expansion in a weak area of operation.
* You might be well known at the executive level of the company for your expertise.

The broadcast letter should be not more than a page, precise and concise in its expressions, starting with a paragraph of your personal identification and field of specialization. Paragraph by paragraph, state your career objective, list some of your notable achievements, indicate your special qualities, mention your educational background, and end your letter asking for a response.

If your broadcast letter leads to requests for your resume or for a possible job interview, it has done its purpose.

NETWORKING AND THE HIDDEN JOB MARKET

Employment networking is a process by which you can reach out to a group of friends and acquaintances to get their support during your job search. Considering the number and diversity of potential employers, the traditional job search techniques are often ineffective to locate the vast resources of a hidden job market. **Richard H. Beaty**, the author of "The Complete Job Search Book", considers networking the "undisputed centerpiece of most, if not all," job search techniques. It is most suited to tap into what is commonly called "the hidden job market".

The technique of building a network is as follows:

1. Start with a selected group of friends or acquaintances (say ten).
2. Tell them your career objective and qualifications.
3. Ask for their help to identify a suitable job.
4. Ask them also to recommend at least two new contacts.
5. Ask this second level group for their assistance as well as for two or more new contacts.
6. Send a thank-you note.
7. Keep the network informed periodically of your progress.
8. Notify them when you accept a job offer.

You must have it in mind that the major drawback of the networking process is that it demands a considerable investment of personal time and discipline to execute it properly and systematically.

* * * * * * *

Chapter 24

ALL ABOUT JOB INTERVIEWS

"The interview is crucially important to both you and the employer because it is the best way for each to determine what the other has to offer".

Sidney F. Austin,
Coauthor of "Career Development for the College student"

TOPICS

1. Preinterview Preparation
2. Dress for Success
3. 3 Stages of an Interview
4. Interviewer's 10 basic questions
5. 10 Basic Questions You Should Ask
6. Don'ts for the Interview
7. Follow up
8. Rejections and How to Handle Them
9. 12 Reasons Why Candidates Receive Rejection Replies
10. Successful Job Offers and How to Handle Them

PREINTERVIEW PREPARATIONS

An approaching job interview invokes feelings of anxiety to varying degrees with different persons, primarily because of the element of uncertainty about the outcome and also due to a subconscious fear of rejection. However, by being aware of the information presented in this section, you can not only learn to cope with the stress of interviewing but even relax and enjoy it. It will help you get the most out of an interview by becoming aware of the whole process.

2 Types of Interviews

There are basically 2 types of interviews:

1. Screening, and
2. Hiring.

The screening interview is usually conducted by a personnel representative of the company to determine:

* If you meet the general requirements for the position, and
* If you will fit into their organization and be productive.

On the other hand, the hiring interview is generally conducted by the person you would be working for, to determine:

* Whether you have the right background to do the job, and
* Whether you will be comfortable working together in the section or department.

In either case, your aim should be to:

* Project yourself as the best candidate for the job.
* Find out for yourself whether the organization and the job are what you want.
* Get a job offer.

Employer's Point of View

Put yourself in the position of the potential employer and view the interview from his/her point of view. This will help you to be ready with the right kind of responses to their questions, and will also help you to ask appropriate questions. The following thoughts are generally entertained by the employer at the interview:

* The candidate with the highest GPA (Grade Point Average) is not necessarily the best candidate.
* Does the candidate possess the ability to solve key problems and perform specific job functions?
* Is he/she motivated enough?
* Is he/she compatible with the organization's culture and goals?
* Can he/she be entrusted with responsibility?

Your Point of View

To make sure you accept only the job that is right for you, you should be asking yourself:

* Is this the right job you are seeking?
* Is the organizational culture compatible to your values and goals?
* Are there opportunities for self-improvement and career advancement?

Assess Yourself before the Interview

On an index card, write down your skills, interests, abilities and past accomplishments. Write down specific examples of past successful activities, academic and otherwise. Also, write down the specific strengths and weaknesses that you are aware of in yourself.

Review this card often prior to the day of interview. This will help boost your self-confidence and keep the key points in your memory for recall during the interview.

Know about the Position

Try to learn before the interview as much as possible about the position for which you are a candidate. Make sure that you have the knowledge and skills called for in the position.

Know about the Organization

It is worth your time and effort to research about the organization—its objectives, products or services, goals, expansion plans, locations, etc. This will help you impress the interviewer with your knowledge of the organization, which, of course, is a plus in your favor.

Rehearse the Interview

Mock interview. The ease with which you can go through an interview can be enhanced by participating in a rehearsal of the interview with a friend or career counselor acting as the employer's representative. After your role-play rehearsal, ask them to critique your performance so that you can do more rehearsals, trying to improve each time. Interviewing workshops are routinely conducted in most colleges by the career centers. Some even have videotaping facilities so you can observe your performance and critique it.

Visualized interview. Visualization has the potential to desensitize the impact of an actual interview. The procedure is as follows:

1. Sit in a secluded place away from interference on a straight-back chair or in a position that keeps your back upright, straight, and relaxed.
2. Close your eyes, and bring yourself to a state of total relaxation bodily and mentally through diaphragmatic deep breathing.
3. Imagine yourself walking into the interviewer's office, greeting him/her, seating yourself in front of him/her and going through an auto-suggested interview with him/her in every detail as if you are taking an actual interview.
4. By repeated vivid visualization your nervous system stores this "experience" in your brain. It becomes a part of your memory and will help face the actual interview with more comfort and ease.

DRESS FOR SUCCESS

Be aware that interviewers take note of your dress as much as your face. Dress has a powerful influence in the first impression of a person. An appropriate business outfit is what you need for interviews. Expensive or fashionable clothes are not required. "Dress conservatively" is the motto here.

A well-tailored dark suit and conservative shirt and tie with polished dark shoes are appropriate for men.

A conservatively worn dress and jacket of dark color and well-polished pumps with a moderate heel are appropriate for women.

3 STAGES OF AN INTERVIEW

All interviews can be considered to consist of the following 3 stages:

The ice-breaker period. This is the time when you make your first impression on the interviewer through your visual impact, and this sets the tone for the interview.

Greeting the interviewer with a smile, looking him/her straight in the eye, sitting on the chair indicated by him/her may be trivial actions but have meaning in assessing your personality. Your aim during this period is to project a confident self.

The exchange period. The bulk of the interviewing time is devoted to the exchange of pertinent information through questions and answers. The interviewer tries to assess you and your qualifications from the employer's point of view. This is the time when you should make the interviewer believe that you are the best candidate for the job. This is also the time when you ask questions about the job and the company.

The closing period. This is the time when you can reiterate your interest in the position, and find out the next step—will they write or call you? Or should you call them?

Your Portfolio

Have your portfolio prepared well ahead of the interview and take it with you to the interview. The portfolio is an aid to "show and tell" your accomplishments in academic and other areas of interest. You can use any format that works best to show the material to your best advantage.

The very fact that you have taken the time and effort to prepare a portfolio and bring it to the interview—and not just a copy of the resume—is a plus point in your favor.

INTERVIEWER'S 10 BASIC QUESTIONS

By way of preparing for an interview you should be ready with answers to many common questions that the interviewer will ask you. It is not possible to anticipate all questions. Nevertheless, you should be ready with impressive answers to the following 10 basic questions:

1. Tell me about yourself.
2. I see from your resume that you have such and such experience. Tell me about it.
3. Do you think that your grades are a good indication of your academic achievement?
4. What were your most significant accomplishments during college life?
5. What are your goals?
6. How did your college experience prepare you for the job you have applied for?
7. What do you know about this job?
8. What do you know about this company?
9. What can you contribute to this organization?
10. What are your strengths? Weaknesses?

10 BASIC QUESTIONS YOU SHOULD ASK

The interview is not a "Yes" or "No" session with the interviewer. It is a time of exchange of information and mutual exploration. To avoid job stress later on, and prevent a "dead-end street" in your career ambitions, this is the time to get some answers to help you decide on accepting the job offer—if it comes through. The following 10 questions are basic among the many more you may like to ask:

1. What are the daily and other responsibilities of the job?
2. What is the most important responsibility?

3. How, and how oft.n, will you evaluate my job performance?
4. Do you have a training program?
5. What type of person are you looking for?
6. What are the departmental goals this year?
7. What are the goals of the organization?
8. What are the expansion schemes of the organization?
9. How would you like me to contribute?
10. Who would I be reporting to?

You don't have to be afraid that asking too many questions related to the job and the company may jeopardize you chance of getting it. In fact, it is the other way. Asking as many right questions as possible about the job and the company's plans and goals is a plus factor in your favor, establishing your interest in the company. No employer wants to hire a person who is not interested in the company's progress.

Questions You Should not Ask

Questions regarding salary, benefits, insurance, vacation, etc., should not be asked at this time. They are premature until you are offered the job.

Be Positive

Your aim during the interview is to project a positive self-image and to relate your skills and abilities to the job and company. Remember that enthusiasm is the key word in job search. If you are not enthusiastic about the job for which you are interviewing, how can you expect the employer to offer you the job?

DON'TS FOR THE INTERVIEW
Do not:

* Be late for the interview.
* Apologize for your background.
* Criticize your past employers.

* Blame others for your past failures.
* Sound desperate.
* Focus on salary and benefits.
* Become emotional.

FOLLOW UP

It will be good ethics to write a thank-you letter following your interview. It will distinguish you from the crowd since few people send it.

If you have not heard from them within a reasonable amount of time, write a second letter to reaffirm your interest. If you have any new information related to your training and experience such as graduating from your college, completion of summer job, etc., you can include it in this letter.

You can also call them by phone after the time period specified for notification to find out where they are in the selection process. Your call is a reminder to the employer that you are still interested in the position.

REJECTIONS AND HOW TO HANDLE THEM

You must realize that for each job search activity there can be only two possible outcomes: success or rejection. Rejection is an integral part of the job search and as such you should know how to handle it. You can learn to live with it if you keep it in its proper perspective.

Matching Process

You must understand that rejection is a by-product of a matching process and has nothing to do with your personal self-worth. It does not mean that you are not qualified. It does not question your capabilities. It simply means that the employer, in his matching process, chose someone else whose personality, experience, goals, etc., were close to what he/she was seeking for this particular position. Do not let your self-confidence be shaken by rejection letters.

Systematic Search

Instead, keep waging an active job search campaign. Approach your job search with the same enthusiasm, preparation, and persistence of a warrior and organize your activities in a systematic manner. An effective campaign requires well-organized and complete records. Job search experts recommend that you keep an index card system, filed by company name, or any similar system to keep track of your ongoing search with many different organizations.

Be Persistent

Accept rejections without becoming emotional about them and prepare yourself for the next search. If necessary prepare different resumes with a different slant. You will gather valuable experience just interviewing with different companies. The best advice is to persevere until you succeed. Don't give up after a few "No's". Remember that it is not the rejection letter that makes you unhappy—it is your attitude toward rejection. So maintain a positive attitude and run an active job search campaign.

12 REASONS WHY CANDIDATES RECEIVE REJECTION REPLIES

1. Lack of proper career planning—objectives and goals poorly defined.
2. Lack of specialty knowledge.
3. Inability to express oneself clearly.
4. Lack of preparation for the interview.
5. No real interest in the company/organization.
6. Lack of enthusiasm and motivation.
7. Interested only in the best dollar offer.
8. Asks no questions about the job or the company.
9. Expects too much too soon.
10. No display of self-confidence.
11. Fails to look interviewer in the eye.
12. Poor personal appearance—inappropriate dress for the interview.

SUCCESSFUL JOB OFFERS AND HOW TO HANDLE THEM

Decision of Acceptance

Sooner or later you will get your first job offer, and then perhaps many more. Whether you have just one or several offers, you have to make the decision of accepting one job. You should consider the following factors before arriving at a decision:

The Job.
* Will this job be emotionally satisfying on a daily basis?
* Will this job provide you with training and experience that are compatible with your goals?
* Will this job provide you with opportunities for further learning and developing new skills?
* Will this job enhance your self-image?

The people.
* Do you like the people you will be working for and with?
* Will you be happy being with them every day?
* Can you learn from them?

The organization.
* Will you be proud of being their employee?
* Do your goals fit with the employer's goals and expansion programs?

Acceptance Letter

Once you have decided to accept an offer from an organization, write them a formal letter of acceptance. A typical acceptance letter is as follows:

502 6th Ave
Montgomery, WV 25136
August 26, 1989

Mr. S. K. Dasan
Personnel Manager
Universe Corporation
New York, NY 10012

Dear Mr. Dasan:

I am very pleased to receive your letter of August 23, 1989 in which you invited me to become a member of your organization. I enthusiastically accept your offer of employment at a monthly salary of $2,050.00.

The description of the duties which will be assigned to me in your Structural Design Department are both interesting and challenging. I am certain that my educational background and previous cooperative work experience will be of value to me, and will enable me to be a contributing member of the Universe Corporation.

I look forward to a lengthy and profitable career with Universe and will report to your office at 8:00 A.M. on October 6, 1989.

Sincerely,

John Neal

More than One Offer

If you had other job offers at the time of your decision, it will be ethical on your part to write a polite thank-you letter to the offering organizations, turning down their offers at this time.

* * * * * * *

Chapter 25

CAREER QUALITY POINTS AVERAGE (CQPA)— AN INDEX OF CAREER EXCELLENCE

"So the formula is to know what you want, test it to see if it is a right thing, change yourself in such a manner that it will naturally come to you, and always have faith".

Norman Vincent Peale,
author of "The Power of Positive Thinking"

TOPICS

1. What is Career Excellence?
2. What Do the Employers Look for?
3. Concept of Career Quality Point Average (CQPA)
4. A New Technique to Evaluate CQPA
5. An Example
6. Significance of CQPA
7. Relation between Academic and Career QPA's
8. How to improve CQPA
9. Self-Image and CQPA
10. Limitations of CQPA

WHAT IS CAREER EXCELLENCE?

As a college student, it will be hard for you to imagine what life will be like in a career. Yet you will have to choose a career at some point in your life in order to make a living. Since your career is such an integral part of your life, you should find one that best suits you and expresses your natural abilities and talents. Leading a life of meaningful satisfaction is important, as is living to your full potentials. You might choose to work for others or for yourself. You might work solely for yourself or employ other people to work for you. Whatever the career you may pursue, certain basic personal and interactive skills are needed for a satisfactory and successful career, apart from your academic skills.

Career excellence implies the development of these skills and characteristics to a degree that will ensure success in your future endeavors. Career excellence, like academic excellence, is both a process of being and becoming. Though it is not amenable for an objective evaluation, it can be assessed subjectively on a relative scale. Psychologically speaking, it is a continuous reflection of your personality, intellectual growth, and management skills.

WHAT DO EMPLOYERS LOOK FOR ?

We already mentioned before why many graduating seniors get rejection letters after their interviews, even though they might have had a decent academic record. The truth of the matter, which they unfortunately don't realize, is that **just the possession of a graduate-diploma is not the only thing that employers are interested in.** To run their company successfully and profitably against stiff competition in not only the domestic but international markets as well they need certain qualities in their executives and employees. These are the qualities that the interviewer is trying to assess in the potential employees and interviewees, and that makes the difference.

Based on a survey of 250 **Fortune 500** firms, asking them to rate the important characteristics which make a graduating college senior desirable as a job candidate, **Bill Osher** and **Sioux Campbell,** authors of "The Blue-Chip Graduate", found that expertise and academic knowledge are not the foremost factors. The deciding factor, then, is the question of what else can you offer a potential employer.

Fortunately, many of the so-called job-winning "qualities" or "characteristics" are cultivable, just like any other skill, to a reasonable degree, when you take an active interest in developing them. You can develop them along with your academic growth through the four years of your college life. A grand strategy for such development is given in a later chapter of this book. In this chapter we will highlight the ten most important characteristics and skills that contribute directly to excellence, and which spell the difference between a job offer or rejection.

CONCEPT OF CAREER QUALITY POINTS AVERAGE (CQPA)

Definition

The Career Quality Points Average is a number reflecting the overall job performance potential of an individual in a career environment, expressed in a scale ranging from zero to a maximum of 4.

Basis of CQPA

It is the experience of most employers that for a fresh college graduate to function effectively in the professional environment mere college graduation is not adequate. He/she needs to have a wide variety of skills and qualities to be productive. The following ten characteristics are considered the pivotal qualities around which all others revolve:

1. Self-confidence
2. Academic excellence and expertise
3. Communication skills
4. Interpersonal relations (Getting along with others)
5. Organizing ability
6. Hard work and willingness to work
7. Leadership qualities
8. Reliability and responsibility

9. Entrepreneurial spirit

10. Good references and contacts.

These factors are considered "the Ten Factors of Career Excellence" (CE Factors).

Point System

It is neither practical nor possible to evaluate these factors for a person on a quantitative basis. At best they can be subjectively, yet arbitrarily, estimated, first on a relative scale varying from "poor" to "excellent", and then assigning arbitrary points. The following point system is adopted to develop the CQPA using a 10-Point scale for any one CE Factor.

Relative Scale	CE Points
Poor	1
Fair	3
Average	5
Good	7
Excellent	9

The points are denoted as "Career Excellence Points (CE Points)".

Thus, the ten factors of career excellence can now be evaluated individually on this 10-Point scale. The sum total of CE Points for all the ten CE Factors is "the Cumulative CE Points", out of a possible maximum of 100 Points.

Cumulative CE Points to CQPA

Figure 5 shows the relationship between Cumulative CE Points and CQPA. It is based on the commonly accepted notion regarding Grade Point Averages that while a GPA of 2.00 is the barest acceptable, a value of 4.00 is the highly desirable maximum. A linear relationship is assumed in producing the graph shown in Figure 5.

It should be noted that the two boundary values for CQPA for meaningful interpretation are 2 and 4, associated with the Cumulative CE Points of 50 and 100 respectively.

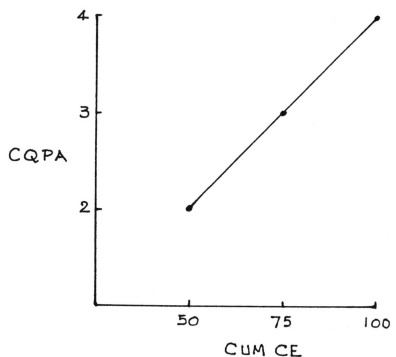

Figure 5. Cumulative CE Points versus CQPA

Once the Cumulative CE Points are estimated, it is simply a matter of reading the corresponding CQPA from the chart.

The results of Figure 5 can also be represented in a tabular form as shown below:

Cumulative CE Points	CQPA
50	2.0
60	2.4
70	2.8
80	3.2
90	3.6
100	4.0

Any other values of Cumulative CE Points can be interpolated to read the corresponding Career Quality Points Average.

Equation for CQPA

The data of Figure 5 can also be given in an equation form as follows:

$$Y = m X$$

where Y represents the desired CQPA,
X represents the Cumulative CE Points, and
m represents a constant number equal to 2/50.

Stated simply,

$$CQPA = 2/50 \times (Cum\ CE\ Po^{i} ts).$$

Interpretation of CQPA

1. CQPA of 3 and above are indicative of a high potential for career success.
2. CQPA of 2 and below are indicative of poor potential from a career point of view; a career counselor's help must be sought to identify and improve the potential areas of weakness.
3. For those with CQPA from 2 to 3 self-analysis will be helpful to improve themselves from a career success point of view.

AN EXAMPLE

Computation of career QPA based on a subjective evaluation of the self (or another person) is fairly simple. The following example demonstrates the process in all its simplicity.

Step 1.

Self-evaluation: Charles College Student
                                    Academic GPA: 2.2

Characteristics	Poor	Fair	Average	Good	Excellent	CE Points
1. Self-confidence			×			5
2. Academic excellence		×				3
3. Communication skills				×		7

4. Interpersonal relations	×			3
5. Organizing ability		×		5
6. Hard work & willingness			×	7
7. Leadership qualities	×			3
8. Reliability & responsibility			×	9
9. Entrepreneurial spirit	×			3
10. Good references & contacts			×	7

Cumulative Career Excellence Points: 52

Step 2.

Use the chart in Figure 5. For the Cumulative CE Points of 52 it is readily seen that the value of career QPA is 2.1.

Step 3. Analysis.

1. Charles's weak areas are:
   Academic excellence,
   Interpersonal relations,
   Leadership qualities, and
   Entrepreneurial spirit.
   He has to start improving himself in these areas right away.
2. He can improve some more in:
   Self-confidence, and
   Organizing ability.
3. His strength is in:
   Reliability,
   Willingness to work hard,
   Communication skills, and Good references and contacts.
4. Academically he may just be able to graduate with his GPA of 2.2. But he should expect it to be very hard to find a good job until he can improve himself to a career QPA of 3 or better.

SIGNIFICANCE OF CAREER QPA

Though, on the face of it, the Career Quality Points Average might appear as a crude technique, its significance can not be underestimated. Since it is basically composed of characteristics sought after by employers in young and fresh graduates from colleges and universities, it is important to understand it.

Even if it is not a completely objective evaluation, it is undoubtedly a good technique of self-evaluation for the college student who is ambitious about his/her career after graduation. At the very least, it shows you where your weaknesses are long before you are ready to interview for a job, thus giving you ample time to improve.

At its best, career QPA is a companion to the academic Grade Point Average in reflecting the skills and strengths not revealed by the latter.

RELATION BETWEEN ACADEMIC AND CAREER QUALITY POINT AVERAGES

A limited study carried out by the author indicates that there is no definite correlation between these two Quality Point Averages. High or low academic QPA does not mean a corresponding high or low career QPA. In fact, often the reverse was observed. Some students with high overall Academic Quality Point Averages, in general, were deficient in many factors of career interest. On the other hand, some with low Academic QPA had also been observed to come out high in their Career Quality Points Average.

It is of interest to note that if there is any "one to one" correspondence between the two QPA's, it is, in general, in the case of academically B+ students. It seems to confirm the notion that B+ students tend to be more successful in later life than straight A students, implying that B+ students are more world-wise and adaptable to the career world.

HOW TO IMPROVE CAREER QUALITY POINT AVERAGE

You probably observed that of the ten factors of career excellence discussed earlier in this chapter, except for one, namely academic excellence, all the others are not "taught" in the formal classroom. They are qualities that you have to develop on your own during your college years. The grand strategy presented in another chapter of this book will show you how you can systematically develop yourself in the factors of career excellence by taking an active interest in extracurricular and campus activities and by building a positive personality.

Becoming aware of your deficiencies is the first step towards any self-improvement. Self-assessment from time to time with reference to these factors will help you to take steps for continuous improvement, not only for career excellence, but also for overall success in your life.

SELF-IMAGE AND CAREER QUALITY POINTS AVERAGE

Career QPA is more than an index. It is reflective of the personality and its development. It also indicates the potential for effective task performance. Since this potential is drawn from the many factors listed under career excellence, the career QPA has psychological significance. It is indicative of the self-image of the person.

"Self-image" is the way a person sees himself/herself intellectually, emotionally, and even spiritually. High career QPA can not be expected from a person with a low level of self-esteem and poor or negative self-image. It can be theorized that as a person develops into a positive personality, his/her career QPA will rise, indicating the emergence of a stronger self-image.

LIMITATIONS OF CAREER QUALITY POINTS AVERAGE

You must realize that career QPA is based purely on subjective evaluation, unlike the academic GPA which is an earned index. However, with all its limitations, career QPA has the merit of reflecting human characteristics and personality factors, and, as such, its use as a self-help tool for personality development is meaningful. It depends only on an honest and sincere evaluation of the self with reference to the so-called factors of executive excellence.

* * * * * * *

Section 6

The Grand Strategy

Chapter 26

TRAINING FOR CAREER EXCELLENCE

"The leaders and managers like what they do and they get enthusiastic about it".

**T. J. Peters and R. H.
Waterman, Jr.,**
authors of "In Search of Excellence"

TOPICS

1. A Bias for Action
2. Two components of Career Excellence
3. Two Characteristics of Career Excellence
4. Values and Attitudes
5. Skills of Importance
6. Interactive Human Relations
7. Self-assessment and Criticism
8. Planned Continuous Learning
9. Share Your Expertise
10. How Good Is the Notion "Greed is Good".

Career excellence, as we had mentioned elsewhere, is a process of being and becoming. It does not happen by itself, just by getting through college and obtaining a degree certificate. Career excellence is a product of many different factors of development that are consciously and wilfully adopted and applied for professional life. It is a cultivated excellence achieved through sheer self-effort. Nobody else can get it for you, except yourself!

This chapter presents all the significant factors you should be aware of for adaptation in the pursuit of career excellence. It is a continuous process and the training for it should start right from your first semester at college.

A BIAS FOR ACTION

A career is an arena for action. You make things happen only through action—of course, appropriate action. Being action-oriented is the key to getting things done. Action is better than inaction, as far as a career is concerned. Being active implies that you are energetic in performing the task of your undertaking. Since your energy level, in turn, will depend on your **enthusiasm** for the task, it becomes obvious that a task approached without enthusiasm can not be expected to be highly productive. Herein lies one of the secrets of career excellence—enthusiasm!

Enthusiasm is not possible if you do not believe in the activity or the objective behind it. It boils down to a simple axiom: If you don't believe in it, don't do it. The statement is equally valid for the simple task of giving instructions to an employee or for trying to put together a complex multi-million dollar deal.

Another aspect of the action-bias is **taking initiative** on your own, without being told, in matters related to your career interest. Taking initiative is indicative of self-confidence, which constitutes the very foundation of career excellence.

TWO COMPONENTS OF CAREER EXCELLENCE

Career excellence has a dualistic nature—**how others look at you related to your career** and **how you look and feel about your-**

self in the career environment. Others look at the careerist through the physical appearance, and his/her career success through material possessions such as a house, car, position occupied in the professional hierarchy and the power wielded thereby, etc.

The other side of career excellence is your own perception and self-fulfillment in the career environment. The emotional satisfaction associated with a successful career is as important as, or even more than, the mundane aspect of the career. How good is a career which is monetarily very rewarding but highly stressful to you? Only when you are physically and emotionally comfortable with your career and the life around it, and only when you are able to achieve all of your career goals, may you consider yourself to have been career-excellent!

TWO CHARACTERISTICS OF CAREER EXCELLENCE

The two basic characteristics of excellence in any career are:

1. Mastery of the career, and
2. Optimum performance of the careerist.

Mastery of the career means staying on top of career-related activities and skills through continuous learning and application. As career experience keeps accumulating, new learning becomes more meaningful than ever before. The counterpart of mastery over the career is optimum performance. The level of career performance is directly related to the maintenance level of the mastery. As this level declines, career productivity also falls.

You should be aware of the fact that it is knowledge that serves as the invisible force in accomplishments. It is a holistic knowledge of the career-related activities and the career environment, and not just learning derived from books that leads to success in a chosen profession. The book knowledge, of course, is needed for task performance, but career excellence is one step farther than that.

VALUES AND ATTITUDES

Career excellence has its roots in your value system and attitudes. No matter what career you have chosen, you will be carrying out your job obligations viewed through **your** own value system and attitudes. Your career success depends on them.

Fortunately individual values and attitudes are subject to changes, modifications and adaptations as one grows intellectually and professionally. Positive attitudes, in general, should be adopted at all times and situations. Following are some of the cultivable attitudes that contribute to career excellence:

1. Be fair to all.
2. Look at career as a service to society.
3. Be courteous and polite to all.
4. Learn to examine your own faults and accept constructive criticism from others.
5. Don't be afraid to admit mistakes and apologize.
6. Be punctual.
7. Be yourself—learn not to put on airs.

THREE SKILLS OF IMPORTANCE

The three basic skills of career excellence are:

1. Communication,
2. Time management, and
3. Decision making.

Communication

The skill of direct communication is the single most important skill for success in the career world. Communication through writing notes, memos and reports, direct one-on-one conversations, group discussions and public speaking are the various means of communication in the career environment in general. It is important that you should have a reasonable mastery over these means of communication, at least in those that are directly related to your chosen career.

Time Management

The ability to manage one's own time is a skill that must be learnt for modern living in general, and for career success in particular. The principles of time management which are valid for career-oriented living are dealt with elsewhere in this book. Goals, activities, the available time and the prioritizing of activities are interdependent, and must be considered together. Effective time management not only gets career activities done on time, but also leaves room for non-professional and other activities for relaxation and self-development. Time management is the very basis of career excellence.

Decision Making

Seldom do people think of decision making as a cultivable skill. Yet, they are confronted with the decision making process constantly at home, the place of work, and elsewhere. It may be the matter of a simple decision in the morning as to what to put on for the day or to decide on a complex business deal. A decision is needed in both cases.

Decision making calls for the rational consideration of all possible courses of action and then deciding which will be the most beneficial. Decision making also calls for the maturity to stick with the decision, once it is made, and to accept the outcome.

Going back on a decision is not only unethical, but also can result in damage to the reputation of the individual or the organization. The reconsideration of a decision is warranted only if a major change in the original situation, or if new factors are involved. Indecision is also equally bad, in the sense that good opportunities might be lost, resulting in monetary and time costs.

INTERACTIVE HUMAN RELATIONS

Commonly referred to as "interpersonal relations", the ability to deal with others, is a basic requirement for all people. It is all the more important for career success. Many graduates develop career difficulties for want of this one quality—not being able to get along with others.

The general principles of good interactive human relations are:

1. Empathy. A feeling for the other person's feelings. Put yourself in the other person's shoes and see how you would respond.

2. A genuine respect for other people. They are as human as you are. Make them feel that you both work as a team.
3. Be a good listener. Listening promotes goodwill and wins friends.
4. Do not criticize anyone in the presence of others. If you must, let him/her know about your feelings in the privacy of your office.
5. If you are at fault, be quick to acknowledge it and ask to be forgiven.
6. Thank people if they did some favor for you, however trivial it may seem.
7. Be quick to reward a person for his/her contribution to the organization in any form.

SELF-ASSESSMENT AND CRITICISM

Career growth needs self-assessment from time to time so that you can know both your strengths and weaknesses. Expanding your career activities along a line of strength paves the way for career success. However, an undetected or unsuspected weakness in the career environment could prove to be disastrous.

A willingness to accept criticism and an open mind to receive new ideas are essential for success in a chosen career. Valid and constructive criticism has a message that something is not right, and keeping an open mind serves as a feedback mechanism to sense the problem and take corrective measures for improvement.

PLANNED CONTINUOUS LEARNING (PCL) AND HANDS-ON EXPERIENCE

Learning and knowledge go together. Learning is the very process of acquiring knowledge. To keep up with new knowledge, continuous learning becomes a necessity. Due to the specialized nature of a career or profession, the selective learning of matters pertaining to the career on a continuous basis becomes essential. Attending seminars and reading journals related to one's career interest will help to keep abreast of new knowledge.

Besides the acquisition of knowledge, hands-on experience through training seminars and workshops must be acquired on a continuous basis for career excellence. There is no better way to acquire the applied skills of any new knowledge from experts in the field than to attend special workshops conducted by them.

SHARE YOUR EXPERTISE

As you become successful in your career by virtue of your diligent work, knowledge and experience, you have learned to do something right that works. At that point of career excellence you do have something which the less fortunate ones in your profession and the young graduates just getting started on the path you once trod do not have.

You owe it to them and to yourself to share your expertise, experience, and the tricks that you have accumulated related to your excellence. You may share it through writing articles or books, or through the presentation of lectures and seminars. Sharing expertise is the ultimate test of career excellence. No knowledge should die with the knower; it should be spread for the welfare of the world at large, because the knower himself/herself has picked it up from others who have helped him/her knowingly or unknowingly. True knowledge in any form is the greatest heritage of mankind.

HOW GOOD IS THE NOTION "GREED IS GOOD"?

Greed, greed for money, is not something new in an environment where materialism rules. "Greed is good"—that is what wheeler-dealer Gordon Gekko tells a stockholder's meeting in the movie "Wall Street". In the real world, financier Ivan Boesky made millions of dollars on Wall Street, apparently using illegal insider information. He was convicted by a federal grand jury to undergo a term in jail and pay a huge fine.

It is essential for any aspirant of success in the business world to differentiate between ambition and greed. Ambition is an eager or strong desire to achieve something, such as fame or fortune, whereas greed is a rapacious desire for more than one needs or deserves, as of wealth or power. Ambition is healthy and lets a person use his/her potentials and abilities to reach great heights in both personal and professional lives within the ethical and legal boundaries of career activities. On the other hand, greed has no such sensitivity to moral and legal boundaries, and it has no difficulty in compromising higher principles of living to go after money or power as if they were the only things in life.

Ambition works within the value-system of the person which in turn is compatible to the values of the society at large. Greed also works within the value-system of the person, who values money or power more than anything else, but it is incompatible to the social values. When money becomes the only focus in life, the person loses sight of other values of humanity in general and loses the perspective of a balanced living. Remember that greed can never do good for you. Greed is antithesis of all humanistic values.

* * * * * * *

Chapter 27

A 4-YEAR PLAN FOR ACADEMIC AND CAREER EXCELLENCE

"A company whose organizational scheme requires planning at every level finds men who have learned how to look ahead because they have been doing it".

Pearson Hunt,
contributor in "Harvard Business Review on Human Relations"

TOPICS

1. Custom-Made Grand Strategy
2. 1st Year of college (Freshman Year)
3. 2nd Year of college (Sophomore year)
4. 3rd Year of college (Junior Year)
5. 4th Year of college (Senior Year)
6. Count Your Assets—Cultivated Skills
7. On to Professional/Graduate School?
8. Job Search and Acceptance
9. Foster the Spirit of Entrepreneurism
10. The Sky is the Limit

CUSTOM-MADE GRAND STRATEGY

In this chapter is presented a comprehensive view of the systematic planning and corresponding actions needed on your part, in a step by step manner, spread out over the four years of your college life. At the least, these steps can serve as guidance for you, and you should work out a modified plan to suit your unique personality, academic major and career interest. That is your custom-made plan for action. Have this plan tabulated on a year by year basis and keep it right on your study table in front of you so that you don't lose sight of it. Review it once a day, at least for a couple of minutes, to make sure that you are progressing according to this plan in your pursuit of academic and career excellence.

Remember that plans on paper always look good. Paper plans do not take anyone anywhere. It is only your commitment and appropriate actions that will take you towards your goals.

1ST YEAR OF COLLEGE (FRESHMAN YEAR)

It is not quite right to draw a clear-cut distinction between academic and career skills. They simply reflect the relative importance of the skills of the same person in two different environments. Transfer of skills from one area of learning to another is a special function of the human brain. What is important is the cumulative learning experience contributing to academic and career excellence. The following listing of skills and action steps is intended to show their relative importance in the hierarchy of your learning through the years in college.

Towards Academic Excellence
Study Skills
  * Learn techniques of fast reading.
  * Learn effective writing.
  * Learn effective note-taking.
  * Learn the SQ3R technique of comprehensive learning.
  * Learn the habit of daily reviewing after class.
  * Learn effective test-taking techniques.

Use of Library

* Learn to search for books and journals.
* Learn to use the study-aids and gadgets in the library.

Towards Career Excellence
Organizational Skills

* Learn the technique of time management.
* Learn to set daily, weekly, and monthly goals.
* Learn to prepare and execute a list of "Things to do" everyday.
* Get the habit of "calendar watching" and marking important future events for the month, semester, and the year.
* Develop a file system for school work, as well as for personal information management.

Career Inquiry

* Make a self-assessment of your likes and dislikes, strengths and weaknesses in the job market areas which you are vaguely aware of at this time.
* With this list, meet the career counselor of your college.
* Find the academic majors of compatibility to your interests and abilities.
* Explore various career fields by trying to learn about them.
* Learn about the skills needed for different career interests.

Towards General Excellence

* Learn and practice a good physical exercise program.
* Learn the techniques of preventive stress management.
* Learn techniques of physical relaxation.
* Learn to eat right.
* Develop friendship among peers.
* Develop contact with your professors.

2ND YEAR OF COLLEGE (SOPHOMORE YEAR)

The skills you developed and the experience you gained during the freshman year form a solid basis for your academic and career excellence which can now be expanded and strengthened during the sophomore year.

Towards Academic Excellence
Major of Study

* Decide on your major of study.
* Meet with your academic advisor.
* Survey the whole load of courses all the way to graduation.
* Plan an optimally-loaded schedule so that you can aim for a semester QPA of 3.5 + .

Use of Library

* Learn to research a topic more effectively.
* Browse through the handbooks in your major area to get a wider and proper perspective of your academic territory.

Towards Career Excellence
Career-related Skills

* Reevaluate your marketable skills.
* Keep learning more about them as a hobby.
* Keep in touch with the Career Office and be informed about forthcoming career workshops and interviews in your area of interest.

Career-related Employment

* Contact Co-op Director for a regular co-op or part-time career-related job.
* Seek work assignments or summer jobs that will help develop skills in your areas of interest.

Towards General Excellence

* Develop a good hobby, preferably in some area of your career interest (such as photography for a journalism major).
* Join campus organizations of your interest.
* Join student chapters of professional organizations affiliated with your major.

* Seek positions of responsibility.
* Volunteer to work on projects to the degree you can spare your leisure time.
* Learn the skill of working and getting along with other people.

3RD YEAR OF COLLEGE (JUNIOR YEAR)

This is a critical year for many students. Psychological career orientation takes place in their minds and they begin to associate themselves with the profession related to their major of study. While trying to maintain good grades in the course work, you should simultaneously get involved in many of the activities listed below to make the most of the junior year.

Towards Academic Excellence

* Meet with your academic advisor and plan a comprehensive study schedule leading to graduation.
* Do not fall into the trap of wanting to take too many courses to "get out" early. Keep a balanced schedule with ample time for career-related activities.
* Refine your skill of report writing.
* Pick an area in your major in which you might like to specialize. Remember that this choice must be based on its appeal to your emotions or intellect.
* Start research on graduate schools of your choice.

Towards Career Excellence

* Talk to your career counselor and reassess the market potentials of your career interest.
* Research your potential employers—companies, corporations, government agencies, etc.
* Learn about the entry level jobs and their academic requirements.
* Learn about the organizational and hierarchial structure of the organizations that interest you, and about the product or service they provide.

* Make field trips to get acquainted with these organizations.
* Assess the compatibility of your skills and interests with the different areas of potential employment in these organizations.
* Find a summer job in the area of your interest.

Towards General Excellence

* Take active interest in the campus organizations of your interest.
* Seek leadership positions.
* Assess your ability to get along with others.
* Develop managerial and communications skill.
* Research on the need and benefits of an advanced degree in your field of interest with a view to go to graduate school.
* Apply for professional or graduate school entrance exams.

4TH YEAR OF COLLEGE (SENIOR YEAR)

This is the year of mixed feelings. You will be glad at the thought that you will be graduating soon; but you will also feel reluctant to leave the familiar places, people, and friends who have been a part of your college life. You may also feel stressful about the uncertainties that await you in the world outside the security of the campus. These are but natural and normal responses of a student in the senior year and are nothing much to be concerned about.

However, you have lot more to do than you may think in getting ready for graduation and stepping into a career, or moving towards an advanced degree. The following will serve as a check list to remind you of the multifarious activities that you should, not just be aware of, but be doing actively to ensure a smooth transition.

Remember that timing is one of the major components of success in any venture, and landing a job that is right for you is not a matter of routine occurrence. You have to make it happen with coordinated effort.

Towards Academic Excellence

* Use all the study skills you have accumulated to your best advantage in every course you take.
* Use your test-taking skills with adequate preparation.
* Plan your daily, weekly, and semester study schedule with

adequate time for the career related activities listed elsewhere.
* Take time to meet with your professors before tests to clarify doubts.

Graduate/Professional School Entrance Exams

* Prepare well for the entrance exams you have decided to take.
* Read preparatory books; attend preparatory seminars and review classes.

Towards Career Excellence

* Be in touch with the career counselor's office.
* Be informed of on-campus interviewing by various employers.
* Arrange for interviews through Placement/Career Counselor's office.
* Write a winning resume, tailoring it to the company or graduate school you are interviewing with.
* Make a library search to know more about the companies/employers you are interested in or the graduate schools you are considering.

Interviewing

* Follow the interview techniques discussed elsewhere.
* Be on time; carry a well-prepared portfolio; dress appropriately; be relaxed but active; highlight what you can offer to the employer.
* Send a thank-you letter to each interviewer.

Visits

* Take plant-trips if you are seeking a job.
* Visit graduate schools if you are planning for an advanced degree.
* Apply for graduate or professional schools.

Get References

* Decide on at least four persons who can serve as references for you both for graduate/professional school admission and for job applications; be sure that you are in their good books.

* Talk to the references beforehand and get their permission to use their names.
* Give them a brief resume highlighting your skills and qualifications.

Towards General Excellence

* Learn the principles of self-excellence for emotional and physical well-being.
* Adopt effective time management as a principle to live by.
* Learn to be sensitive to other people's feelings in your interpersonal relations.
* Let enthusiasm be the code word in all your activities—academic, career-related, or personal.

COUNT YOUR ASSETS (CULTIVATED SKILLS)

By sincerely following the ideas and suggestions presented in this book, you will find that your life will be enriched in many ways by your own self-effort. You can not only graduate with honors and distinction, but also accumulate many skills and characteristics important for career success and for life in general, which are not taught in the formal classrooms of the college. It is these skills that make the difference in finding the right job and becoming successful in your chosen career. Following is a list of some of the important skills and characteristics you can acquire:

1. Academic excellence.
2. Effective speaking.
3. Getting along with others.
4. Organization of data and activities.
5. Effective time management.
6. Expertise in the area of your career interest.
7. Goal-setting and achievement.
8. Leadership.
9. Effective report writing.
10. Reputation for reliability.

ON TO PROFESSIONAL/GRADUATE SCHOOL?

It is an inevitable decision that you must make during your senior year whether to go to professional or graduate school, or to go for a job. If you decide to go to professional/graduate school, the following information will be of help. You should consult your library and career counselor for more detailed information.

The MBA

Major admission criteria:

1. Grades
2. GMAT scores
3. Practical experience.

GMAT Facts

4-hour test to assess:
Basic mathematics
Quantitative reasoning
Problem solving
Graph interpretation
Reading and writing ability.

Law School

Major admission criteria:

1. Grades
2. LSAT scores
3. Personal accomplishments.

LSAT Facts

Emphasis is on:
Reading and writing
Comprehension
Analytical reasoning
Evaluation of facts.

Medical School

Major admission criteria:

1. Grades
2. MCAT Scores

MCAT Facts

The six areas of testing are:

Biology
Chemistry
Physics
Reading
Quantitative
Scientific problem solving.

Other Graduate Programs

Major admission criteria:

1. Grades
2. GRE, MAT and other graduate admissions test scores. The GRE and the MAT are widely used.

Other specified areas are:

1. Dental Admission Test
2. National Teacher Examination
3. Optometry College Admission Test
4. Pharmacy College Admission Test.

JOB SEARCH AND ACCEPTANCE

If you followed the job search techniques presented earlier in this book, chances are that you should be able to find a job that is right for you. The right job can pave the way for the fulfillment of your career and personal goals. However, you should exercise caution, restraint, and discretion in accepting your first job when you get more than one offer. Evaluate each job from your perspective and also from the employer's perspective. Try to assess potential conflicts in an offer in relation to your sense of values and goals and those of the employer.

A wrong job can cause perennial problems. Money and nearness of location to one's home are often the reasons for many to accept one job in preference to another. However, job-satisfaction at the emotional level should be the governing factor in your final choice and acceptance.

Remember that your job is not just a bread-winning occupation, but an opportunity for the expression of your innate potentials and a gateway to work towards your cherished personal ambitions and aspirations.

FOSTER THE SPIRIT OF ENTREPRENEURSHIP

Entrepreneurs are not born. They are self-made. Entrepreneurship is in fact the spirit of creativity which is dormant in every individual. In many this potential is never awakened and goes to the grave with them.

Of course, it takes energy and effort to become an entrepreneur, but it is not beyond your means. When you become aware of this fact, you may consider becoming an entrepreneur as another career option. It has its own advantages and disadvantages, just like any other option. But, the greatest thing about entrepreneurship is that it is creative and productive. It has a marked influence on the economic welfare of the individual and the community at large.

Entrepreneurship is not just starting a new business. It calls for an ability to comprehend and implement the following ideas among others:

* The psychology of risk-taking and its encouragement.
* The diffusion of innovation.
* The development and implementation of novel approaches to problems.
* Realistic goal-setting and achieving.
* The mobilization of energy around new and creative ideas.
* The creation of innovative enterprises or other organizations.

Of course, you don't become an entrepreneur overnight. Entrepreneurship is both a process of being and becoming. If the above mentioned ideas are appealing to your intellect and satisfying to your emotions, you may well consider becoming an entrepreneur.

THE SKY IS THE LIMIT

The college degree you have earned for yourself after years of academic maturation has the potential to infuse confidence in you in all of your future undertakings, professional and personal. It also opens up a wide array of employment possibilities which are denied for one who did not go through college.

In a democratic country like ours adhering to the principles of freedom of speech and action within the framework of the law, and to the capitalistic philosophy of economic development there is no dearth for opportunities for self-unfoldment. It is up to you to set your direction and fix the target. The sky is the limit!

Of course, mere words and dreams will not take you anywhere. You need action—planned action with faith, dedication and the self-discipline of a mountain climber. Remember that you can do it only when you think you can, and only when you actually try.

* * * * * * *

Chapter 28

WHAT EVERY COLLEGE STUDENT SHOULD KNOW ABOUT MANAGEMENT

"More importantly, a basic knowledge of management is a useful steppingstone to productive and
gainful employment in a highly organized world in
which virtually everything is managed".

Robert Kreitner,
author of "Management"

TOPICS

1. What is Management?
2. Managerial Functions
3. Managerial Roles
4. How to Become a Successful Manager
5. The Management Pyramid
6. Management By Objectives
7. Importance of Communication in Management
8. Career and Job Stress Management
9. Life Management
10. International Management
11. Personal Financial Management

WHAT IS MANAGEMENT?

The word "management" is used so often these days under varying contexts, such as time management, stress management, office management, organizational management, etc., that it has acquired a simplistic connotation, while actually being quite complex in its meaning. It is important for you to have a clear perception of what management is because it has a direct bearing on your job search, employment, career excellence, and the quality of your life itself.

Management implies the utilization of all available resources most effectively and efficiently to achieve whatever that is desired in a changing environment. Your personal life objectives and your potential employing organization's objectives must have common ground for mutual benefit. Hence it is important for you to realize how the organization views management.

Whereas time and energy are your resources, people and capital are the organization's resources. As much as you would like to optimize the use of your resources for maximum benefit, the organization will aim at maximizing its profits through the utmost utilization of its employees and capital. The organization calls this process "management". Central to this process is the employee's ability to work with and through other people to achieve the organization's objectives. Your career success depends on your understanding management from this perspective; how it is carried out and where you fit in if you had been given a position with them are factors of vital interest in your career life.

MANAGERIAL FUNCTIONS

The process of management has basically the following eight functions, which are carried out by managers.

* **Planning**

Effective planning and the objectives on which it is based provide purpose and direction to the organization and its employees.

* Organizing

Establishing a hierarchy for an effective chain of command, division of labor, and assignment of responsibility so that all human resources are utilized efficiently is part of this function.

* Decision Making

Making the right choice among alternate courses of action is an important function of the management.

* Staffing

An organization is a collection of individuals working toward the same goal. Recruiting the right people and training them to contribute to the objectives of the organization is a distinct function generally referred to as staffing.

* Communicating

Effective communication vertically and laterally, within and outside the organization, is an important function for its optimum performance.

* Motivating

Motivating themselves and other individuals to pursue collective objectives by satisfying needs and expectations with challenging work and appropriate rewards is one of the major functions for organizational success.

* Leading

Managers are leaders within their organization. Functionally, they provide leadership not only by serving as role models but also by adapting their management style to the demands of changing situations.

* Controlling

Keeping an organization moving toward its objectives, even under adverse conditions, by taking the necessary actions is a control function which the managers are expected to exercise.

MANAGERIAL ROLES

The above mentioned managerial functions are, in fact, a useful categorization of the diverse nature of the manager's tasks. However, in trying to carry out these various functions they tend to play certain key roles. **Henry Mintzberg** has isolated the various roles which are common to managers at all levels, and has grouped them into the following major categories:

1. Interpersonal roles,
2. Informational roles, and
3. Decisional roles.

Interpersonal Roles

By virtue of their relative position, status, and formal authority, managers engage in a good deal of interpersonal contact, especially with subordinates and peers. The three interpersonal roles most often played by them are those of a figurehead for the organization, a leader in motivating subordinates to get things done, and a link in a horizontal, as well as vertical, chain of command.

Informational Roles

Information is the lifeblood of organizations and every manager acts as a clearing house for information relating to the organization. They play the role of a disseminator when transmitting selected information to subordinates, and that of a spokesperson when giving selected information to outsiders.

Decisional Roles

Vital to the success of an organization are the decisions its managers make under widely different situations. While initiating changes within the organization they are entrepreneurs; in deciding about the distribution of resources to various divisions of the organization they are resource allocators; in deciding on corrective measures they are trouble shooters, and in representing the organization's interests they serve as negotiators.

HOW TO BECOME A SUCCESSFUL MANAGER

It is hard to prescribe a formula for successful managership because successful managers have been observed to come from a wide variety of backgrounds and possess an equally wide variety of traits and skills. However, it is possible to isolate at least some basic preconditions for achieving success as a manager. **Robert Kreitner,** author of "Management", considers three key preconditions needed for managerial success. They are:

1. Ability to manage (A),
2. Motivation to manage (M), and
3. Opportunity (O).

The basic formula for managerial success (S) is then given by

$$S = A. M. O.$$

Be sure to note that success depends upon a **balanced combination** of ability, motivation, and opportunity. The absence of one factor can cancel out the strength of the other two.

Ability to manage can be acquired through the successful integration of theoretical knowledge obtained from formal classroom instruction and textbooks and practical experience gained in actually managing an organized endeavor. Motivation to manage is basically an emotional trait in the individual. The third element, the opportunity for managerial growth, has two requirements: a suitable managerial job and a supportive climate once on the job.

There is no dearth for opportunities in modern times; this can be seen in the steadily rising demand for managerial talent in both the public and private sectors.

THE MANAGERIAL PYRAMID

As a college student you will, of course, be interested in entry level jobs in various organizations which are generally in the lower levels of the managerial pyramid. Unit managers, supervisors, and foremen are the different job designations for people working at this level. Their function is to contribute to the operational planning of the organization and to carry out specific tasks on time using available resources.

Above this level is middle management. Functional managers, product managers, and departmental heads are the job designations at this level. In the overall planning process they are responsible for determining the contributions that subunits can make with allocated resources.

On top of this group is the upper management, who formulate strategic planning and run the organization. It is strategic planning that provides the direction and target for the entire organization on a

Figure 6. The Managerial Pyramid

long-term basis. Chief Executive Officer, President, Vice President, General Managers, and Division Heads are some of the job designations at this level. They are often referred to as executives.

It is important for you to become aware of the fact that moving up the career ladder is not an automatic process, but is something you have to work at. There may even be reverses and set-backs along the way. However, by learning what is needed for career success and then applying this knowledge diligently to your career life, you should be able to reach your career objectives. Climbing up the managerial pyramid certainly requires a systematic integration of management theory, practice and personal experience into meaningful and pragmatic ways of managing. It is a process of conscious and willful self-development to acquire effective managerial abilities.

MANAGEMENT BY OBJECTIVES (MBO)

Though **Management by Objectives** has come to mean a comprehensive management system based on measurable and participatively set objectives meaningful for business organizations, a knowledge of MBO has direct application for the goal-directed college student. Since objectives are targets to steer toward, all goal-oriented ventures, personal or organizational, need certain specific steps for their achievement. MBO combines planning and control through the following four step-cycle:

* Step 1. Setting objectives:
    clearly decide what you wish to accomplish.
* Step 2. Developing action plans:
    plan specific steps toward achieving your objectives.
* Step 3. Periodic review:
    periodically assess the steps you have taken for their effeciveness and efficiency.
* Step 4. Evaluation:
    periodically evaluate the progress you have made toward your main objectives.

The cycle should be repeated for as long as it takes to reach the final objectives. A single-minded commitment to the objective and a whole-hearted motivation to achieve are the personal factors that need to complement MBO for success.

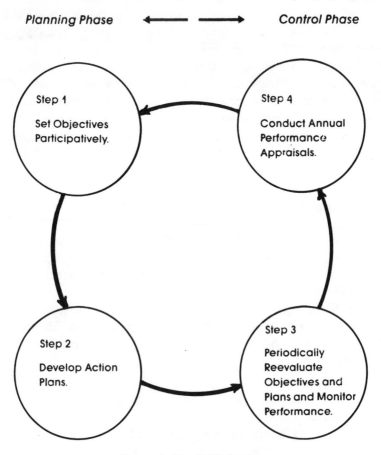

Figure 7. The MBO Cycle

IMPORTANCE OF COMMUNICATION IN MANAGEMENT

Effective communication to let individuals within the organization understand and voluntarily pursue organizational objectives is the greatest challenge for managers. To a large extent the success of an organization is dependent on the quality of its managerial communication.

Effectiveness of the organizational communication must be viewed from two perspectives:

1. System communication, and
2. Personal communication.

System Communication

This refers to the structured form of communication within and outside of the organization. Advertising, promotion, relations with shareholders, consumers, community, government, media, etc., fall within the realm of external communication. These are best handled through a specialized section of the organization who can provide centralized and coordinated communication such as a department of public relations.

The internal communication, on the other hand, flows in accordance with established lines of authority and structural boundaries. Media for formal and official communication may include memos, letters, telephones, bulletin boards, in-house publications, and "electronic mail".

Besides this formal internal communication you should be aware of the fact that an unofficial and informal communication system exists superimposed on the formal network in every organization, large or small, commonly known as the **grapevine.** As an aspiring effective manager it will be to your advantage if you learn to handle grapevine information with discrimination not giving undue importance to it but at the same time not ignoring it.

Personal Communication: How to Become a Better Communicator

Communication skill, as many erroneously believe, is not dependent only on effective speaking. In fact, the three most important skills for effective communication in today's highly organized world, besides effective speaking, are:

1. Listening,
2. Writing, and
3. Running a meeting.

Listening

Successful mangers are invariably effective and sympathetic listeners. Attentive listening gives time for comprehension, and at the same time wins the friendship of the speaker. Following are five basic rules for more effective listening:

* Be sincerely attentive to the speaker and do not fake listening.
* Show your emotions and feelings of sympathy through facial expressions.
* Do not show negative emotions of anger or distrust to the speaker.
* Encourage the speaker with eye contact and an alert posture.
* Tolerate silence and pauses of the speaker, giving him/her time to express the situation in his/her own words.

Writing

Writing as a managerial communication tool can not be overemphasized. As a learned skill, effective writing is a product of regular practice. College students who do not get the necessary writing practice in college are seriously handicapped when they step up to the managerial firing line. Five basic rules for good writing are:

* Keep your words simple.
* Express your idea with clarity.
* Write concisely and precisely.
* Be specific and to the point.
* Use words and phrases that have some punch.

Running a Meeting

Meetings have become an integral part of modern organizational life, whether corporate, governmental, professional or community service. They are convened for many reasons, such as to find facts, devise alternatives, formulate action plans, to vote on issues, to pass along information, etc.

In the career world, meetings occupy a good deal of a manager's time, and hence it is important that his/her time not be wasted in these meetings. Well-conducted meetings use the participants' time and talents efficiently and contribute positively to the organization's objectives. On the contrary, poorly conducted meetings are not only a direct waste of company resources, but also can foster ill-will among the participants. The final responsibility for the outcome of a meeting, its success or failure, rests with the person who chairs the meeting.

Kreitner lists the following principles for conducting successful meetings:

1. Make certain that a meeting is necessary.
2. Develop an agenda and send it out in advance.
3. Give careful consideration to special invitees to the meeting.
4. Give the meeting your undivided attention.
5. Be well prepared. Anticipate questions and issues that may arise.
6. Ask the right questions to stimulate discussion. Encourage everyone to get involved.
7. Keep to the agenda. Don't allow members to wander off the subject.
8. Conclude the meeting on time by summarizing the highlights.
9. Distribute a set of accurate and detailed minutes to all members before the next meeting.

CAREER AND JOB-STRESS MANAGEMENT

Stress and Personal Productivity

All careers call for continuous and effective personal productivity in carrying out the various functions and role-playing aspects associated with the career. Human beings are not heartless machines made to pursue productivity targets with mechanical efficiency. Being human, they will be emotionally affected by the nature of their career environment, and being human, they will also have the potential to constructively deal with their environment. However, career-environment factors affect people differently, due to differences in individual perception and abilities to deal with them.

Stress, up to a point, can act as a motivator and energizer, contributing to increased and effective personal productivity. However, beyond a certain limit, stress can become destructive, affecting the individual's physical and mental health as well as career productivity.

Career Stressors

It is important that you be aware of the various career stressors you are likely to encounter when you adopt a career. The following are a few:

* Role conflict
* Role ambiguity
* Role overload
* Conflict in interpersonal relations
* Competition
* Unreasonable deadlines
* High risk job situation
* Job dissatisfaction
* Failure in getting promotions
* Salary dissatisfaction.

Symptoms of Destructive Stress

It is equally important that you be aware of the physiological symptoms of destructive stress on individuals so that you can take preventive measures before being affected negatively by career stress. Following are some of the tell-tale symptoms of stress overload:

* Sleeplessness
* Headaches
* Sudden changes of mood
* Unexplained irritability
* Dependence on alcohol
* Dependence on drugs
* Apathy and lack of interest
* Stomach ulcer
* Hypertension (high blood pressure).

How to Cope with Career Stress

In attempts to cope with stress it is worth remembering the following three facts:

1. There is no short-cut or magic cure for dealing with stress and stress-related ailments.
2. Since stress is a non-specific response of the body to a stressor, imagined or real, the root cause of the stressor must be identified to appropriately counter the stress-related symptoms.
3. Through learning to function at or just below one's optimum level of stress, one can not only reach maximum personal career productivity, but also lead an active and healthy life.

The best way to cope with stress is through a program of preventive stress management, which calls for some **attitude and behavior modification** on the part of the individual. The following 10-point program is recommended by career stress experts:

1. Self assessment. Assess your individual situation, strength and limitations. Identify your stressful situations and the stressful people in your career; limit your exposure to them.
2. Do not bottle up your emotions—especially anger, fear, grief and frustrations. Talk them out with a trusted friend, pastor or counselor. Letting someone else know the worries in your mind has an almost magic effect in making worries lighter and defusing stress.
3. Avoid working against unrealistic deadlines. A reasonable deadline can stimulate personal productivity to get things done. On the other hand, an unreasonable deadline can have detrimental results on personal health and productivity.
4. Learn to apply the principle of "Planned Priority Activity" (PPA) to your daily life. PPA requires that you plan your daily activities on a flexible but prioritized basis, so that you can get things done in a systematic manner. Low priority unfinished activities must be carried over to the next day, but must be reprioritized in the light of developments during the day.
5. Be organized and stay organized. Keep your office and work environment in an organized manner.
6. Develop excellence in interpersonal relations. By being sensitive and sympathetic to the other person's feelings and sentiments you can gain their friendship and goodwill. This is the best insurance against people stress.

7. Your smile is your best asset. Use it. At the psychological level, every human being desires to be accepted by others as they are. A smile conveys that acceptance, and prepares the ground for better relationship.

8. Learn to relax physically and mentally. Relaxation is the antidote to stress. Meditation and visualization are among the many techniques for effective relaxation, anytime, anywhere. Learn to use them on the job, as well as off.

9. Exercise for fitness. Make a regular non-competitive physical activity such as walking, aerobic dancing, swimming, running, etc., a part of your daily life for at least 30 minutes. The exercise not only improves your cardiovascular efficiency and relaxes you physically, but also can help you withstand career stress better.

10. Throw some enthusiasm into your activities. Enthusiasm has the potential to eliminate negative stress. An activity carried out with genuine enthusiasm can not be stressful; in fact, it becomes an enjoyable activity.

LIFE MANAGEMENT

Many people do not have a clear plan for their life, nor for their career. As a result they drift along in life, taking whatever comes their way. They do not make full use of their potential strengths due to a lack of clear objectives, and for the same reason they do not take measures to overcome their weaknesses. Behavioral psychologists keep telling us that the human mind works like a goal-seeking machine; once a goal is defined, it sets the direction of motion towards the goal. It is for the individual to plan his/her life and career around personally challenging goals and objectives.

By defining personal goals for growth and development starting from your college years, you should be able to integrate a career plan with a plan for your life. Discussions with a career counselor will be of great help to you in formulating meaningful objectives, based on your strengths, weaknesses, value-system and cultural background. For planning purposes, life should be visualized as a continuous journey from birth to death, assuming that you will live well beyond "retirement" from your career. "Management By Objectives" can be used effectively for personal life and career management, just as well as it applies to organizational management.

INTERNATIONAL MANAGEMENT

Think Internationally

It is important for today's college student to think more and more internationally. Fast air travel services and modern telecommunications are turning the world into a global community. Interactions between countries have increased dramatically since World War II. Manufactured goods from one country are routinely marketed in another country. The whole world has become interconnected economically, and is rapidly moving towards a global economy. More and more large corporations and companies are going international, expanding their operations around the world.

This opens up a whole new avenue for job seekers coming out of colleges and universities—job assignments in foreign countries with different social, political, and cultural environments.

Career with Multi-national Corporations (MNC)

The corporations that have expanded their business operations beyond national boundaries into other countries have new problems and challenges to overcome. The pursuit of organizational objectives in an international and intercultural setting requires the ingenious and effective adaptation of conventional management techniques. International management strategies, of course, are based mainly on profit potential rather than national boundaries. The supply of capital, technology, goods and services, information and managerial talents may be drawn from different countries for a true MNC operation. International management, to be successful in its objectives, needs a new breed of managerial talent who are trained to deal with the many and complex challenges faced by the MNC operating on alien soil.

If international management excites you, now is the time to get prepared. Following are some helpful tips for your preparation:

1. Develop foreign language skills. Learn the language of the country where you want to work. Language tops the list of desirable talents for the international manager.
2. Learn the history and geography of the host country and develop an understanding of its social values and needs.
3. Develop cultural sensitivity. Culture is the unique system of perceptions, beliefs, and behavioral patterns of a given population. It is important that you learn to view the host country through its culture, rather than from just your cultural background.
4. Learn the political history and the system of government of the host country. It is essential for the international manager to know how their government functions so that he/she can deal with them effectively and appropriately.
5. Learn about labor management and labor's attitudes.
6. Learn about the marketing and distribution system of the host country.

PERSONAL FINANCIAL MANAGEMENT

Managing personal finances is not as simple as it looks, and can be a good training ground for managerial principles. Few people realize that just by earning "a lot" of money, one does not automatically solve all his/her financial problems. They also don't realize that there are principles to understand and follow in the handling of money once it is lawfully earned. A knowledge of these principles will not only help you make effective use of your money for present living, but also for future financial independence when you are older and retired from your career. Besides, the same principles are valid for many situations in organizational financial management.

The seven principles of personal financial management are:

1. Budget your expenses
2. Save with objectives

3. Invest with objectives
4. Protect your investments
5. Provide for home ownership
6. Provide for your retirement years
7. Explore further avenues of income.

Budget Your Expenses

Learning to spend for your needs within your available income is the basic principle of financial management, and the tool for this is a budget. A monthly budget can regulate your expenditures in a controlled manner, providing for your needs and some luxuries. A typical personal budget is given below:

Food and Miscellaneous	$250
Home (rent/mortgage)	250
Transportation (car/gas)	150
Utilities	100
Credit payments	200
Other (Savings, Insurance, etc.)	250

A Personal Budget

Save with Objectives

Developing a positive attitude towards saving and including a systematic provision in your monthly budget for savings towards meaningful objectives are vital for sound financial management and pave the way for better living. The reasons for saving can be listed in three major categories:

1. To create investment reserves,
2. To meet emergency needs, and
3. To meet non-routine expenses such as a vacation, etc.

David West and **Glenn Wood,** authors of "Personal Financial Management", state that the failure to build up a savings fund is a serious financial mistake. Having a solid savings reserve to fall back on is indispensable for one's financial freedom.

Invest with Objectives

Assets create income, and learning to acquire assets in life will help you improve your financial position. Of course, your ability to earn an income is your most important asset, which you can improve through acquiring additional educational and technical skills. In effect, you are investing your natural resources of time and effort to acquire them.

In addition, there are other investments you should consider which can give you financial returns. They include:

1. Real estate (physical assets),
2. Stocks and bonds (financial assets), and
3. Franchises and the like (intangible assets).

Protect Your Investments

It is not enough to simply invest in whatever form of assets you have chosen; it is important that you should be constantly examining their soundness and validity. The disposal of unsound assets and reinvestment in better ones should be done diligently and with care on a continuing basis. Market trends, socio-political and technological impact, and other risk factors must be taken into consideration as well.

Provide for Home Ownership

As a young college student you may not realize the importance of this step in personal financial management. Owning a home is not just an American dream, but is a major factor in career and life planning. Home ownership increases financial security, improves one's credit standing, encourages saving, provides an identity, and above all, contributes to better citizenship and a sense of pride.

Provide for Retirement Years

Though retirement seems quite far away for the young college student, it is a wise person who realizes the importance of starting a retirement program at an early age. When you start investing early in retirement income, you get all the advantages of the power of compound interest over a long period of time. Look at what a modest saving and investment of $500 a year at 7% compound interest will grow into in 20 and 45 years. See Figure 8.

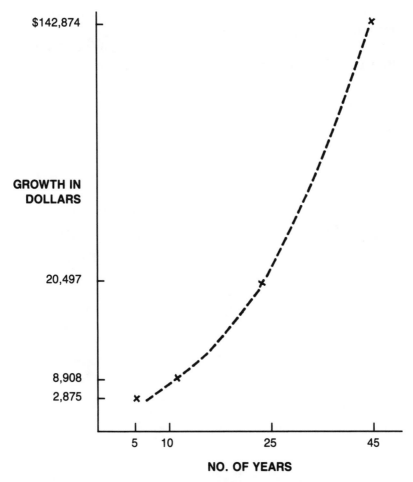

Figure 8. Long-term Investment Growth.

Explore Further Avenues of Income

The seventh principle requires that you constantly explore additional avenues of income flow. It may be through acquiring new educational and technical skills by attending graduate school, specialized skill development seminars and evening classes, by taking a part-time job, or by starting a business venture cashing in on a hobby-skill you might possess. The additional income generated means more money for personal enjoyments or for new investments.

The reader is referred to George Clason's book "Richest Man in Babylon", for a fascinating illustration of the principles discussed above.

* * * * * *

Chapter 29

PRINCIPLES OF SUCCESS IN PERSONAL, FAMILY, AND PROFESSIONAL LIFE

"Success is his who can act after a thorough investigation of the five elements: resources, equipment, time, place, and the action itself".

Thiruvalluvar,
3rd century B.C. philosopher, poet, and saint of India, author of "Thirukural"

TOPICS

1. Three Principles of Mind Pertaining to Success
2. Seven Steps to Success
3. Role-playing and the Individual
4. Need to Understand Human Behavior
5. Self-Excellence
6. Five Principles for Successful Personal Life
7. Five Principles for Successful Family Life
8. Five Principles for Successful Professional Life
9. Stress—the Price of Success
10. Five Principles of Stress Management

Life is the process of living. It is not a destination but a journey. The more you prepare for this journey of life, the more rewarding your experiences will be. Few people realize the importance of such preparation. When hardships are encountered in their lives they quickly put the blame on others or ascribe their difficulties to circumstances. Some put the blame on their astral signs, horoscopes, or fate. What they don't realize is that by knowing and applying certain principles to their lives, they can not only lead rewarding and successful lives, but can also avert many stressful situations and make their lives more fulfilling. This chapter presents some of the principles worth knowing for happy and creative living.

THREE PRINCIPLES OF MIND PERTAINING TO SUCCESS

Central to human living is "a sound mind in a sound body". Why human beings behave the way they do is still an enigma, even to behavioral psychologists. The mind is at the center of all activities, providing the thought processes needed for appropriate behavior. Though we have not fully understood the working of the human mind, psychologists have unearthed some subjective truths about the mind which have been found useful in successful living. Though they are quite subjective in nature, they are understandable and applicable for personal living.

Principle No.1.

"Human thought processes crystallize around emotionally satisfying goals and stimulate action towards these goals". This the principle of **auto-suggestion**.

Every self-proposed goal is an auto-suggestion. Once an emotionally satisfying goal is selected, the thought processes of the person begin to orient themselves toward the goal, stimulating the mind to initiate actions, which then make the goal achievable. For this chain reaction to take place the goal must, of course, be emotionally satisfying to the individual, and he/she must be willing to make the sacrifices demanded by the action part of the chain.

Goals play an important role in the life of an individual. Without meaningful goals one will drift aimlessly. As the popular saying goes, "If you don't know where you're going, you'll probably end up somewhere else".

Principle No.2

"The human nervous system can not distinguish between real and visualized experiences; its response is the same in both cases". This is the principle behind the technique known as "visualization" in modern psychology.

Visualization is not only a good stress management technique, but is also a powerful tool for the enhancement of performance in almost any activity. It is also very effective in the planning and execution of any project, small or large. Most, if not all, highly successful people in all fields make effective use of visualization in their lives, whether they are aware of it or not. From champion athletes to Nobel-prize winning scientists, from expert surgeons to successful businessmen, all highly developed individuals seem to have perfected their capacities for visualization.

Visualization is the use of mental images to simulate a situation or activity. The images used should be not only visual, but, for greater effectiveness, should also be as multi-sensory as possible, including sound, smell, touch, taste and feelings. Using these images in a state of physical and mental relaxation, a business-person can plan out how to conduct a meeting, and work out different courses of action based on projected changes in the situation; an athlete can work on technique, form, and strategy; a pianist can rehearse a piece of music; and a student can review for examinations, all by mental simulation and projection. Reputable and widely-accepted studies have shown that mentally rehearsing a technique or situation can have almost as much effect as performing it physically.

Although many different techniques and methods of visualization have been developed, the use of mental imagery is a highly creative endeavor and, as such, can not really be taught. Visualization, a very subjective and individual process, should be experimented with and applied to your own life in the ways that are most suitable to you, keeping in mind the fundamental principle that your subconscious mind and your nervous system are not capable of distinguishing between experiences in the physical world and lucid, realistic imagined experiences. A trained psychologist or counselor can guide you in various methods of visualization, or you can turn to the many self-improvement books on the subject to get started.

An example of this principle is the REM sleep phase. REM stands for Rapid Eye Movement, the name researchers have given to the stage of sleep in which dreams occur, during which the eyes make quick and rapid movements with the eyelids closed. In this period the body responds to dreaming by increases in heart-rate, blood pressure, eye movements and other physical reactions. Fortunately, motor activity is inhibited during this period, otherwise the arms and legs would react to the dream by acting it out. The importance of visualization lies in the fact that we are capable of learning from visualized experiences as well as from "real" ones. It has the potential to enrich your life, if you can learn and apply it to your unique life situations.

Principle No.3

"Enthusiasm is emotional energy; it is the driving force behind all activities that leads to success". This is the principle of mental energy.

Enthusiasm is inspiration from within. Any activity undertaken without enthusiasm will seem like pure drudgery, and will not bring out the best in the individual. It is a feeling of excitement and exhilaration in working toward a goal which is emotionally satisfying. No one can become enthusiastic unless he/she associates himself/herself with the objective or the goal. Enthusiasm brings quality to living; it lifts one from the monotony of routine living and charges one with the energy to undertake new activities, however difficult they may appear.

Infusing your activities with enthusiasm is the surest way to living with satisfaction and fulfillment. If you are unable to evoke enthusiasm and emotional interest in an activity, you should carefully examine your reasons for doing it. You may have negative attitudes and beliefs that hold you back, which can be changed if you so desire. Otherwise the activity just may not be for you, in which case you should find something you do feel enthusiastic about. Of course, in the real world you must often do many things you may not particularly like, for various reasons, but even then, unless you have deep enthusiasm for at least one aspect of your life, you will not have any sense of fulfillment or satisfaction, and life will seem more negative than positive, which is perhaps the ultimate tragedy. However, you do have the power to develop enthusiasm in your activities, and lead a life of greater vitality and enjoyment.

SEVEN STEPS TO SUCCESS

In Chapter 7 of this book we discussed the principles of goal setting and achievement. Success is a magic word. It conveys a sense of the accomplishment of something that is desired, planned, and attempted. That something need not be a goal that others might consider important, or historical, but should be a goal that you find meaningful, and satisfying, whatever it may be.

Success is the outcome of activities undertaken towards a predetermined goal. The seven steps constituting the action part, based on the principles of goal achievement, are listed below. When they are applied systematically to any undertaking, you will be successful.

1. Keep the objective in sight.
2. Keep studying about the goal.
3. Make adequate preparation.
4. Work with enthusiasm.
5. Be ready for due sacrifice.
6. Do not mind the opinions of others.
7. Get continuous feedback.

Keeping the objective at the uppermost level of your mind at all times while working towards a goal is the first and foremost thing to remember. It acts as a catalyst, mobilizing your thoughts and actions and steering them towards your objective. It should be followed by a continuous effort on your part to learn everything possible about the goal you seek. This study helps to bring to light the nature of the road ahead, the impediments on the way, the pitfalls to be aware of, and above all, your own shortcomings relative to the goal.

The next step is to make preparations. This is, in effect, to get control over the prerequisites essential to the objective and the goal. Many people fail in their ventures, not for a lack of hard work, but because they overlooked the need to master fundamentals and prerequisites first. With prerequisites taken care of, only now are you actually ready to embark on the action part of the goal-seeking game. Motivated, consistent, and systematic work is called for now. It is not the persistent drudgery of the sullen workaholic, but the excellence of an enthusiastic athlete in training.

It is inevitable that a certain amount of sacrifice of your personal time and comforts will be needed in the achievement of any worthwhile goal. There is no compromise on this fact. However, an enthusiastic goal-seeker does not consider it a sacrifice because for him/her working towards the goal becomes a way of life, willingly adopted. While the opinions of others whom you live and work with count, you should not pay attention to any discouraging or distracting comments about your goal. We mentioned before that your faith in yourself and in your objective is the seed of success, and you should learn to discount the opinions of others that are not founded on facts.

Finally, getting continuous and periodic feedback about the results of your effort on a measurable scale is a necessary condition for success. An evaluation of the feedback lets you know how well you are doing relative to your objective and the time frame for its completion. It lets you decide on changes and modifications in the approach and nature of execution, if needed. Periodic evaluation of the feedback serves as both a monitoring and a warning device. It is a forecast of what is yet to come. Its message is loud and clear for the goal seeker.

When any goal, small or big, short-range or long-range, is tackled systematically in accordance with these seven steps, the chances of achieving the goal are very high.

ROLE PLAYING AND THE INDIVIDUAL

It is essential for you to realize that there is no sharp division of personal, family, and professional living for any person. Family, personal, and professional living are only extensions of one's living in different environments. The personality is the same, but the roles are different in each case. To use a simple, mathematical analogy, the totality of your life can be considered as 3-dimensional space, stretching out along personal, family, and professional axes, each running perpendicular to the other. Your time and energy being limited, you must distribute them in a balanced manner among these different dimensions to be successful in all the three phases of your life.

Of course, there will invariably be conflicts and contradictions among the interests and goals in each of these spheres. It is your ability to resolve them while maintaining a judicious balance that will determine how happy and satisfying your life is going to be.

NEED TO UNDERSTAND HUMAN BEHAVIOR

Success in life, particularly in the family and professional aspects, is largely dependent on one's ability to understand human behavior in one's sphere of involvement. Human behavior, including one's own, is a complex phenomenon, and is not amenable for easy analysis and interpretation. However, certain patterns and characteristics are distinctly noticeable to the keen observer. Behavioral psychologists have tried to associate these traits with "personalities" with the objective of studying the behavioral patterns of people under varying circumstances. But even this approach has severe limitations, especially when one tries to apply the theories of behavioral psychology to everyday life and "real" people, who are too complex to neatly fit the limited theoretical models.

Person to person interaction is a tremendously intricate and complex process, as can be seen by the long amount of time a psychoanalyst or therapist needs to spend with a client before any lasting or meaningful progress is made, anywhere from several months to several years. In spite of all the progress that has occurred, and there has been much, the field of human behavior remains largely unknown territory, full of controversy, especially at its farthest reaches.

To be able to get along well with others is not only a sign of maturity, but also a prerequisite for successful family and professional life. The so-called "leadership qualities" imply an ability to inspire others, to win them over to your way of thinking, and to have a sustained hold on their loyalty to you and your institution. The more you educate yourself on human behavior, the more successful you can be in dealing with people. An understanding of human behavior is the basis of good interpersonal relationship. It is also essential for harmonious living in general.

SELF-EXCELLENCE

Self-excellence is a dynamic and continuous state of inner growth. It is also an innate drive to excel oneself for continuous progress in one's chosen field of activities. Self-excellence can be considered the very foundation of successful living. There is no yardstick to measure it, yet it is self-realizable and achievable through self-effort. Success is indeed a manifestation of self-excellence.

How does one attain self-excellence? There are two aspects to the answer to this question. The first deals with a set of seven negative factors which are literal stumbling blocks in the path of self-excellence. You have to rid yourself of these negative factors before you can attempt to move towards self-excellence. The second aspect deals with a set of seven positive characteristics. These are the mainsprings of self-excellence, and they need to be cultivated by the individual.

The Stumbling Blocks to Self-Excellence

1. Lack of purpose in life
2. Lack of will and discipline
3. Laziness and procrastination
4. Lack of self-respect and respect for others
5. Lack of patience
6. Emotional turbidity
7. Cognitive distortion.

The Mainsprings of Self-Excellence

1. Self-confidence
2. Planned continuous learning
3. Commitment and willingness to work
4. Motivation and enthusiasm
5. Willingness to forego immediate pleasures
6. Emotion management
7. Reaching out to help others.

Remember that lasting success in all of your ventures has its origin in striving for self-excellence. For a detailed discussion of self-excellence, the reader is referred to this writer's book "Self-Excellence".

FIVE PRINCIPLES FOR SUCCESS IN PERSONAL LIFE

Whether you have a family or not, whether you are in a profession or not, you still have a life of your own which needs to be lived. To get the most from your personal life, and to live it to a high degree of satisfaction, you can make use of the following five principles:

1. Recognize your inner personality.
2. Develop honesty and contentment.
3. Care for others.
4. Recognize and unleash your creative potential.
5. Practice "Planned Continuous Learning".

Your Inner Personality

Discover who you are, your strengths and weaknesses, your natural talents, innate interests, and emotional values. Get to know yourself. The process can be done through techniques like self-psychoanalysis and meditation, and by questioning yourself honestly and directly, which is harder than it may seem. You will find success in your life by following your innate desires and potentials—doing what you naturally like and avoiding what you don't.

Two Basic Values

Successful personal living revolves around two basic human values, namely honesty and a sense of contentment. Honesty eliminates mental conflicts and promotes self-acceptance. Contentment, brings a sense of satisfaction to your living.

Caring for Others

Sensitivity and consideration for the needs of others is essential for the welfare and harmony of any society. Caring for others and reaching out to help them in times of need are indications of a truly successful person. Besides, there can be genuine happiness in the act of giving and sharing. The pleasant feeling that you are helping someone less fortunate than you is enough to kindle the flame of self-esteem in you. Reaching out to help others is a sign of self excellence.

Creative Potentials

You must realize that you have a tremendous reservoir of creative potential which can be released only through your own self-effort. To make this happen you must have faith in yourself. Skill development in any or all of your chosen activities is the true manifestation of your creative potential. A well developed skill can be maintained as a hobby for your own pleasure and satisfaction, or, if need be, it can be used as an extra source of income, or even as an occupation.

Planned Continuous Learning (PCL)

Learning implies acquiring knowledge; the practice of knowledge makes one skillful. In today's world of constant change, it is absolutely essential for one to keep abreast of the latest knowledge in one's field of specialization, and it is just as important to stay up to date on the various events and trends that are shaping our world. For a balanced life one also needs a hobby activity, be it reading, golf, music, etc. Since your time and energy are limited, it is important that you apportion them among your various interests. Here lies the importance of planned continuous learning, which is the systematic and continuous organization of the various materials you wish to learn, along with a plan that breaks the material down into sub-units that are to be mastered on a periodic basis. PCL brings mastery over your hobbies and professional interests, as well as any other activities you might like to undertake. PCL holds the key to creative and meaningful living.

FIVE PRINCIPLES FOR SUCCESS IN FAMILY LIFE

Family living is shared living. It is not a mechanical sharing. The underlying fabric of successful family life is interwoven with love, care, and consideration. Though these characteristics are often innate in most people, they need to be cultivated and kept in a state of awareness in a family. The following five principles, when practiced sincerely and conscientiously, have the potential to strengthen the emotional ties of the family members for successful family living.

1. Be willing to relegate your personal interests to the back seat. Keep the interests of other family members on par with yours, and work out your activities accordingly.
2. Keep the channels of communication with other family members open at all times and at as pleasant a level as possible. Let communication be two-way and settle all the differences of opinion with a willingness to give more and take less.
3. Let other family members live by their own standards. Give them guidance, where needed in your opinion, but not by force.
4. Help them plan and prepare for their future. Children, of course, need help and advice in this process. Your spouse, too, needs to get prepared for the uncertainties of life and for the possible loneliness of old age.
5. Plan and go for periodic family vacations, and visit places far and near. Vacations are great fun for children and stress-breakers for adults. Besides reducing the monotony of routine living, they infuse new enthusiasm among family members.

FIVE PRINCIPLES FOR SUCCESS IN PROFESSIONAL LIFE

Success in professional life is more complex and demanding than success in personal and family living. Nevertheless, there are principles to guide you for a successful and satisfying professional life. Though many others may also be considered as important factors, there can be no success in any profession without the following five basic principles.

1. Set short-term and long-term goals for your professional growth and keep working towards them.
2. Eliminate procrastination. Putting off for tomorrow what you can do today is the single most important negative factor pre-

venting success in any field of activity. Change your perspective on time and learn to appreciate its value. Learn the techniques of effective time management to plan and prioritize activities for the day.

3. Apply the principle of "Planned Continuous Learning" to your professional interests.
4. Develop excellent interpersonal relations with all the people whom you come into contact with in your professional world.
5. Learn the techniques of effective communication. Remember that you also need to share your time with your family and your personal interests.

STRESS—THE PRICE OF SUCCESS

Success does not come easy. It is inevitable that you will have to work hard and long. You will also encounter many conflicts along the way. These conflicts may come in the form of deadlines, unfinished deals, personality clashes with peers and bosses at the workplace, and tensions with your spouse at home. Conflict may also come from the pressure to achieve for both survival and prestige in the professional jungle, the wish to advertise your "success" through possession of the best things money can buy, which may be just barely affordable, and similar reasons. The result is stress. Of course, stress is not always bad. It can act as a motivator and a stimulant to achieve your goals, if you know how to handle it.

However, when not properly managed, stress, though psychological in origin, can and will manifest through physiological symptoms, impairing your physical health. Headaches, sleeplessness, stomach ulcers, high blood pressure and related ailments are but a few that have been attributed to stress.

FIVE PRINCIPLES FOR STRESS MANAGEMENT

The following are five basic principles of stress management, both preventive and curative.

1. Learn to relax.
2. Attitude and behavioral modifications.

3. Time management.
4. Exercise, aerobically.
5. Eat right.

Learn to Relax

Relaxation is the antidote to stress. It implies the calming down of the nervous system, relieving the tensions in the mind and body without resorting to drugs or alcohol. The ability to relax at will, any place, any time, is a skill that can be developed like any other. There are many techniques of relaxation, both for the body and mind, such as diaphragmatic deep breathing, meditation, visualization, and simple physical exercises of many kinds to name a few. It is important to choose a method of relaxation that is emotionally appealing to you and that is most suited to your way of living.

Attitude and Behavior Modifications

Stress is subjective in nature. It originates at the psychological level of a person and is related to his/her attitudes and values in life. Unresolved conflicts in the mind often become a perennial source of stress. Self-assessment and self-psychoanalysis are techniques that are helpful in recognizing the sources of stress so that you can deal with them appropriately.

Stress management calls for willful adaptation to stress to eliminate or minimize its effects. Such an adaptation is possible only through attitude and behavioral changes relevant to the stress. Of course, not all people respond to a given stressor in the same way, nor are they affected in the same manner. It is up to the individual to bring about appropriate modifications in his/her attitudes and behavior to manage the stress.

Time Management

Modern life revolves around the clock, and as such it is essential to learn to live with the clock. The inability to manage one's own time is a serious source of stress for many, no matter what profession one is in. Effective time management is again a learnable skill.

Time management and the prioritization of activities go hand in hand. The priorities, in turn, must be related to the objective or goals for the day, week and month from the immediate and short-term perspective. Effective time management needs planning, the organization of activities, priority-assignment, and self-discipline on the part of the individual. A strategy planning session of ten minutes in the morning before starting the day's work is the key. It is also important to include relaxation breaks in your list of activities.

Exercise Aerobically

Though aerobic exercises are well known for their positive influence on cardiovascular excellence, few people realize that they are potential stress relievers, both physical and emotional. When carried out systematically and regularly, preferably every day, these exercises relax all the muscles of the body by making them work in a rhythmic manner. The increased blood flow through the capillaries of the circulatory system brings oxygen and vital nutrients to every cell of the body muscles. It is this new flow of energy that counteracts the ill-effects of stress, often preventing them from developing into serious physical illness.

Aerobics differ from recreation, isometrics, and isotonics in that you gradually build your body up to demanding large amounts of oxygen for a sustained length of time, at least ten minutes, during which no significant oxygen debt is incurred. Of all the aerobic exercises, rope-jumping, or skipping, and swimming seem to be considered the best by most experts. However, each aerobic exercise is more suited to different people, depending on body structure, past injuries, and personal interest. Walking, jogging, running, cycling, rowing, and climbing stairs are some other popular aerobic exercises.

Eat Right

Continued stress can affect a person's eating and drinking habits. Some respond by eating more than they need to, and some by eating less. If unresolved stress persists over a long period of time, the person may end up with a changed eating habit and pattern as a subliminal defense against the unpleasant consequences of stress. This may lead him/her to medical problems through either overeating or undereating. Besides, stress has been known to increase the cholesterol level of the blood, which, in turn, tends to get deposited on the walls of the blood vessels. The excess cholesterol deposit causes a hardening of the arteries, known as atherosclerosis, the forerunner of a possible heart attack and stroke.

The fifth principle of stress management emphasizes excellence in eating and drinking habits as a preventive measure. Your aim should be to have a balanced diet with all the proper nutrients, vitamins, minerals, proteins, carbohydrates and low-saturated fats. Avoid high cholesterol and high saturated fat products such as red meat and pork, and have poultry, fish, and vegetables instead. Avoid alcoholic beverages altogether if you can; otherwise be moderate and limit yourself reasonably to maintain your optimum physical and mental health.

* * * * * * *

Chapter **30**

GRADUATION AND COMMENCEMENT

"Educational philosophy can be as trivial or as deep as one wishes to make it. The foundation course, however, can only be the beginning of a study of a very extensive field".

James Monroe Hughes,
author of "Education in America"

TOPICS

1. Graduation
2. Commencement
3. What to Expect
4. In Pursuit of Excellence
5. Goal-Oriented Living

GRADUATION

At last the great day has arrived! It is time for you to go through the ceremonies. You have put on the attire of a by-gone era, the cap and gown—still used ceremoniously to mark great occasions in the academic world today. It is a symbol of academic excellence which can not be bought by money, but can only be earned by devotion to learning. It symbolizes all the hard work and sacrifices over the years since you started your college program. It also establishes a new identity for you as a "graduate".

To the world it announces that you have matured enough academically and mentally so that potential employers can consider you for gainful employment. To you, it serves as a passport to a job when you seek one—not just any job, of course, but one in your area of specialization.

Besides the new identity, graduation brings with it feelings of joy and elation at your own achievement. It is indeed an achievement worthy of the admiration and happiness of your friends and family. It is more than a passing feeling of excitement—it is an event of personal fulfillment that culminates in a state of self-confidence, adding positive reinforcement to your self-image.

Time for Reminiscence

Graduation is a time for reminiscence. It is similar to a mountain climber's reaching the peak and looking back at the vast expanse of the rugged mountain he/she has just climbed. Your own success at reaching your goal, that is, to graduate from college, is no less spectacular, as far as your personal experiences are concerned. You did pass test after test, though not without worry and anxiety. There were times when you thought you had surely failed, only to find that it was not that bad after all.

Remember that painful weekend when you stayed behind in your room to prepare for a major test the following Monday, when you would have rather joined your friends at the big party? Remember that late night when you were still working on the term paper you thought you could finish in a couple of hours? Remember the sound of music, rather the din of noise, that blasted through the corridors of the dormitory the day you most needed to study, and so you had to leave for the library in search of a quiet corner to work on the most difficult assignment of a required course you didn't care much about.

Well, the list can go on and on. It is good to remember that all these and other experiences in your college life have helped you to grow in your learning process. It is also good to remember that nothing worthwhile in life comes easy. Success has its own price tag. Success eludes those who are unwilling to pay the right price at the right time. Let us now look forward—a look at the road ahead.

COMMENCEMENT

Now that you are a graduate, "What next?" is the big question that looms before you. It is not just a question of what you plan to do next, but also calls for the careful deliberation of what you want your life after graduation to be like in the long run, both professionally and personally. If graduation marked the end of a chapter in your life, commencement marks the beginning of another. Commencement also implies the beginning of life's journey outside the walls of the college which have protected you from the harsh realities of the real world during your college life, giving you time to mature intellectually and emotionally.

When you think about life ahead you can't help but wonder what lies over the horizon, and how much control you will have over the events of your own life. While there is no satisfactory answer to this question, you will also find that you can not allow yourself to drift without direction. It is here that commencement plays a vital role; it lets you become aware of the need for your setting the direction and pace of your life ahead. Nobody else can do it for you! And, nobody else should, if you want to lead a life of developing to your full potential and finding self-fulfillment.

You will find that there is a lot of truth in the statement that you are the architect of your own destiny. This only emphasizes the fact that you still hold the reins of your life in your own hands, as far as initiating the activities to improve and enrich your life are concerned. The time to start is **now.** That is commencement.

WHAT TO EXPECT?

Commencement is also the time to reflect and learn more about the outside world in which you will be spending the rest of your life. You will find that the knowledge you have gained in your college years plays but a minor role in your future, and that you have to keep learning in many different areas throughout the rest of your life for both success and happiness.

Besides being aware of the limitations of your knowledge, you should also become aware of the opportunities and pitfalls awaiting you. It is this lack of foresight on the part of many enthusiastic graduates that prevents them from attaining their highest career aspirations, which remain unrealized dreams.

Also, you will find that the single most important area of future learning for success and happiness in your personal and professional lives is in the domain of interpersonal understanding and relationships. Being able to understand the behavior and responses of other people in your life, whether in your own family, neighborhood, place of employment or elsewhere, will make it possible for you to deal with others appropriately and effectively, with dignity and respect.

Understanding others is a myth if you don't understand yourself as a person. It is this knowledge of the self, reflected in the maxim **"know thyself"**, that should be your guide through the complex maze of interpersonal relationships.

Opportunities abound in the outside world for personal and professional development, especially in our modern technological era, if you are willing to explore them and adapt yourself to the rigors needed for their fulfillment.

There are many opportunities to earn money, and to spend even more; there are opportunities to build new businesses and to create wonderful works of art, to make marvelous scientific discoveries and to help improve the lives of others. There are opportunities to travel all over the world, to learn about other cultures and make new friends. In short, there are opportunities to do almost anything that you have the interest, inclination and energy to do. Even if opportunities are not readily apparent, then there will be opportunities to make the opportunities you desire.

Of course, you can not expect life to be a bed of roses all the way. There will be setbacks, disappointments, and even heartbreaks. What is important for you to know is that behind every crisis awaits an opportunity for recovery, rebuilding, and improvement. Remember the old saying "Success lies not in never falling, but in rising up every time you fall".

IN PURSUIT OF EXCELLENCE

If **stress** was the password of the eighties, **excellence** is the password of the nineties and beyond. Excellence has, of late, been the focal point of large corporations, educational institutions, product manufacturers, the defense services, and the federal and state governments. Why this sudden surge of interest in excellence?

Competition is the basis of survival in a free-enterprise society such as ours. It can be internal or external to an organization. To withstand this competition, whether internal or external, the competing departments or organizations must necessarily evolve towards excellence in their operation. In general, excellence is distinctly manifest in three categories, namely management, product, and marketing. The long-term survival of organizations, large or small, private or governmental, depends on the degree of excellence attained in their areas of competition.

There is magic in the word excellence. It is generally thought of in an objective sense, associating excellence as a visible component of the end product. The excellence of organizations is judged by their profit margins, by the quality of service rendered, or by the quality of the consumer goods produced.

Self-Excellence

To expect excellence from an organization whose members and executives are not motivated to excel is not realistic. Excellence requires commitment on the part of the members of the organization. The desire to excel should emanate from the individual, though a certain degree of motivation can be provided from the outside.

Psychologists and anthropologists have found that the desire to excel exists in all organisms, including humans; however, it does not appear till a certain degree of motivation is present. This motivation can be self-induced or externally imparted. Self-excellence is an improved state of excellence through self-effort in the mental, intellectual, and physical planes of a person. Self-excellence is manifest through the person's attitudes, behavior patterns and interpersonal relations with others. The self-excellent person projects an aura of confidence around himself/herself, and he/she is capable of creating objective excellence in his/her undertakings, personal or professional.

Commencement is the time to reflect on the deficiencies and shortcomings which prevent you from becoming self-excellent. Remember that self-excellence holds the key to making all your ambitions and aspirations come true.

GOAL-ORIENTED LIVING

Having decided on a path to pursue in your professional and personal life, the next thing to do is to set meaningful goals to achieve

as you go along. You will discover that working towards these goals is a source of pleasure when the goals are of your own choice. Of course, you will have many goals in your life. When you organize them into immediate, short-term, and long-term goals, in both personal and professional life, you will find that achieving them is not as difficult as it might have seemed.

The organization of your actions by goal-setting directs your effort in a more efficient way, letting you do more in less time with

less energy. The clear planning of goals also reduces stress and anxiety. Once you examine a goal, think through the various steps needed to achieve it, and then whole-heartedly decide to pursue it. This reduces anxiety and worry about what to do next at every step of the way, leaving you free to deal with unforeseen changes or circumstances, and to devote greater intensity to work toward your goal, whatever it may be. The secret of creative and happy living lies in making it goal-oriented.

EPILOG

EMERGENCE OF THE GOAL-DIRECTED GRADUATE

Can you imagine the plight of a ship in mid-ocean with no rudder or navigational instruments to steer the vessel toward its port of destination? Being left to the mercy of the wind and waves, the ship will drift and be thrown off course, and it will be a miracle if it lands safely anywhere. On the other hand, a ship equipped with a rudder and all the necessary navigational equipment can be expected to reach its port of destination, barring calamities beyond human control.

Herein lies the secret of the three components of success for the college student—**strategy, technique** and **a goal**. Strategy is similar to the ship's navigational map, which charts the best course from the ship's present location to its desired destination. Technique is analogous to the effective management and execution of everyday work on board, keeping the ship running efficiently and maintaining its course toward the destination. The goal, of course, is the ship's destination, and you, as the ship's captain, must determine a destination and then keep the ship proceeding smoothly on course until the port of destination is reached. As a college student, you can translate this into these three parts: a comprehensive strategy or overall plan for your entire college program; an efficient system for the organization of time, information, and work, along with effective techniques for study; and a major of study that fits your long-term educational and career plans.

When you understand and apply this fundamental principle of success while still in college, you are not only assured of graduation, but you will also be laying the foundations of a highly successful career. You have learned to become a **goal-directed** person, one who sets realistic goals, develops effective strategies and plans to reach them, and then works efficiently and systematically toward them. It is the goal-directed graduate that employers and professional schools are seeking. It is the goal-directed person who leads the academic and career worlds.

The goal-directed person is not born; he/she is evolved. The potential for self-evolution is dormant in every student, no different from the emergence of a beautiful butterfly from the clumsy caterpillar. However, this evolution is not necessarily a natural process, so intrinsic motivation and self-effort must come from you to break through the barriers of inaction and procrastination.

The sky is the limit for the goal-directed person. You owe it to yourself to become not just a graduate, but a goal-directed graduate.

REFERENCES

PART 1—ACADEMIC EXCELLENCE

1. Samuel Smith, et el., "Educational Psychology", Barnes & Noble, inc., New York, 1967.
2. Geoffrey A. Dudley, "Increase Your Learning Power", Wilshire Book Co., N. Hollywood, California, 1966.
3. Jack A. Adams, "Learning and Memory", The Dorsey Press, Homewood, Illinois, 1976.
4. J. A. Rickard, "A Student's Guide to Better Grades", Wilshire Book Co., N. Hollywood, California, 1964.
5. Thomas M. Sherman and Terry M. Wildman, "Proven Strategies for Successful Test Taking", Charles E. Merrill Publishing Co., Columbus, Ohio, 1982.
6. Dennis B. Jackson, "The Exam Secret", Wilshire Book Co., N. Hollywood, California, 1965.
7. Sara Jane Coffman, "How to Survive at College", College Town Press, Bloomington, Indiana, 1986.
8. Lana J. Chandler and Michael D. Boggs, "The Student Loan Handbook", Betterway Publications, White Hall, Virginia, 1987.
9. P. H. Nowell-Smith, "Ethics", Penguin Books, Ltd. 1954.
10. Rosalind Ekman, "Readings in the Problems of Ethics", Charles Scribner's Sons, New York, 1965.
11. James Monroe Hughes, "Education in America", Harper & Row, Publishers, New York, 1970.
12. Taisen Deshimaru, "The Zen Way to the Martial Arts", E. P. Dutton, New York, 1982.
13. Fritjof Capra, "The Tao of Physics", Shambhala Publications, Colorado, 1975.

14. Reader's Digest, "Write Better, Speak Better", The Reader's Digest Association, Inc., Pleasantville, New York, 1972.
15. Karin Mack and Eric Skjei, "Overcoming Writing Blocks", J. P. Tarcher, Inc., Los Angeles, 1978.
16. Richard W. Smith, "Technical Writing", Barnes & Noble, New York, 1963.
17. Jonathan Price, "Thirty Days to More Powerful Writing", Avenel Books, New York, 1982.
18. A. Craig Baird and Franklin H. Knower, "Essentials of General Speech", McGraw Hill Book Co., New York, 1968.
19. E. F. Elson and Alberta Peck, "The Art of Speaking", Ginn & Co., Boston, 1952.
20. Albert J. Beveridge, "The Art of Public speaking", Nash Publishing, Los Angeles, 1974.
21. Herman Holtz, "The Business of Public Speaking", John Wiley & sons, New York, 1985.
22. Abraham H. Lass and Eugene S. Wilson, "The College Student's Handbook", David White Co., New York, 1970.
23. Fred B. Millett, "Professor", The Macmillan Company, New York, 1961.

PART 2—CAREER EXCELLENCE

24. Mary J. Hicks, C.S.J., "Assessing and Applying Your Gifts", A Job Campaign Handbook, Career Services, WV Institute of Technology, Montgomery, West Virginia, 1988.
25. Bill Osher and Sioux Henley Campbell, "The Blue-Chip Graduate", Peachtree Publishers, Ltd., Atlanta, Georgia, 1987.
26. Susan Bernard, "Getting the Right Job", A T & T's College Series, 1988.
27. Burdette E. Bostwick, "Finding the Job You've Always Wanted", John Wiley & Sons, New York, 1977.

28. Ben Greco, "How to Get the Job That is Right for You", Dow Jones-Irwin, Inc., Homewood, Illinois, 60430.
29. Arthur R. Pell, "The College Graduate Guide to Job Finding", Simon & Schuster, New York, 1973.
30. Philip W. Dunphy, Sidney F. Austin and Thomas J. McEneaney, "Career Development for the College Student", The Carroll Press, Cranston, Rhodes Island, 1976.
31. Richard H. Beatty, "The Complete Job Search Book", John Wiley & Sons, New York, 1988.
32. Ramon J. Aldag and Timothy M. Stearns, "Management", South-Western Publishing Co., Cincinnati, Ohio, 1987.
33. Robert Kreitner, "Management", Houghton Mifflin Co., Boston, 1986.
34. Richard T. Pascale and Anthony G. Athos, "The Art of Japanese Management", Warner Books, New York, 1982.
35. David E. Dougherty, "From Technical Professional to Corporate Manager", John Wiley & sons, New York, 1984.
36. George Mazzei, "Moving Up", Poseidon press, New York, 1984.
37. Donald Sanzotta, "The Manager's Guide to Interpersonal Relations", AMACOM, New York, 1979.
38. Terence R. Mitchel, "People in Organizations: Understanding Their Behavior", McGraw-Hill, Inc., New York, 1978.
39. S. A. Swami, "Self-Excellence", Minibook Publishing Co., Montgomery, West Virginia, 1987.
40. Harvard Business Review "On Human Relations", Harper & Row, Publishers, New York, 1979.
41. Thomas J. Peters and Robert H. Waterman, Jr., "In Search of Excellence", Warner Books, New York, 1983.
42. Diane Lento-McGovern, "Life After College", Betterway Publications, White Hall, Virginia, 1987.
43. David A. West and Glenn L. Wood, "Personal Financial Management", Houghton Mifflin Co., Boston, 1972.
44. Hap Vaughan, "Your Career Game", John Wiley & Sons, New York, 1987.
45. George S. Clason, "The Richest Man in Babylon", Hawthorn Books, Inc., New York, 1955.

INDEX

ABOUT THE AUTHOR

S. A. Swami, Ph.D., P.E.,

Dr. Shanmugam A. Swami, born on May 30, 1928 in India, received his formal education in three continents. He holds a bachelor's degree in civil engineering from the University of Madras, India, a master's degree from the University of New South Wales, Sydney, Australia, and a doctorate degree from Purdue University, Lafayette, Indiana, USA.

He has served in the industry, Government, and educational institutions over his long career of more than 38 years. Currently, he serves as a professor of civil engineering in the West Virginia Institute of Technology since 1968. A self-taught educational psychologist, he is familiar with the various study techniques and their applications most suited for college education leading to academic excellence.

Recognizing that college education is invariably a passport to a job and a career, Dr. Swami has counselled his students over the years on the various phases of job search and career excellence. This book is an outcome of his desire to pass on to the student generation the pertinent information on how to be successful in college and in career.

A registered professional engineer, he is also the author of "Self-Excellence", published by the Minibook Publishing Co., Montgomery, WV.

COLOPHON

THE COLLEGE STUDENT'S HANDBOOK

FOR
BETTER GRADES, JOB SEARCH,
AND CAREER SUCCESS

This book was designed by the author and produced by Minibook Publishing Co., Montgomery, WV.

The text type is 11 on 13 Times Roman.

The typesetting was done by BookMasters, Inc.

The printing and binding was done by BookCrafters, Inc.